George W. Patten

Patten's Army manual:

Containing instructions for officers in the preparation of rolls, returns and accounts required of regimental and company commanders, and pertaining to the subsistence and quartermasters' departments, etc., etc

George W. Patten

Patten's Army manual:

Containing instructions for officers in the preparation of rolls, returns and accounts required of regimental and company commanders, and pertaining to the subsistence and quartermasters' departments, etc., etc

ISBN/EAN: 9783337814601

Printed in Europe, USA, Canada, Australia, Japan

Cover: Foto ©ninafisch / pixelio.de

More available books at **www.hansebooks.com**

PATTEN'S
ARMY MANUAL:

CONTAINING

Instruction for Officers

IN THE

PREPARATION OF ROLLS, RETURNS AND ACCOUNTS

REQUIRED OF

REGIMENTAL AND COMPANY COMMANDERS,

AND PERTAINING TO THE

SUBSISTENCE AND QUARTERMASTERS' DEPARTMENTS,

ETC., ETC.

Fourth Edition, Revised, with Additions to the present time.

By GEORGE PATTEN,
LATE OF THE U. S. ARMY.

New York:
PUBLISHED BY J. W. FORTUNE,
No. 102 CENTRE STREET.
1864.

Entered according to Act of Congress, in the year 1861,
BY J. W. FORTUNE
In the Clerk's Office of the District Court of the United States for the Southern
District of New York.

Entered according to Act of Congress, in the year 1863,
BY J. W. FORTUNE,
In the Clerk's Office of the District Court of the United States for the Southern
District of New York.

PREFACE TO FOURTH EDITION.

THE many changes which have been made in the *time* of rendering the returns of the Quartermaster's Department, as well as in the *persons* to whom many of them are to be made; together with the fact that the regulations governing the Quartermaster's and Subsistence Departments have been materially amended since the publication of the Revised Army Regulations in 1861, have rendered a thorough revision of the ARMY MANUAL necessary, in order that its instruction may agree in every particular with the latest regulations of the War Department. Pursuant to this necessity, the *forms*, as well as the text, have been so revised as to exhibit the several papers required by the regulations of the Departments to which they relate, in the exact condition prescribed for them by the latest orders and regulations. Being in this respect in advance of the edition of the *Army Regulations* now in use, where the old forms are retained, and the amendments indicated by notes alone in another portion of the book.

Since its appearance, the *Army Manual* has supplied a want long felt in the regular service, and made pressingly evident by the requirements of officers called into the army from civil pursuits. It is devoted to the instruction of officers in the preparation of all the *Rolls, Returns,* and *Reports* they are required to make; with forms of each, and full information concerning the manner of filling them. All the accounts to be rendered by officers are fully explained, and the manner of preparing them clearly set forth.

Officers acting in the Subsistence and Quartermaster's Departments will here find full information concerning the several *Abstracts* and the *vouchers* required for each, together with the character of transactions pertaining to these abstracts, and the manner of classifying them.

The regulations of the general and regimental *recruiting service* are here given, with rules for examining recruits, and instruction in the preparation of all accounts and returns required of officers on the recruiting service, together with the rules governing the enlisting of volunteers and instruction in the preparation of their *muster-in* and *muster-out rolls*.

Much of the information which it has been the endeavor of the author to impart has heretofore been acquired by the usages of service alone, there being no work to which the newly-made officer may apply for instruction in the preparation of the various papers prescribed by the army regulations.

It is as a guide in the preparation of papers and accounts that the following pages are laid before the officers of both the regular and volunteer services, with the hope that they may contribute to the efficient performance of these duties and the consequent benefit of the service.

NEW YORK,
January 1st, 1864.

TABLE OF CONTENTS.

ORGANIZATION,

EMBRACING:

RANK — REGIMENTS — COMPANIES, ... Page 5-10

SUBSISTENCE,

EMBRACING:

THE ARMY RATION — PROVISION RETURNS — ACTING ASSISTANT COMMISSARIES OF SUBSISTENCE — ISSUES TO HOSPITAL — WASTAGE — MONTHLY SUMMARY STATEMENT — MONTHLY RETURN OF COMMISSARY PROPERTY — VOUCHERS — ABSTRACT OF PROVISIONS SOLD TO OFFICERS—ABSTRACT OF PURCHASES — ABSTRACT OF DISBURSEMENTS ON ACCOUNT OF CONTINGENCIES — ACCOUNT CURRENT — THE HOSPITAL RATION — COMMUTATION OF RATIONS — ABSTRACT OF PROVISIONS ISSUED TO TROOPS — ABSTRACT OF PROVISIONS ISSUED TO MEN IN HOSPITAL—ABSTRACT OF EXTRA ISSUES, ... 10-64

CLOTHING, CAMP, AND GARRISON EQUIPAGE,

EMBRACING:

ISSUES OF CLOTHING — EXTRA ISSUES OF CLOTHING — ALLOWANCE OF CLOTHING — COST OF CLOTHING — COST OF CAMP AND GARRISON EQUIPAGE — ALLOWANCE OF CAMP AND GARRISON EQUIPAGE — CLOTHING RECEIPT ROLL — SPECIAL REQUISITION — MONTHLY RETURN OF CLOTHING, CAMP AND GARRISON EQUIPAGE, ... 65-72

QUARTERMASTER'S DEPARTMENT,

EMBRACING:

HORSES — FORAGE — STRAW — STATIONERY — FUEL AND QUARTERS — TRANSPORTATION — EXPENSES OF COURTS MARTIAL — POSTAGE — ACTING ASSISTANT-QUARTERMASTERS, ... 73-82

Returns of the Quartermaster's Department,

CONSISTING OF

SUMMARY STATEMENT — REPORT OF PERSONS AND THINGS — ROLL OF EXTRA DUTY MEN — REPORT OF STORES FOR TRANSPORTATION — RETURN OF ANIMALS, WAGONS, HARNESS, ETC. — REPORT OF FORAGE — REPORT OF FUEL AND QUARTERS COMMUTED — REPORT OF PAY DUE — ESTIMATE OF FUNDS FOR THE CURRENT MONTH — TRANSFER ROLL — ACCOUNT CURRENT OF DISBURSEMENTS ON ACCOUNT OF THE QUARTERMASTER'S DEPARTMENT — ACCOUNT CURRENT OF MONEY RECEIVED AND DISBURSED UNDER APPROPRIA-

CONTENTS.

TIONS FOR CONTINGENCIES OF THE ARMY — RETURN OF PROPERTY — STATEMENT OF ALLOWANCES PAID TO OFFICERS — ABSTRACT A — ABSTRACT B — ABSTRACT B b — ABSTRACT C — ABSTRACT D — ABSTRACT E — ABSTRACT F — ABSTRACT G — ABSTRACT H — ABSTRACT I — ABSTRACT K — ABSTRACT L — ABSTRACT M — ABSTRACT N — VOUCHERS TO ABSTRACT A — VOUCHERS TO ABSTRACT B — VOUCHERS TO ABSTRACT C — VOUCHERS TO ABSTRACT D — VOUCHERS TO ABSTRACT E — VOUCHERS TO ABSTRACT K — VOUCHERS TO ABSTRACT L — REQUISITION FOR FORAGE — REQUISITION FOR STRAW — REQUISITION FOR STATIONERY — REQUISITION FOR FUEL — COMMUTATION OF FUEL AND QUARTERS — OFFICERS TRANSPORTATION ACCOUNT — ACCOUNT OF ACTUAL TRANSPORTATION EXPENSES — TRANSPORTATION ACCOUNT OF A PAYMASTER'S CLERK — ACCOUNT FOR COURT MARTIAL EXPENSES — ACCOUNT FOR POSTAGE PAID — BILL OF PURCHASE — INVOICE — LIST OF ARTICLES LOST — LIST OF QUARTERMASTER'S STORES EXPENDED — ACCOUNT SALES OF PROPERTY — BILL OF MEDICINE PURCHASED BY AN OFFICER OF THE QUARTERMASTER'S DEPARTMENT — EXTRA DUTY PAY ROLL — REPORT OF PAY DUE — 82–148

ORDNANCE,

EMBRACING:

ARMS AND ACCOUTREMENTS — SALES OF ARMS TO OFFICERS — PRICES OF SMALL ARMS — PRICES OF ACCOUTREMENTS — COMPOSITION AND EQUIPMENT OF A BATTERY FOR WAR — COMPRISING: COMPOSITION OF A 12-POUNDER BATTERY — COMPOSITION OF A 12-POUNDER BATTERY (LIGHT) — COMPOSITION OF A 6-POUNDER BATTERY — AMMUNITION FOR A 12-POUNDER BATTERY — AMMUNITION FOR A 12-POUNDER (LIGHT) — AMMUNITION FOR A 6-POUNDER BATTERY — HARNESS REQUIRED FOR EACH HORSE OF A FIELD-BATTERY — IMPLEMENTS AND EQUIPMENTS FOR FIELD-PIECES — SMITH'S TOOLS AND STORES REQUIRED FOR A FIELD-BATTERY — CARRIAGE-MAKER'S TOOLS — SADDLER'S TOOLS AND STORES — REQUISITION FOR A BATTERY AND ITS EQUIPMENT — REQUISITION FOR ORDNANCE FOR MILITIA — RETURN OF ORDNANCE AND ORDNANCE STORES, 149–163

PAY,

EMBRACING:

TABLE OF PAY, SUBSISTENCE, FORAGE, ETC., OF THE U. S. ARMY — COMMUTATION OF SUBSISTENCE — PAYMENT OF DISCHARGED SODIERS — PAYMENT OF SOLDIERS — PAYMENT OF VOLUNTEERS, ... 164–177

ROLLS, RETURNS, AND REPORTS,

EMBRACING:

Rolls, Returns, and Reports required from Company Commanders.

MUSTER ROLLS — MUSTER AND PAY ROLLS — MUSTER AND PAY ROLLS OF DETACHMENTS — INVENTORY OF EFFECTS OF DECEASED SOLDIERS — FINAL STATEMENT OF DECEASED SOLDIERS — RETURN OF DECEASED SOLDIERS — RETURN OF CLOTHING, CAMP, AND GARRISON EQUIPAGE — RETURN OF ORDNANCE AND ORDNANCE STORES — CERTIFICATE OF INVENTORY ON RETURN OF ORDNANCE AND ORDNANCE STORES — REPORT OF DAMAGED ARMS — DESCRIPTIVE LIST OF MEN JOINED — COMPANY RETURN — TRANSCRIPT OF ORDERS MAKING TEMPORARY APPOINTMENTS OF NON-COMMISSIONED OFFICERS, AND REDUCING NON-COMMISSIONED OFFICERS — MORNING REPORT OF COMPANY — RETURN OF COMPANY FUND, ... 178–190

CONTENTS. vii

Rolls Returns and Reports required of Regimental Commanders.

RETURN OF THE REGIMENT — MUSTER ROLL OF THE FIELD, STAFF, AND BAND — RECRUITING RETURN OF THE REGIMENT — QUARTERLY RETURN OF DECEASED SOLDIERS — ANNUAL RETURN OF CASUALTIES — REPORT BY LETTER OF APPOINTMENT OR CHANGE OF STAFF OFFICERS — ACKNOWLEDGMENT OF BOOKS AND BLANKS — REPORT OF PRIZEMAN OF TARGET PRACTICE — ACCOUNTS OF REGIMENTAL AND COMPANY FUNDS — REPORT OF DAMAGE TO ARMS — MORNING REPORT, ... 190-194

Rolls, Returns, and Reports required from Post Commanders.

POST RETURN — REPORT OF ARRIVAL AND DEPARTURE OF TROOPS — REPORT OF CHANGE OF OFFICERS ACTING IN STAFF DEPARTMENTS — ACKNOWLEDGMENT OF BOOKS AND BLANKS — QUARTERMASTER'S REPORT OF CONDITION OF BUILDINGS — RETURN OF ORDNANCE — RETURN OF COMPANY AND POST FUNDS — POST FUND — COMPANY FUND — DIRECTIONS FOR REGIMENTAL FUND ACCOUNTS — DIRECTIONS FOR POST FUND ACCOUNTS, ... 194-207

Monthly Return of Departments, Army, Corps, Divisions, and Brigades.

RECRUITING SERVICE,

EMBRACING:

RECRUITING PARTIES — RECRUITS — CONSENT IN CASE OF A MINOR — FORM OF EXAMINING A RECRUIT — ACCOUNTS, RETURNS, AND ROLLS TO BE RENDERED BY OFFICERS ON RECRUITING SERVICE — RECRUITING ACCOUNT CURRENT — ABSTRACT OF DISBURSEMENTS ON ACCOUNT OF CONTINGENCIES OF RECRUITING SERVICE — VOUCHER FOR DISBURSEMENTS — QUARTERLY RETURN OF PROPERTY — MONTHLY SUMMARY STATEMENT — TRI-MONTHLY REPORT — MUSTER ROLL — MONTHLY RETURN OF RECRUITS — RETURN OF CLOTHING, CAMP, AND GARRISON EQUIPAGE, AND QUARTERMASTER'S PROPERTY — RETURN OF ARMS AND ACCOUTREMENTS — ESTIMATES FOR FUNDS — MUSTER AND DESCRIPTIVE ROLLS OF RECRUITS SENT TO DEPOT OR TO REGIMENTS — ACCOUNT OF CLOTHING — FORM OF ENLISTMENT — TRANSPORTATION — BLANKETS — BOARDS OF INSPECTION — RETURNS FROM OFFICERS COMMANDING RECRUITS — DESCRIPTIVE LIST, ... 208-222

REGIMENTAL RECRUITING SERVICE,

EMBRACING:

MONTHLY RETURN OF REGIMENTAL RECRUITING PARTY — QUARTERLY RETURN OF RECRUITS — ACCOUNT CURRENT — RECRUITING OF VOLUNTEERS, 222-238

MILITIA IN THE SERVICE OF THE UNITED STATES,

EMBRACING:

MUSTER-IN ROLLS — MUSTER-OUT ROLLS — ALLOWANCES TO VOLUNTEERS, 239-248

RETIRED LIST,

SHOWING:

HOW FILLED — MANNER OF RETIRING OFFICERS — PROMOTIONS CONSEQUENT ON THE RETIRING OF AN OFFICER, ... 249-250

DISCHARGE OF SOLDIERS,

EMBRACING:

OATH OF IDENTITY — DISCHARGE FOR DISABILITY — FORM OF DISCHARGE — CERTIFICATE OF DISABILITY — DISCHARGE OF VOLUNTEERS — DISABILITY EXISTING PREVIOUS TO MUSTERING INTO SERVICE — DISCHARGE OF COMMISSIONED OFFICERS OF VOLUNTEERS — CERTIFICATE TO BE GIVEN TO VOLUNTEERS AT THE TIME OF THEIR DISCHARGE, ... 251-254

MEDICAL DEPARTMENT,

EMBRACING:

SURGEONS — ASSISTANT-SURGEONS — MEDICAL CADETS — HOSPITAL STEWARDS — EMPLOYMENT OF PRIVATE PHYSICIANS — CONTRACT WITH A PRIVATE PHYSICIAN — LIST OF INSTRUMENTS ISSUED TO MEDICAL OFFICERS — MEDICAL SUPPLIES — STANDARD SUPPLY TABLE FOR FIELD SERVICE — MUSTER ROLLS OF HOSPITAL ATTENDANTS — SURGEON'S CALL — RETURN OF MEDICINES — ACCOUNT OF ARMS, ETC., OF PATIENTS — MORNING REPORT — RETURN OF CAMP AND GARRISON EQUIPAGE — ACCOUNT CURRENT — CORRESPONDENCE, 255-275

JURISDICTION AND DUTIES OF BOARDS OF SURVEY.

SETTLEMENT OF ACCOUNTS.

ASSIGNMENT OF PAY BY VOLUNTEERS.

CAMP AND GARRISON EQUIPAGE REQUIRED FOR A REGIMENT.

UNIFORM, DRESS, AND HORSE EQUIPMENTS PRESCRIBED FOR THE ARMY.

THE

ARMY MANUAL.

ORGANIZATION.

THE Army of the United States is composed of the following Regiments and Corps, ranking in the order in which they are placed:

Corps of Engineers.
Corps of Ordnance.
Six Regiments of Cavalry.
Five Regiments of Artillery.
Nineteen Regiments of Infantry.

The several Regiments of Cavalry, Artillery and Infantry are designated as the 1st, 2nd, etc. Regiment of Cavalry, Artillery or Infantry, as the case may be.

The Army is supplied with provisions by the Subsistence Department, under direction of the Commissary-General of Subsistence, at Washington, through Assistant Commissaries of Subsistence and Officers *acting* in that capacity.

The Quartermaster's Department presided over by the *Quartermaster-General* at Washington provides the Army with clothing, camp and garrison equipage, transportation, forage, fuel, quarters, and every thing required for the *equipment* of an Army that does not properly belong to any other Department.

The duties of the Department are performed by Assistant Quartermasters, Regimental Quartermasters, and other Officers acting as such.

The Army is paid by the Pay Department, presided over by the Paymaster-General, through its officers, denominated Paymasters.

The Medical Department, under the charge of the Surgeon-General, has the supervision of the sick and wounded through its Surgeons and Assistant Surgeons.

The Adjutant-General's Department, under the supervision of the *Adjutant-General*, has charge of the organization of the army, promulgation of orders, reception of all rolls, reports and returns, and the superintendence of the recruiting service.

The army is supplied with arms, accoutrements, and all ordnance and ordnance stores by the Ordnance Department, under the supervision of the Chief of Ordnance, who is the colonel of the ordnance corps, and has his office at Washington.

RANK.

The foundation of military discipline requires that all inferiors shall strictly obey and execute with alacrity and good faith the lawful orders of the superiors appointed over them, therefore, *obedience* is the first thing to be learned by the officer.

Military authority should be exercised with firmness, but with kindness and justice; and punishment should be made in strict conformity to military law.

The following is the rank of officers and non-commissioned officers:

1st. Lieutenant-General.
2d. Major-General.
3d. Brigadier-General.
4th. Colonel.
5th. Lieutenant-Colonel.
6th. Major.
7th. Captain.
8th. First Lieutenant.
9th. Second Lieutenant.
10th. Cadet.
11th. Sergeant-Major.
12th. Quartermaster-Sergeant of a Regiment.
13th. Ordnance Sergeant and Hospital Steward.
14th. First Sergeant.
15th. Sergeant.
16th. Corporal.

And in each grade by date of commission or appointment.

When commissions are of the same date, the rank is to be decided, between officers of the same regiment or corps by the order of appointment; between officers of different regiments or corps: 1st. by rank in actual service when appointed; 2d. by former rank and service in the army or marine corps; 3d. by lottery among such as have not been in the military service of the United States. In case of equality of rank by virtue of a brevet commission, reference is had to commissions not brevet.

Officers having brevets, or commissions of a prior date

to those of the regiment in which they serve, may take place in courts-martial and on detachment, when composed of different corps, according to the ranks given them in their brevets or dates of their former commissions; but in the regiment, troop, or company to which such officers belong, they shall do duty and take rank both in courts-martial and on detachments which shall be composed only of their own corps, according to the commission by which they are mustered in the said corps.

If, upon marches, guards, or in quarters, different corps of the army shall happen to join, or do duty together, the officer highest in rank of the line of the army, marine corps, or militia, by commission, there on duty or in quarters, shall command the whole, and give orders for what is needful to the service, unless otherwise specially directed by the President of the United States, according to the nature of the case.

An officer not having orders from competent authority can not put himself *on duty* by virtue of his commission alone.

Officers serving *by commission* from any state of the Union take rank next after officers of the like grade *by commission* from the United States.

Brevet rank takes effect only in the following cases: 1st. by special assignment of the President in commands composed of different corps; 2d. on courts-martial or *detachments* composed of different corps. Troops are on *detachment* only when sent out temporarily to perform a special service.

In regularly constituted commands, as garrisons, posts, departments; companies, battalions, regiments; corps, brigades, divisions, army corps, or the army itself, brevet rank can not be exercised except by special assignment.

The officers of Engineers are not to assume nor to be ordered on any duty beyond the line of their immediate profession, except by the special order of the President.

An officer of the Pay or Medical Department can not exercise command except in his own department.

Officers of the corps of Engineers or Ordnance, or of the Adjutant-General's, Inspector-General's, Quartermaster-General's, or Subsistence Department, though eligible to command according to the rank they hold in the army of the United States, and not subject to the orders of a junior officer, shall not assume the command of troops unless put on duty under orders which specially so direct by authority of the President.

An officer in a temporary command shall not, except in urgent cases, alter or annul the standing orders of the regular or permanent commander without authority from the next higher commander.

In time of war, or with an army in the field, resignations shall take effect within thirty days from the date of the order of acceptance.

Leaves of absence shall not be granted by commanding officers to officers on tendering their resignation, unless the resignation be unconditional and immediate.

REGIMENTS.

On the organization of a regiment, the companies receive a permanent designation by letters, beginning with A, and the officers are assigned to companies; afterward, company officers succeed to companies, as promoted to fill vacancies. Companies take place in the battalion according to the rank of their captains.

Captains must serve with their companies. Though subject to the temporary details of service, as for courts-martial, military boards, etc., they shall not be detailed for any duty which may separate them for any considerable time from their companies.

It is enjoined upon all officers to be cautious in reproving non-commissioned officers in the presence or hearing of privates, lest their authority be weakened; and non-commissioned officers are not to be sent to the guard-room and mixed with privates during confinement, but be considered as placed in arrest, except in aggravated cases, where escape may be apprehended.

Non-commissioned officers may be reduced to the ranks by the sentence of a court-martial, or by order of the commander of the regiment, on the application of the company commander. If reduced to the ranks by garrison courts, at posts not the headquarters of the regiment, the company commander will immediately forward a transcript of the order to the regimental commander.

Every non-commissioned officer shall be furnished with a certificate or warrant of his rank, signed by the colonel and countersigned by the adjutant. Blank warrants, on parchment, are furnished by the Adjutant-General's office.

The books for each regiment are as follows:

1. *General Order Book*, of three quires of paper, to contain all orders and circulars from general department, division, or brigade headquarters, with an index.
2. *Regimental Order Book*, to contain regimental orders, with an index.
3. *Letter Book*, to contain the official correspondence of the regiment, with an index.
4. *An Index of Letters*, required to be kept on file in the following form:

No.	Name of Writer.	Date.	Subject.
1	Captain A. B....	July 15, 1860	Appoin't non-com. officers.
2	Adjt.-Gen. R. J...	Sept. 4, 1860	Recruiting service.
3	Captain F. G....	Oct. 11, 1860	Error in company return.
4	Lieutenant C. D..	Nov. 2, 1860	Application for leave.

The date of receipt should be indorsed on all letters. They should be numbered to correspond with the index, and filed in regular order, for easy reference.

5. *Descriptive Book*, of five quires of paper, 16 inches by $10\frac{1}{2}$ inches, to contain a list of the officers of the regiment, with their rank, and dates of appointment, and promotions; transfers, leaves of absence, and places and dates of birth. To contain, also, the names of all enlisted soldiers, entered according to priority of enlistment, giving their description, the dates and period of their enlistment, and, under the head of remarks, the cause of discharge, character, death, desertion, transfer; in short, every thing relating to their military history. This book to be indexed.

One copy of the monthly returns will be filed.

COMPANIES.

The captain will cause the men of the company to be numbered, in a regular series, including the non-commissioned officers, and divided into four squads, each to be put under the charge of a non-commissioned officer.

1*

Each subaltern officer will be charged with a squad, for the supervision of its order and cleanliness; and captains will require their lieutenants to assist them in the performance of *all* company duties.

As far as practicable, the men of each squad will be quartered together.

The utmost attention will be paid by commanders of companies to the cleanliness of their men, as to their persons, arms, accoutrements, and equipments, and also as to their quarters or tents.

Where conveniences for bathing are to be had, the men should bathe once a week. The feet to be washed at least twice a week. The hair *kept short*, and beard neatly trimmed.

Non-commissioned officers, in command of squads, will be held more immediately responsible that their men observe what is prescribed above; that they wash their hands and faces daily; that they brush or comb their heads; that those who are to go on duty put their arms, accoutrements, dress, etc., in the best order, and that such as have permission to pass the chain of sentinels are in the dress that may be ordered.

Commanders of companies and squads will see that the arms and accoutrements in possession of the men are always kept in good order, and that proper care be taken in cleaning them.

When belts are given to a soldier, the captain will see that they are properly fitted to the body; and it is forbidden to cut any belt without his sanction.

Cartridge-boxes and bayonet-scabbards will be polished with blacking; varnish is injurious to the leather, and should not be used.

All arms in the hands of the troops, whether brown or bright, are to be kept in the state in which they are issued by the ordnance department. Arms will not be taken to pieces without permission of a commissioned officer. Bright barrels will be kept clean and free from rust without polishing them; care should be taken in rubbing not to bruise or bend the barrel. After firing, wash out the bore; wipe it dry, and then pass a bit of cloth, slightly greased, to the bottom. In these operations, a rod of wood with a loop in one end of it is to be used instead of the rammer. The barrel, when not in use, will be closed with a stopper.

SUBSISTENCE.

THE ARMY RATION.

A RATION is the established daily allowance of food for one person. For the United States army it is composed as follows: Twelve ounces of pork or bacon, or, one pound and four ounces of salt or fresh beef; one pound and six ounces of soft bread or flour, or, one pound of hard bread, or, one pound and four ounces of corn meal; and to every one hundred rations fifteen pounds of beans or peas, and ten pounds of rice or hominy; ten pounds of green coffee, or, eight pounds of roasted (or roasted and ground) coffee, or, one pound and eight ounces of tea; fifteen pounds of sugar; four quarts of vinegar; one pound and four ounces of adamantine or star candles; four pounds of soap; three pounds and twelve ounces of salt; four ounces of pepper; thirty pounds of potatoes, when practicable, and one quart of molasses.

The Subsistence Department, as may be most convenient or least expensive to it, and according to the condition and amount of its supplies, shall determine whether soft bread or flour, and what other component parts of the ration, as equivalents, shall be issued.

Desiccated compressed potatoes, or desiccated compressed mixed vegetables, at the rate of one ounce and a half of the former, and one ounce of the latter, to the ration, may be *substituted* for beans, peas, rice, hominy, or fresh potatoes.

Beans, peas, salt, and potatoes (fresh) shall be purchased, issued, and sold by weight, and the *bushel* of each shall be estimated at *sixty pounds*. Thus, 100 rations of beans or peas will be fifteen pounds, the equivalent of eight quarts; 100 rations of salt will be three pounds and twelve ounces, the equivalent of two quarts; and 100 rations of potatoes (fresh) will be thirty pounds, the equivalent of half a bushel.

ISSUES EXTRA.

The issues authorized under this head shall be made on returns signed by the officer in charge of the guard, by the Assistant Adjutant-General or Adjutant of the headquarters, by the Quartermaster or other officer accountable for the animals, by the officer in charge of the working party, etc., as the case may be, and approved by the commanding officer of the post or station.

Extra issues will be allowed as follows, viz.:

Adamantine Candles.—To the principal guard of each camp or garrison, per month.. 12 pounds.
And when serving in the field, not exceeding the following rates per month, viz.: -
To the headquarters of a regiment or brigade............................ 10 pounds.
To the headquarters of a division... 20 pounds.
To the headquarters of a corps.. 30 pounds.
To the headquarters of each separate army, when composed of more than one corps.. 40 pounds.

Salt.—Two ounces a week to each *public* animal. The *number* of animals to be supplied, and *the period* drawn for, will be stated on each return for extra issues, and so entered on the Abstract. (Form 6.)

Whisky.—One gill per man daily, in cases of *excessive* fatigue, or *severe* exposure. The *number* of men issued to will be stated on each return for extra issues, and so entered on the Abstract. (Form 6.) Under "Remarks," on the return and on the Abstract, the letters of companies to which the men belong, *number* and designation of regiment, etc., will be given.

Oil, candles, or gas, with which to light a fort, barrack, or stable, are not allowed from the Subsistence Department. *Extra* issues of subsistence, except as prescribed above, are forbidden.

WASTAGE.

Wastage on issues, or from evaporation or leakage, will be ascertained monthly, or when it can be most conveniently done, and the actual deficiency, and no more, will be charged on the monthly return. Loss from whatever cause, exceeding ordinary waste, must be accounted for by the officer's certificate, or other satisfactory evidence. Ordinary wastage on issues, etc., should not exceed, say three per cent. on pork, bacon, flour in sacks, sugar, vinegar, and soap; and one per cent. on hard bread, beans, rice, coffee, and salt. Any surplus gained will be taken up. No wastage is admitted on issues of fresh beef, furnished a command directly from the butcher; but in beef on the hoof, errors in estimated weight, or absolute decrease of weight, and losses of cattle strayed, stolen, or died, will be accounted for by the certificate of the officer, or other satisfactory evidence. When cattle are received on contract, or purchased, their net weight will be ascertained as nearly as practicable, and entered on the return.

This wastage is entered in the return below the issues. Gain on issues is taken with provisions received.

RATION RETURN.

Form 1, p. 31.

Soldiers' rations are issued by the issuing *Commissary of Subsistence* on returns made agreeably to Form 1, p. 31.

It is the duty of commanders of companies, on arriving at a depot to ascertain the number of days' rations on hand, and, previous to exhausting them, to make a requisition for an additional supply. This requisition, after approval by the commanding officer of the post, is taken to the issuing Commissary, and the provisions drawn.

It is advisable, when practicable, to consolidate the provision returns of a regiment agreeably to Form 2, p. 32. This return will be signed by the commanding officer of the regiment, and approved by the post commander.

Provisions are never issued except in this manner, upon returns properly made out; all officers should therefore immediately on entering the service, acquaint themselves with the rules governing the issuing of provisions.

Regiments and separate commands of one or more companies have frequently an acting Assistant-Commissary of Subsistence with them. This officer receives from the Depôt Commissary a suitable quantity of provisions in bulk, and issues to the command upon provision returns as before prescribed.

There should be a man detailed from the command to act as commissary sergeant, whose duty shall consist in making the issues ordered by the A. C. S.

When men leave their company the rations they have drawn and left with it will be deducted from the next return for the company; a like rule when men are discharged from the hospital will govern the hospital return.

Four women are allowed to each company as laundresses, and are each entitled to one ration a day; rations are not, however, to be drawn for them unless they are present with the company.

The provision return will be made out for the *actual* strength of the company, soldiers in hospital and other absentees not being included therein.

Commissioned officers do not draw rations, but are allowed to *purchase* of the issuing commissary such articles as they may require at cost price, paying cash on delivery.

ACTING ASSISTANT COMMISSARY.

An acting assistant commissary of subsistence may be any subaltern detailed to the duty of issuing provisions to a command. Where it is practicable the regimental Commissary performs this duty.

The A. A. C. S. on a requisition, approved by his commanding officer, receives from the Depôt Commissary of Subsistence a suitable quantity of provisions in bulk, for which he gives duplicate receipts, and then becomes responsible for the property. Duplicate invoices, corresponding with these receipts, are furnished by the Depôt Commissary at the time he receives the provisions.

As these invoices and receipts constitute the basis of the officers' accountability to the government, he should be careful to verify their accuracy on receiving the property.

This is a general rule which will be well for all officers to follow when receipting for any species of property.

The A. A. C. S. likewise receives from the Depôt Commissary a suitable number of scales, weights, measures scoops and other articles needed to facilitate the issuing of provisions, which are denominated *Commissary property*.

Should it be deemed necessary, the A. A. C. S. will, on a requisition approved by his commanding officer, receive from the Depôt Commissary a suitable sum of money for expenditures on account of the subsistence department. He will give duplicate receipts for the funds, and never part with any portion thereof without like vouchers.

The following form may be adopted for a receipt:

FORM 3.

Received at ———, *this* ——— *day of* ———, 186 , *from Lieut. A*——— *B*———, ——— *Regiment of* ———, *A. C. S., the following Subsistence Funds, for which I am accountable at the Treasury of the United States, viz.:*

$2,900\frac{61}{100}$. Twenty-nine hundred dols. and sixty-one cts.

C——— D———,

(Signed in duplicate.) *Lieut.* ———, *Regt. of* ———, *A. C. S.*

The regular provision returns received by the A. A. C. S. will be duly filed, and at the end of every month will be embodied in an *abstract of provisions issued*, in accordance with Form 4, p. 33. The quantity in bulk will be as-ascertained from the Table annexed.

This abstract will be compared with the original returns by the commanding officer, who will certify to the correctness of the abstract, which will then become the voucher of the commissary for the provisions issued.

All extra issues will be made on special returns, which at the end of the month will be *embodied* in the *abstract of extra issues*.

This abstract will be certified by the commanding officer after examining the returns, and will also receive the certificate of the SURGEON if any of the extra issues were made on his recommendation. Form 6, p. 35, shows the abstract.

These abstracts are to be made in duplicate, one to accompany the monthly return, and one to be retained by the commissary.

Should the commissary issue to both *regulars* and *militia* or *volunteers*, their returns will be embodied in separate abstracts. Should he issue to volunteers alone, the fact of the issues being made to that character of troops will be specified in the abstract.

Issues to citizens will be embodied in a separate abstract. Form 5, p. 34.

Issues to the hospital will be on returns by the medical officer for such provisions only as are actually required for the sick and the attendants. The costs of such parts of the ration as are issued will be charged to the hospital at contract or cost prices, and the hospital will be credited by the whole number of complete rations due through the month, at contract or cost prices, the balance constituting the *Hospital Fund;* or any portion of it may be expended by the Commissary, on the requisition of the medical officer, in the purchase of any article for the subsistence or comfort of the sick not authorized to be otherwise furnished.

The articles purchased for the hospital, as well as those issued from the subsistence store-house, will be included in the surgeon's certificate of issues to the hospital, and borne on the monthly return of provisions received and issued. Vouchers for purchases for the hospital must either be certified by the surgeon or accompanied by his requisition.

Abstracts of the issues to the hospital will be made by the commissary, certified by the surgeon, and countersigned by the commanding officer. See Form 7, pp. 36 & 37

The commissary will each month enter the sales to officers in an abstract made agreeably to Form 8, p. 38, which will be compared by the commanding officer with the certified lists of the officers purchasing, and certified to, as shown in Form 8.

The foregoing abstracts constitute the Commissary's vouchers for his monthly issues. They will be entered in his monthly return of provisions received and issued, and forwarded with it to the Commissary-General.

The monthly return is shown in Form 12, p. 43a.

The invoices of provisions received are first entered according to date, and next the purchases made during the month, as shown by the abstract, Form 9, p. 39.

The abstracts of provisions issued, and property receipted for, are entered as indicated in Form 12.

Besides the return of provisions, and the abstracts which accompany it, every Commissary must forward the following Returns to the Commissary-General *monthly*.

Return of all property in the Department, except provisions and forage, with the invoices and receipts thereto belonging..................................Form 11.
Summary statement of funds received, expended, etc., in the month...... " 10.

MONTHLY RETURNS TO THIRD AUDITOR.

The following are the usual accounts, abstracts, etc., to be rendered to the Third Auditor of the Treasury *monthly*, or forthwith, when a disbursing officer, for whatever cause, ceases to be such, viz.:—

Account current..Form 15.
Abstract of provisions and forage purchased and paid for in the month, with vouchers.. " 13.
Abstract of all expenditures in the month, except for provisions and forage, with vouchers.. " 14.
Abstract of sales to officers.. " 8.
Receipts for funds transferred.. " 8.

In transmitting official papers to the Commissary-General and Third Auditor for examination or other action, the following rules will be observed, viz.:—

I. Invoices and receipts for subsistence stores, bills of

company savings, abstracts of issues, abstracts of sales, boards of survey, inspection reports, summary statements, return of commissary property (with its invoices and receipts, etc.,) will be *officially* signed, *properly* endorsed, *carefully* assorted, and put up (by a wrapper of strong paper, for example) *with* the return of provisions for the same month.

II. Receipts for funds, abstract of purchases, and abstract of contingencies (each with its appropriate vouchers), abstract of sales to officers, etc., will be *officially* signed, *properly* endorsed, *carefully* assorted, and put up in like manner *with* the Account Current for the same month.

III. In all cases, official papers will be accompanied by a letter of advice, enumerating them, and briefly giving necessary explanations.

MONTHLY SUMMARY STATEMENT.

Form 10, p. 40.

This is a statement of all money received and expended during the month. No vouchers will accompany it.

The money value of subsistence supplies sold must be entered on the Summary Statement for the month in which the sales are made.

RETURN OF COMMISSARY PROPERTY.

Form 11, p. 41.

This return embraces all property, except provisions and forage, and is to be sent to the Commissary-General *monthly*.

With this return will be enclosed one copy of each invoice and receipt for commissary property received and transferred in the month.

Dates of purchase, *names* of persons from whom procured, and *all articles* and *quantities* of commissary property bought in the month, *must be entered* on this return, in order that the *property* may be accounted for.

Vouchers for purchases of commissary property accompany Abstract of Contingencies. (Form 14.)

ACCOUNT CURRENT.

ABSTRACT OF PROVISIONS SOLD TO OFFICERS.
Form 8, p. 38.

This abstract will contain a statement of all sales made to officers during the month. It will be made out in *quadruplicate;* one copy to accompany the Account Current, one the Return of Provisions, and two to be filed with the corresponding retained papers. The amount of this abstract is to be credited on the Summary Statement and on the Account Current.

ABSTRACT OF PURCHASES.
Form 13, p. 42.

This abstract includes all provisions purchased for the hospital and for issue. Also the purchase of provisions from the savings of companies, the amount being paid to the captains thereof, on their receipt.

These savings go to the COMPANY FUND, and to that end, where practicable, returns may be made for back rations undrawn, and the provisions paid for by the Commissary.

ABSTRACT OF DISBURSEMENTS ON ACCOUNT OF CONTINGENCIES.
Form 14. p. 43

The form indicates the nature of this abstract. This and the foregoing abstract are entered on the debtor side of the account current.

ACCOUNT CURRENT.
Form 15, p. 44.

This account will show on the Dr. side the amount of expenditures made during the month, as shown by the two abstracts of Disbursements. The Cr. side will show the amount of money on hand when the last account was rendered, together with such sums as may have been received from officers, or in any other way, on account of army subsistence.

The account current will be accompanied with its abstracts, each supported by its proper vouchers.

The abstract of disbursements will be supported by

vouchers similar to that shown in Forms 16 to 19, according to the nature of the case.

These monthly papers will all be prepared as soon as practicable after the expiration of each month, and forwarded by mail.

The abstracts of issues will show the corps or detachment. When abstracts require more than one sheet, the sheets will be numbered in series, and not pasted together; the total at the foot of each carried to the head of the next, etc., etc.

All lists of subsistence shall run in this order: meat, bread-stuff, rice and beans, coffee, sugar, vinegar, candles, soap, salt, anti-scorbutics, purchases for hospitals, forage for cattle.

No charge for printing blanks, as forms, will be allowed.

A book will be kept by the commissary at each post, in which will be entered the monthly returns of provisions received and issued. It will show from whom the purchases have been made, and whether paid for. It is called the Commissary's book, and will not be removed from the post.

When any officer in the commissariat is relieved, he will close his property accounts; but money accounts will be kept open till the end of the month, unless he ceases to do duty in the department.

Stores longest on hand will be issued first.

Armorers, carriage-makers, and blacksmiths, of the Ordnance Department, are entitled to one and a half rations per day; all other enlisted men, one ration. Laundresses, one ration. No hired person shall draw more than one ration.

In order that the authorized women of companies may draw their rations while temporarily separated from their companies, the officer commanding the company must make a report to the commanding officer of the post where the women may be left, designating such as are to draw rations as attached to his company. Their rations are not commuted, and they can only draw them at a military post or station where there are supplies.

One ration a day may be issued to any person employed with the army, when the terms of his engagement require it, or on paying the full cost of the ration when he cannot otherwise procure food.

Lamps and oil to light a fort or garrison are not allowed from the Subsistence Department.

As soldiers are expected to preserve, distribute, and cook their own subsistence, the hire of citizens for any of these duties is not allowed, except in extreme cases. The expenses of bakeries are paid from the post fund, to which the profits accrue by regulations, such as purchase of hops, yeast, furniture; as sieves, cloths, &c., and the hire of bakers. *Ovens* may be built or paid for by the Subsistence Department, but not bake-houses.

Mode of ascertaining the cost at which the ration shall be credited the hospital, and commuted to soldiers while on furlough, cost of transporting stores not included; 100 complete rations consist of, say—

100 rations of pork or bacon are 75 pounds, at 6 cents............... } ¼ is	$4 75
100 rations of fresh beef are 125 pounds, at 4 cents..................	5 50
100 rations of flour are 187½ pounds, at 4 cents.....................	60
100 rations of beans or peas are 15 pounds, at 4 cents..............	
100 rations of rice are 10 pounds, at 5 cents............................. } ¼ is	40
100 rations of hominy are 10 pounds, at 3 cents.....................	
100 rations of coffee are 10 pounds, at 15 cents...................... } ¼ is	1 11
100 rations of tea are 1½ pounds, at 48 cents.........................	
100 rations of sugar are 15 pounds, at 8 cents........................	1 20
100 rations of vinegar are 4 quarts, at 4 cents........................	16
100 rations of adamantine candles are 1¼ pounds, at 20 cents..........	25
100 rations of soap are 4 pounds, at 5 cents...........................	20
100 rations of salt are 8½ pounds, at 1 cent...........................	4
100 rations of pepper are 4 ounces, at 1¼ cents......................	7
100 rations of potatoes are 30 pounds, at 2 cents.....................	60
100 rations of molasses are 1 quart, at 12 cents......................	.12
Cost of 100 rations...	$15 00

Or, one ration costs 15 cents.

The *proportions* here given are *fixed*, but the *prices* of the component parts of the ration are *variable*. The Commissary's invoices of stores received in the month will give the prices from which to calculate the cost of the ration for that month.

COMMUTATION OF RATIONS.

When a soldier is detached on duty, and it is impracticable to carry his subsistence with him, it will be commuted at seventy-five cents a day, to be paid by the commissary when due, or in advance, on the order of the commanding officer. The officer detaching the soldier will certify, on the voucher, that it is impracticable for him to carry his rations, and the voucher will show on its face the nature and extent of the duty the soldier was ordered to perform (see Form 16, p.   ).

Commutation will be allowed to soldiers while on furlough *by competent authority*, to medical cadets, to female nurses employed in permanent or general hospitals, and to persons entitled to rations when stationed where the Government has not provided subsistence for them, on satisfactory evidence that they have not received rations, or an equivalent therefor, during the time for which commutation is claimed. (Form 17.) The rate of commutation in these cases shall be *the cost* of the ration *at the station* where it is due. The authority competent to give a furlough is indicated in the General Regulations of the Army, or is announced from time to time in orders from the War Department. Payment of commutation to a soldier while on furlough shall not be made until he has returned to duty, or until he is discharged from the military service, when furloughed to that date; and when the voucher for payment is not accompanied by the furlough, the fact of payment, fully and officially attested, shall be entered *on the furlough*.

SPECIAL SERVICE.

The commanding officer will detail a suitable non-commissioned officer or private soldier for special service in the Subsistence Department, when such service is needed. The soldier so detailed will be under the orders of the Commissary, and will be exempt from company or garrison duty. No extra pay for this service is allowed.

VOUCHERS.

Purchases paid for.

Disbursements made for supplies and Commissary Property will be secured by duplicate vouchers shown by Form 22, p. 51.

Commissary Property purchased is entered on vouchers *separate* from those for the purchase of subsistence stores.

Subsistence supplies purchased by a Commissary or or agent, whether paid for or not, must be accounted for by him on the proper returns. (Forms 11 and 12.)

Receipts for money paid must be signed by a principal, and not by his clerk or any deputy.

Purchases not paid for.

The voucher for this class of purchases is shown by Form 23, p. 52.

In this voucher, the certificate will be signed by the officer making the purchase, and the receipt taken in the name of the officer who pays for the stores.

This voucher accompanies Abstract of Contingencies. (Form 14.)

Purchases for use of Hospital.

Purchases for a hospital may be paid for by a Commissary *to the extent* of its hospital credit, and must be confined to

1st. *Food*, solid or fluid, to be used for the diet of the sick, and not furnished by the Subsistence Department or Medical Department.

2d. Articles to be used in either *the preparation or serving* of the food, embracing principally cooking utensils and table furniture, and not furnished by the Quartermaster's Department or Medical Department.

3d. Gas, oil, and *other means of illumination*, to be used instead of candles, which are part of the soldier's ration.

No officer or agent in the military service shall purchase from *any other person* in the military service.

Form 20, p. 49, shows the voucher for this class of purchases.

Purchases of Savings from the Ration.

Form 21, p. 50, shows the voucher for purchase of company savings. It is signed in quadruplicate, and two copies used with Property Returns, the other two, with the receipt in duplicate, are to accompany the Account Current if the officer receiving the property pays for it. But if he should not pay for the purchase, the company commander retains two of the vouchers and presents them with the receipt to a Commissary having funds for such payments.

Sales of company savings, except to the Subsistence Department, are prohibited.

Molasses, green or desiccated vegetables, and all articles

furnished as a cure for or preventive of scurvy, *are not to be purchased as company savings.*

Disbursement for Services Rendered.

Form 18, p. 47, shows the receipt to be taken for payment made to the persons employed in the Commissary Department.

Period of service, rate of pay per day or month, nature of duty, etc., should be stated in this voucher.

When several persons (citizens) are employed by an officer during a month, the number of vouchers for payment of services rendered by them may be diminished by using Form 19.

A tax of three per cent on sums exceeding $50 a month must be deducted from the salaries of employees, and paid to the Commissioner of Internal Revenue.

This voucher, as well as that shown by Form 19, must be entered on the *Abstract of Contingencies.*

When a receipt on a Pay-roll or account is not signed by the hand of the party, the payment must be witnessed—the witness to be a commissioned officer when practicable.

When a hired person is discharged and not paid, a certified statement of his account, in duplicate, shall be given to him.

When practicable, persons hired in the military service shall be paid at the end of the calendar month, and when discharged.

Separate Pay-rolls shall be made for each month.

Receipt for Funds Transferred.

This is to be made out as shown by Form 3, p. 14.

The *amount* of funds received should always be expressed *in words.*

Receipts for Subsistence funds transferred (*one* receipt in each case of transfer) will be enclosed *with* the Account Current.

When there is a large number of receipts for funds transferred during a month, they may be entered on an Abstract, and the total amount of Abstract entered in Account Current, instead of the separate vouchers. The receipts accompany the Abstract and Account Current.

Stores Transferred to an Officer at the Same Station.

Subsistence Stores and Commissary Property transferred to an officer at the same post must be receipted for in duplicate according to Form 24, p. 53.

One copy of *each* receipt most accompany the "Return of Provisions."

Commissary Property must be *separately* receipted for.

The property will be *invoiced* to the officer receiving it, according to Form 25, p. 54, when transferred from one Commissary to another, at the same post or station.

Commissary Property must be *separately* invoiced.

Prices of stores must be expressed on the Invoice.

One copy of *each* Invoice must accompany the Return of Provisions.

Stores Transferred to a Quartermaster for Transportation.

Subsistence stores and Commissary property delivered to a Quartermaster for transportation to a Commissary of subsistence, will be receipted for in duplicate by the Quartermaster receiving them, according to Form 26, p. 55 the *Subsistence stores* and *Commissary property* being separately receipted for.

When the receipt of an officer to whom supplies have been sent is not received in time to accompany the issuing Commissary's Return of Provisions (or Return of Commissary Property), the Quartermaster's receipt for the packages shall accompany the Return, and the Commissary's receipt be forwarded to the Commissary-General as soon as received.

The stores so transferred will be Invoiced in quadruplicate by the transferring officer, pursuant to Form 27, p. 56. Two of the invoices will be delivered to the Quartermaster receiving the property, and two sent to the officer for whom they are intended. On receipt of the stores he will receipt to the transferring officer for them. *Commissary property* must be *separately* invoiced.

When supplies are to be conveyed to a distance by water, the name of the vessel carrying them should be stated on the Invoice. When the transportation is by land, it should be so stated on the invoice, and the route designated.

REQUISITION FOR SUBSISTENCE STORES.

This requisition will be made by the Commissary for the necessary subsistence required for his command for such number of days as he may deem necessary. The number of persons to be supplied will be given with such approximation to accuracy as may be practicable. It will be examined and approved by the post commander. Form 28, p. 57, shows this requisition.

SUBSISTENCE OF RECRUITS.

When subsistence cannot be advantageously issued by the Commissariat to recruiting parties, it will be procured by the officer in charge, on written contracts for complete rations. When a contract is for board *and* lodging, the amount to be paid for each must be *separately* mentioned therein; *board only* will be paid by the Subsistence Department.

Under circumstances rendering it impossible to make a contract, the recruiting officer may pay from subsistence funds the actual necessary expenses of *subsisting* his party.

When the recruiting officer does not disburse subsistence funds, the contractor will send to the Commissary-General for payment, monthly, his accounts for rations issued, accompanied by the Abstract of Issues, certified to by the recruiting officer. In that case, the expense of subsistence at branch rendezvous, and of advertising for proposals, etc., will be paid for by the contractor at the principal station, and included in his accounts.

Issues of subsistence will be made on the usual ration returns, and board will be furnished on a return showing the number of men and of days, dates, etc.

Contractors' Account for Complete Rations.

Form 30, p. 59, shows this account, which will be paid by the recruiting officer, if he have funds for that purpose. Otherwise the contractor will send his account to the Commissary-General with his Abstract of Issues. The Commissary paying this account will enter it on his Abstract of Contingencies.

Contractors' Abstract of Issues.

Form 31, p. 60, shows this abstract, which is to be made out monthly, and sent to the Commissary-General, when the recruiting officer has not funds to pay the account. The Abstract will be compared with the original Ration Returns by the recruiting officer, who will certify thereto.

CONTRACT FOR COMPLETE RATIONS.

Form 32, p. 61, shows the manner of preparing this contract.

CONTRACT FOR FRESH BEEF.

This contract is made out in accordance with Form 33, p. 62.

When a firm is contracting, the full names of the individuals composing it will be stated in the contract, together with the business name or style of the copartnership.

FORM OF BOND.

Bonds for the faithful performance of contracts will be prepared, as shown in Form 34, p. 63.

Bonds to contracts for subsistence supplies shall be executed *in duplicate;* one copy *to be retained* by the contracting officer or agent, and the other to be sent to the Commissary-General of Subsistence with the copies of the contract required to be furnished him.

The name of the contractor (or names of contractors, as the case may be) will be inserted in the bond, *in addition* to the names of at least two sureties thereto.

The foregoing forms will be observed in all contracts for subsistence supplies, with the variations which circumstances may make necessary.

ESTIMATE OF FUNDS FOR PURCHASING FRESH BEEF, ETC.

This estimate will be made pursuant to Form 29, p. 58, and will be examined and approved by the *Commander of the Post.* In making the estimate, the approximate number of troops that will have to be supplied must be arrived at as accurately as practicable, and the number of issues of fresh beef per month, considered.

ABSTRACT OF PURCHASES.
Form 9, p. 39.

This abstract, which is to accompany the Return of Provisions, must contain all the provisions purchased during the month, whether paid for or not. If not paid for, it must be so stated in the "Remarks." The vouchers for purchases do not accompany this abstract

Should the purchases made by the Commissary be but few, and easily entered on the "Return," then this Abstract will not be required, and consequently need not be prepared.

The Abstract of *purchases paid for* (Form 13, p. 42) contains only those purchases for which disbursements have been made, and must, of course, be accompanied by the vouchers for the payments. This Abstract is to accompany the Account Current.

Vouchers to this Abstract embrace stores purchased by an officer or agent, *and paid for by him*. Vouchers for the *payment*, on a certificate, of articles purchased *by another officer*, should be entered on Abstract of Contingencies. (Form 14.)

DUPLICATE PAPERS.

All of the foregoing Abstracts, Returns and Accounts are to be prepared in *duplicate*. One set for transmission to the Commissary-General of Subsistence, and the other set to be retained by the officer rendering the accounts. To this end all vouchers will be taken in duplicate, except those for purchase of company savings, which will be made out in *quadruplicate*.

CORRESPONDENCE, ETC.

Disbursing officers and agents of the Subsistence Department are required *to retain* one complete set of official papers for reference or other use.

No charge for printing blank forms will be allowed. When practicable to provide them, these forms will be furnished officers by the Subsistence Bureau. When officers are not thus furnished, they must *rule out* forms for use from the public stationery to correspond with those prescribed. The want of printed blanks will furnish no excuse to an officer for delay or failure in the rendition of his Returns or Accounts.

The envelops of all *official* communications to the Commissary-General of Subsistence will be marked "Official," with the signature thereto of the officer writing the communication.

Under existing laws, packages to the Commissary-General of Subsistence on official business are carried in the United States mail *free of postage*, and should be intrusted to the Post Office Department for delivery whenever practicable. Packages for the Commissary-General of Subsistence, on official business, will not be committed to express agencies for delivery unless all charges for the service are *prepaid*.

Postage and dispatches by telegraph on public business, paid by an officer, will be refunded to him *by the Quartermaster's Department*. These expenses are not to be paid for with subsistence funds.

Officers doing duty in the Subsistence Department should be particular to forward with their Returns and Accounts, in addition to the required vouchers, all orders of commanding officers, and other papers, upon which they may rely to relieve themselves from responsibility.

An official letter addressed to the Commissary-General of Subsistence, whenever its length will permit, shall be written on a half-sheet of letter paper, and shall refer to one matter only.

The *post-office* address of an officer's station shall be given in his official letters. "In the field," "Headquarters ———," "Camp ———," and other similar indefinite expressions of locality, do not of themselves indicate *the place* at or near which an officer is stationed.

Persons in the military service, when signing official letters, Returns, Accounts, etc., should write their names *plainly*. Underneath the name, their rank, company, and regiment, corps, or other official designation, should be written *legibly*. Official papers shall be signed *by the officer* to whom they belong, and not by his clerk or any deputy. A *regimental* officer on staff duty (a Commissary to a brigade or division, for example) should not omit to write under his signature *the number* of his regiment, and the *State, District,* or *Territory* to which it belongs.

LETTER ENCLOSING RETURNS, ETC., TO THE COMMISSARY-GENERAL OF SUBSISTENCE.

Hagerstown, Washington County, Md.,
February 10, 1863.

SIR:

I have the honor to transmit herewith the following papers pertaining to duty in the Subsistence Department for the month of January, 1863.

Return of Provisions, received, issued, etc.
Abstract of Purchases.
Abstract of Issues to Volunteers.
Abstract of Issues to Hospital.
Abstract of Sales to Officers.
Summary Statement of Funds.
Return of Commissary Property.

Very respectfully, sir,
Your obedient servant,
JOHN W. SMITH,
Lieut. and R. Q. M.
31st Reg't Ohio Vols., A. C. S.

To ——— ———,
Commissary-General of Subsistence,
Washington City, D. C.

MISCELLANEOUS ITEMS.

A box, 24 by 16 inches square, and 28 inches deep, will contain one barrel, or 10,752 cubic inches.

A box, 16 by 16.8 inches square, and 8 inches deep, will contain one bushel, or 2,150 cubic inches.

A box, 8 by 8.4 inches square, and 8 inches deep, will contain one peck, or 537.6 cubic inches.

A box, 5 by 5 inches square, and 4.6 inches deep, will contain a half gallon, or 115.5 cubic inches.

A box, 4 by 4 inches square, and 3.6 inches deep, will contain one quart, or 57.75 inches.

The army wagon being 22 x 42 x 114 inches, inside measurement, boxes for bacon, made 20 x 20 x 28 inches outside measurement (which will contain 225 pounds of bacon) are convenient for *field* transportation. The boxes should be strapped, and the material be one and one-fourth inch thick, tongued and grooved.

Rate per bushel at which certain cereals, esculent roots, etc., shall be estimated.

One bushel of corn (on the cob) at 70 pounds.
" " corn (shelled) at 56 "
" " corn-meal " 50 "
" " hominy " 45 "
" " rye " 56 "
" " buckwheat " 52 "
" " barley " 48 "
" " wheat ⎫
" " beans ⎪
" " peas ⎪
" " onions ⎪
" " beets ⎬ " 60 "
" " carrots ⎪
" " turnips ⎪
" " potatoes ⎪
" " fine salt ⎭
" " bran " 20 "
" " malt " 38 "
" " dried apples " 24 "
" " dried peaches ⎫ " 32 "
" " oats ⎭
Ten gallons pickled onions " 83 "
" sour krout " 81 "

RATION RETURN.

FORM 1.—RATION RETURN.

Ration Return for Captain A. B's, Company A, 3d Regiment of Artillery, for ten days, commencing 21st day of June, 186 , and ending 30th day of June, 186 .

POST OR STATION.	Number of men.	Number of women.	Total.	Number of days.	Number of rations.	RATIONS OF— Pork.	Salt beef.	Fresh beef.	Bacon.	Hard bread.	Flour.	Beans.	Rice.	Coffee.	Tea.	Sugar.	Vinegar.	Candles. Sperm.	Candles. Adamantine.	Candles. Tallow.	Soap.	Salt.	Desic'd potatoes.	Mixed vegetables.	REMARKS.
Camp Scott........	60	3	63	10	630	630	630			630		630			630	630	630		630		630	630			

The A. C. S. will issue agreeably to the above return.

A. B., *Commanding Company.*

Commanding Post.

NOTE.—A similar return is made for detachments and hospital; and if rations are drawn for a commissioned officer, his name, rank, and regiment or corps must be mentioned under Remarks.

FORM 2.—CONSOLIDATED RATION RETURN.

Consolidated Ration Return for Second Regiment of Cavalry, for Ten days, commencing 21st June, 186 , and ending June 30th, 186 .

POST OR STATION.	Number of men.	Number of women.	Total.	Number of days.	Number of rations.	RATIONS OF— Fresh beef.	Pork.	Flour.	Beans.	Rice.	Coffee.	Sugar.	Vinegar.	Candles.	Soap.	Salt.	REMARKS.

The A. C. S. will issue on the above return.

————, *Commanding Officer.*

————, *Commanding Regiment.*

ABSTRACT OF PROVISIONS ISSUED.

FORM 4.—ABSTRACT OF PROVISIONS ISSUED.

Abstract of Provisions issued from the first day of June, 186 , to the 30th day of June, 186 , to the Troops of the United States stationed at the post of Fort Pike, by Captain A. B., A. C. S.

Date.	No. of return.	No. of men.	No. of women.	Total.	No. of day's drawn for.	Commencing.	Ending.	Rations of pork.		Rations of fresh beef.		Rations of bacon.		Rations of flour.		Rations of hard bread.		Rations of beans.		Rations of rice.		Rations of coffee.		Rations of sugar.		Rations of vinegar.		Rations of candles (sperm or tallow).		Rations of soap.		Rations of salt.		REMARKS.
								bbls	lbs	lbs	oz	lbs	oz	bbls	lbs	lbs	oz	bush	qts	lbs	oz	lbs	oz	lbs	oz	gals	qts	lbs	oz	lbs	oz	bush	qts	

Total No. of rations..........

Quantity in bulk..........

I hereby certify that I have carefully compared the above abstract with the original returns now in my possession, and find that they amount to rations of fresh beef, rations of pork, rations of flour, rations of hard bread, rations of beans, rations of bacon, rations of coffee, rations of sugar, rations of vinegar, rice, rations of soap, rations of salt. candles (sperm or tallow),

——————, Commanding.

ISSUES TO CITIZENS.

FORM 5.—ABSTRACT OF PROVISIONS ISSUED TO CITIZENS.

Abstract of Provisions issued to citizens employed with the Army at ——————, in the month of ——————, 186—, by Lieut. A —————— B ——————, Regiment of ——————, A. C. S.

186_.	No. of return.	No. of men.	No. of days.	Commencing.	Ending.	RATIONS OF—																Remarks.
						Pork.		Fresh beef.		Flour.		Beans.		Rice.		Coffee.		Sugar.		Vinegar.	Adamantine candles.	Soap.	Salt.	Pepper.	
						lbs.	ozs.	lbs.	ozs.	lbs.	ozs.	lbs.	ozs.	lbs.	ozs.	lbs.	ozs.	lbs.	ozs.	galls.	lbs. ozs.	lbs. ozs.	lbs. ozs.	lbs. ozs.	
	1	5	5	Jan. 1..	Jan. 5..																				Teamsters in Q. M. Department.
	2	4	5	3..	7..																				Laborers in Q. M. Department.
	3	2	3	10..	12..																				Laborers in Subsistence Dep't.

No. of Rations: ....

Quantity in bulk.......

I certify that I have carefully compared the above "Abstract" with the original ration returns now in my possession, and find that they amount to —————— rations of Pork, —————— rations of Fresh Beef, —————— rations of Flour, —————— rations of Beans, —————— rations of Rice, —————— rations of Coffee, —————— rations of Sugar, —————— rations of Vinegar, —————— rations of Adamantine Candles, —————— rations of Soap, —————— rations of Salt, —————— rations of Pepper.

C ——————, D ——————, Col.— Reg't of ——————, Com'g Post.

ABSTRACT OF EXTRA ISSUES.   35

FORM 6.—ABSTRACT OF EXTRA ISSUES.

Abstract of Extra Issues at ——, in the month of ——, 186 , by Lieut. A. B., — Regiment of ——, A. C. S.

186 .	No. of return.	No. of men.	No. of animals.	No. of weeks.	Adam'ntine Candles. lbs.	Salt. lbs.	Salt. ozs.	Whiskey. galls.	Whiskey. qts.	Remarks.
	1	48	49	4	12	24	8	1	2	Company H, 2d Ohio Volunteer Infantry.
	2				12					Mules belonging to the Quartermaster's Dep't.
	3				10					Guard at Fort ——, Virginia.
	4				40					Guard at Camp ——, District of Columbia.
	5									Headquarters, 3d Regiment, Pennsylvania Cavalry.
	6									Headquarters, Army of the Potomac.

Quantity..............

I certify that I have carefully compared the above "Abstract" with the original returns for Extra Issues now in my possession, and find that they amount to —— pounds of Adamantine Candles, —— pounds and —— ounces of Salt, —— gallons and —— quarts of Whiskey.

D. D., Col. — Reg't of ——,Com'g Post.

FORM 7.—ABSTRACT OF PROVISIONS ISSUED

Abstract of Provisions issued during the month of October, 186 , to men in ———— ————, Assistant Surgeon, U. S. Army, by

Number of return.	Number of men.	Number of days drawn for.	Commencing.	Ending.	Total number of rations due hospital.	RATIONS ACTUALLY REQUIRED FOR CONSUMPTION IN THE HOSPITAL											
						Rations of pork.	Rations of fresh beef.	Rations of flour.	Rations of hard bread.	Rations of rice.	Rations of coffee.	Rations of sugar.	Rations of vinegar.	Rations of candles.	Rations of soap.	Rations of salt.	Gallons of molasses.
1	5	8	Oct. 18	Oct. 25	40	40	...	80	10	40	40	40	40	40	40	40	...
2	...	..	" 18	....	.....	.....	...	......	..	.....	....	.....	.....	.....	.....	.....	2
3	27	4	" 20	" 23	108	108	...	108	..	108	108	108	108	108	108	108	..
4	78	6	" 20	" 25	468	100	168	468	..	368	200	468	300	468	468	200	..
5	46	4	" 22	" 25	184	.....	84	130	..	84	184	184	.....	184	184	.....	..
6	122	6	" 26	" 30	732	130	300	697	..	.....	402	732	.....	732	732	400	10
7	...	..	....	....	.....	.....	...	......	..	.....	....	.....	.....	.....	.....	.....	..
8	...	..	....	....	.....	.....	...	......	..	.....	....	84	.....	.....	.....	100	..

Total rations due hospital	1532

Total quantity issued........		378	552	1433	10	700	934	1616	448	1532	1532	848	12

		Barrels.	Pounds.	Ounces.	Pounds.	Barrels.	Pounds.	Ounces.	Pounds.	Pounds.	Pounds.	Ounces.	Gallons.	Quarts.	Gills.	Pounds.	Ounces.	Pounds.	Ounces.	Quarts.	Gills.	Gallons.
Quantity in bulk......... ...		1	83	8	690	8	44	2	10	70	56	198	14	4	1	7	15	5	61	4	16	7	12

I certify, on honor, that I have carefully compared the above "abstract" with the original .... enty-eight rations of pork, five hundred and fifty-two rations of fresh beef, fourteen hundred and .... rice, nine hundred and thirty-four rations of coffee, sixteen hundred and sixteen rations of sugar, ... rations of candles, fifteen hundred and thirty-two rations of soap, eight hundred and forty-eight .... to two dollars and seventy-eight cents, were required by me for, and issued to, the sick; and that Compared with returns of men in hospital, and found correct.

——— ————, *Commanding.*

TO MEN IN HOSPITAL.

hospital at , under the charge of —— ——, Lieutenant J. T. J., 3d Infantry, A. C. S.

REMARKS.

A MONTHLY STATEMENT OF THE HOSPITAL FUND.

Dr. To balance due hospital last month					$0	00
1532 rations, being whole amount due this month, at 9½ cents per ration					145	54
ISSUED.						
Cr. By the following provisions, at contract prices:						
283½ pounds of pork, at 6 cents per pound			$17	01		
690 pounds of fresh beef, at 4 cents per pound			27	60		
1612¼ pounds of flour, at 2 cents per pound			32	24½		
10 pounds of hard bread, at 3½ cents per pound				35		
70 pounds of rice, at 6 cents per pound			4	20		
56 pounds of coffee, at 9 cents per pound			5	04		
193⅞ pounds of sugar, at 8 cents per pound			15	51		
17⅛ quarts of vinegar, at 5 cents per quart				85⅝		
15 5/16 pounds of candles, at 12 cents per pound			1	83¾		
61⅛ pounds of soap, at 6 cents per pound			3	67¼		
16⅞ quarts of salt, at 3 cents per quart				50⅝		
12 gallons of molasses, at 28 cents per gallon			3	36		
			112	18¾		
PURCHASED.						
2 pairs of chickens, at 87½ cents per pair	$1	75				
4 quarts of milk, at 7 cents per quart		28				
3 doz. oranges, at 25 cents per dozen	..	75	2	78		
Total expended	..	..	......	......	114	96¾
Balance due this month					30	57¼

returns now in my possession, and find that they amount to three hundred and sev- thirty-three rations of flour, ten rations of hard bread, seven hundred rations of four hundred and forty-eight rations of vinegar, fifteen hundred and thirty-two rations of salt, and twelve gallons of molasses; and that the purchases, amounting the rations drawn in kind were actually required for consumption in the hospital.

J. C. J., *Asst. Surgeon U. S. Army.*

(Duplicates.)

FORM 8.—ABSTRACT OF PROVISIONS SOLD TO OFFICERS.

Abstract of Provisions sold to officers at Camp Scott, during the month of June, 186 , by Captain A.B., A.C.S.

Articles and quantities sold.	Amount.	
	Dollars.	Cents.
——pounds of pork...............		
——pounds of fresh pork........		
——barrels of flour...............		
——bushels of beans.............		
——pounds of soap...............		
——pounds of candles............		
——bushels of salt................		
——gallons of vinegar............		
——pounds of sugar..............		
——pounds of coffee..............		
Total...............		

I certify that the above is a correct statement of all sales of subsistence stores made to officers at this post during the month of June, 1861.

————————, A. C. S.

I certify that I have compared the above abstract with the officers' certified list of purchases for their own use and the use of their families, and find the abstract correct.

————————, Commanding.

ABSTRACT OF PURCHASES.

FORM 9.—ABSTRACT OF PURCHASES.

Abstract of Purchases made on account of Subsistence of the Army, by Captain A. B., A.C.S., at Camp Scott, in the month of June, 186 .

Date.	Number.	From whom purchased.	Fresh Beef. Pounds.	Pork. Barrels.	Flour. Barrels.	Beans. Bushels.	Rice. Pounds.	Coffee. Pounds.	Sugar. Pounds.	Vinegar. Gallons.	Candles. Pounds.	Soap. Pounds.	Salt. Bushels.	Pairs of Chickens.	Hay. Pounds.	Corn. Bushels.	Amount. Dollars.	Cents.	Remarks.
		Total amount......																	

I certify that the purchases were made agreeably to the above "Abstract," and at the lowest market-price; also, that I am wholly uninterested in them, and that the "Remarks" opposite to each are correct.

A——— B———,
Captain, and A. C. S.

Form 10.—Monthly Summary Statement.

Monthly Summary Statement of Funds received and disbursed at Camp Scott, in the month of June, 186 .

To amount disbursed this month.......	760	00	By balance as per last statement.......	150	00
			By cash received from the treasury of the United States this month	800	00
To balance due the United States.......	300	00	By cash from agents, sales, &c.	110	00
	1060	00		1060	00

I certify that the above is a true statement of all moneys received and expended by me on account of subsistence during the month, and the balance is in

————, *Assistant Commissary of Subsistence.*

FORM 11.—RETURN OF COMMISSARY PROPERTY.

Return of Commissary Property, received, issued, and remaining on hand, at Camp Scott, during the month of ———, 186–, by Captain A. B., A. C. S.

FROM WHOM RECEIVED.	Date.	No. of voucher.	STATIONERY.	OFFICE FURNITURE.	SCALES, WEIGHTS, ETC.	TOOLS.
On hand per last return						
Total to be accounted for......						
Total issued and expended.....						
Remaining on hand........						

I certify that the above return is correct, and that the articles specified were actually and necessarily expended in the public service.

A. B., *A. C. S.*

FORM 13.—ABSTRACT OF PURCHASES. PAID FOR.

Abstract of Purchases made on account of Subsistence of the Army, by Captain A. B., A.C.S., at Camp Scott, in the month of January, 186 .

Date.	Number.	From whom purchased.	Fresh Beef. Pounds.	Pork. Barrels.	Flour. Barrels.	Beans. Bushels.	Rice. Pounds.	Coffee. Pounds.	Tea. Lbs.—oz.	Sugar. Pounds.	Vinegar. Gallons.	Candles. Pounds.	Soap. Pounds.	Salt. Bushels.	Hay. Pounds.	Corn. Bushels.	Chickens. Pairs of	Amount. Dollars.	Cents.
		Total amount..																	

I certify that the purchases were made agreeably to the above abstract, and that the sums were actually paid as charged; and also that I was wholly uninterested in the purchases, and that the articles were purchased at the lowest market price

A. B., *Captain, and A. C. S.*

PAGE

Retu:

DATE.

186 .

Oct. 16
" 20
" 31
" 31
" 31
" 31

To

Oct. 31
" 31
" 31
" 31
" 31
" 31
" 15
" 13
" 23
" 31

To

FORM 12.—RETURN OF PROVISIONS.

Return of Provisions received, issued, and remaining on hand at ———, during the month of ———, by ———, Assistant Commissary of Subsistence, United States Army

I certify, on honor, that the above return is correct and just.

A. C. S.

FORM 14.—ABSTRACT OF DISBURSEMENTS ON ACCOUNT OF CONTINGENCIES.

Abstract of Disbursements, on account of Contingencies, by Lieut. A. B., Assistant Commissary of Subsistence, in the month of ———, 186–.

Date.	No. of voucher.	To whom paid.	On what account.	Remarks.	Amount.
			Commutation of rations.		
			Weights and measures.		
			Clerk...............	By authority, May 16, '61	
			Stationery.		
			Per diem to extra-duty men.		
					$

I certify that the above is correct.   A. B., *Lieut., 3d Regiment Artillery*,
  Assistant Commissary of Subsistence.

FORM 15.—ACCOUNT CURRENT.

Dr. The United States, on account of Army Subsistence, in the month of ———, 186 , **Cr.**
in account with Lieut. A. B., 3d Regiment Artillery, A. C. S., at Camp Scott, Va.

Date.		Dolls.	Cts.	Date.		Dolls.	Cts.
186 .	To Abstract No. 1. " " 2.			186 .	By Cash on hand last account. By Cash received from Lieut. A. D., *A. C. S.*		
	Balance due U. S.						

I certify that the above account current exhibits an accurate and true statement of all money received and expended by me on account of the subsistence of the army, not heretofore accounted for; and that the balance of   dollars and   cents is due from   , and is deposited in   in   funds.

A. B., *Assistant Commissary of Subsistence.*

Form 16.—Account for Commutation.

The United States,

To Sergeant James H. McMullen, Dr.

Date.		
186 . June 30.	For commutation of rations while on detached service, returning to his branch rendezvous, en route from ———— to ————, from the 8th to the 12th June, 1861 —five days, 75 cents per day..........	$3 75

I certify that the above account is correct; that the commutation was made by my order, and was necessary for the public service, it being impracticable to take rations in kind.

————, *Recruiting Officer.*

Received at ————, 30th June, 186 , from ————, three dollars and seventy five cents, in full of the above.

JAMES H. McMULLEN.

NOTE.—A similar form to the above will be used without a certificate for all purchases for services rendered; a similar form with a certificate signed A. C. S., stating that the services were rendered as charged for, and where necessary for the public service.

COMMUTATION OF RATIONS.

FORM 17.—COMMUTATION OF RATIONS FOR SOLDIER ON FURLOUGH.

The United States

To Private JAMES WELCH, of Company F, 6th Infantry,   Dr.

	Dolls.	Cts.
186 .		
February 5.. For commutation of rations while on furlough, from Jan. 27 to February 5, 186 , inclusive, ten days, at fifteen cents per day, the cost of the ration.............	1	50
(NOTE.—The soldier's furlough should be attached to the voucher for payment of commutation. When this is not practicable, the Commissary who pays the commutation will endorse on the furlough, over his official signature, the *date* and *amount of* payment.)		
	1	50

I certify that the above account is correct and just; that Private James Welch has not received rations in kind, or an equivalent in money therefor, during the time above specified, and that he was on furlough for the period mentioned, by authority of ——.

A. B., *Captain Company F, 6th Infantry.*

Received, at ——, this — day of ——, 186 , from Lieutenant C. D. —— Regiment of ——, A. C. S., — dollars and cents, in full of the above account.
(Signed in duplicate,) .

JAMES WELCH, *Private Company F, 6th Infantry.*

PAYMENT FOR SERVICES.

FORM 18.—VOUCHER FOR PAYMENT FOR SERVICES.

The United States

To ———— ,   DR.

186 .		Dolls.	Cts.
May 6......	For services in the Subsistence Department, as Clerk to Capt. H. N., C. S. Vols., from May 1 to include June 6, 186 , one month and six days, at seventy-five dollars a month.........	90	00
	Deduct direct tax..		90
		89	10

I certify that the above account is correct and just; that the services were rendered as stated, were necessary for the public service, and have been paid for by me as charged.

H. N., *Captain and C. S. Vols.*

Received, at ————, this ———— day of ————, 186 , from Captain H. N., C. S. Vols., ———— dollars and ———— cents, in full of the above account.
(Signed in duplicate.)

Form 19.—Pay Roll of Men Employed.

We, the subscribers, do hereby acknowledge to have received at ——, from Lieut. A. B., —— Regiment of ——, A. C. S., the amounts set opposite to our names, respectively, in full of our pay for services in the Subsistence Department during the period herein expressed, having signed duplicates hereof.

No.	Names.	Occupation.	Period of service.				Compensation.				Amount.				Signers' names.	Witnesses.
			From——	To——	Days.	Months.	Per day.		Per month.		Stoppages.		Received.			
							Dolls.	Cts.	Dolls.	Cts.	Dolls.	Cts.	Dolls.	Cts.		
186.																
Month.																
													Amount........			

I certify that the above is a correct Pay-Roll of citizens employed in the Subsistence Department, under my direction, in the month of ——, 186 ; that their services were rendered as stated, were necessary for the public service, and that the "amount" was actually paid by me to each, as charged.

Examined and approved.
C. D., *Colonel* — Reg't of ——, *Comand'g Post.* (Signed in duplicate.)

A. B., *Lieut.* — Reg't of ——, A. C. S.

PURCHASES FOR HOSPITAL. 49

FORM 20.—VOUCHER FOR PURCHASES FOR HOSPITAL.

The United States

To ———,   Dr.

186 .		Dolls.	Cts.
	For four chickens, at twenty-five cents each........	1	00
	two dozen eggs, at eighteen cents per dozen........		36
	two pounds of butter, at twenty-five cents per pound........		50
	twelve common cups and saucers........		50
	four quarts of milk, at seven cents per quart........		28
	three dozen oranges, at twenty-five cents per dozen........		75
		3	39

I certify that the above-specified articles were purchased, on my requisition, for the use of the sick in hospital, under my charge, and that the expenditure was warranted by the amount of hospital credit due at the time.

E. E., *Surgeon* ———.

Received at ———, this — day of ———, 186 , from Lieut. A. B.. —— Regiment of ———, A. C. S., —— dollars and —— cents, in full of the above account.

(Signed in duplicate.)

FORM 21.—VOUCHER FOR PURCHASE OF COMPANY SAVINGS.

The United States To ——— Company, ——— Regiment of ———.

	Dolls.	Cts.
186 . For		

I certify that the articles above specified are the actual savings of my company for the month of ———, 186 .
Examined.
                H. R., *Capt.* ——— *Reg't of* ———, *Comd'g Company.*
  C. D., *Col.* ——— *Reg't of* ———, *Com'g Post.*

I certify that the above account is correct and just; that the articles and quantities specified have been taken up on my Return of Provisions for the month of ———, 186 , and that I have not paid the account.
(Signed in quadruplicate.)   M. N., *Capt. and C. S. Vols.*

Received at ———, this ——— day of ———, 186 , from Capt. R. T., C. S., ——— dollars and ——— cents, in full of the above account.
(Signed in duplicate.)   E. F., *Lieut.* ——— *Reg't of* ———, *Com'g Company.*

SUPPLIES PAID FOR.   51

FORM 22.—VOUCHER FOR SUPPLIES PAID FOR.

The United States   DR.

To LEONARD WALLACE

186 .		Dolls.	Cts.
January 1...	For ten barrels pork, at twelve dollars per barrel.............................	120	00
	five beef cattle, aggregate net weight 2,500 pounds, at four cents per pound, net.....	100	00
	one hundred pounds of sugar, at eight cents per pound............................	8	00
	twenty pounds of adamantine candles, at twenty cents per pound...................	4	00
	five tons of hay, at fifteen dollars per ton.....................................	75	00
		307	00

Received, at Baltimore, Md., January 1, 1863, of Capt. B. N., C. S., three hundred and seven dollars, in full of the above account.

LEONARD WALLACE.

(Signed in duplicate.)

Form 23.—Voucher for Supplies not Paid for.

The United States

To James Parker, Jr.   Dr.

186 .		Dolls.	Cts.
January 3...	For one hundred pounds of fresh beef, at four cents per pound............. two barrels of flour, at seven dollars and eighty-four cents per barrel............. four gallons of vinegar, at sixteen cents per gallon............. one hundred pounds of salt, at one cent per pound.............	4 15 1	00 68 64 00
		21	32

I certify that the above account for twenty-one dollars and thirty-two cents is correct and just, and has not been paid by me for want of funds; that the articles specified were purchased at the lowest market price, and will be accounted for on my Return of Provisions for the month of January, 186 . The purchase was necessary for the following reasons: ——

Approved: A. B., *Lieut. 4th Reg't of Infantry, A. C. S.*
　　　　C. D., *Col. 4th Reg't of Infantry, Com'g Post.*
Received, at ——, this —— day of ——, 186 , from Capt. ——, C. S., —— dollars and —— cents, in full of the above account.
(Signed in duplicate.)

FORM 24.—RECEIPT FOR STORES TRANSFERRED.

Received at ————, this ——— day of ———, 186—, from Lieut. A. B., ——— Regiment of ———, A. C. S., the following Subsistence Stores.

No. of packages.	Articles and quantities.
————	Pork............................ ———— pounds..
————	Bacon........................... ———— pounds..
————	Ham............................. ———— do.....
————	Salt beef........................ ————
————	Flour............................ ————
————	Corn meal....................... ———— pounds..

C. D., Lieut. ——— Reg't of ———, A. C. S.

(Signed in duplicate.)

FORM 25.—INVOICE OF STORES TRANSFERRED.

Invoice of Subsistence Stores transferred at ———, this ——— day of ———, 186 , by Lieut. A. B., ——— Regiment of ———, A. C. S., to Lieut. C. D., ——— Regiment of ———, A. C. S.

No. of packages.	Articles and quantities.	Cost.	
		Dolls.	Cts.
	Pork................................ per barrel....		
	Bacon........ ——— pounds .... " pound....		
	Ham........ ——— pounds .... " "		
	Salt beef............................ " barrel....		
	Flour................................ " "		
	Corn meal........ ——— pounds .... " pound....		

A. B., *Lieut.* ———, *Reg't of* ———, A. C. S.

(Signed in duplicate.)

FORM 26.—QUARTERMASTER'S RECEIPT FOR STORES.

Received at ———, this ——— day of ———, 186—, from Capt. C. D., C. S., in good order and condition, the undermentioned packages of Subsistence Stores, for transportation and delivery to Lieut. A. B., ——— Regiment of ———, A. C. S., at ———.

Mark.	No. of pages.	Articles and quantities.
A. C. S., Fort ———.	100 barrels	Pork..
	50 sacks	Bacon.. 5,000 pounds.
	50 barrels	Flour..
	75 sacks	Beans... 9,000 "
	25 boxes	Soap.. 1,000 "
	10 kegs	Molasses....................................... 80 gallons.

E. F., *Capt. and A. Q. M.*

(Signed in duplicate.)

FORM 27.—INVOICE OF STORES TO QUARTERMASTER.

Invoice of Subsistence Stores transferred at ——, this —— day of ——, 186 , to Capt. E. F., A. Q. M. for transportation and delivery to Lieut. A. B., —— Regiment of ——, A. C. S., at ——.

Mark.	No. of packages.	Articles and quantities.	Cost.		Gross Weight in lbs.
			Dollars.	Cents.	
A. C. S., Fort ——.	100 barrels	Pork................................ per barrel..			
	50 sacks	Bacon........ 5,000 pounds........ " pound..			
	50 barrels	Flour................................ " barrel..			
	75 sacks	Beans........ 9,000 pounds........ " pound..			
	25 boxes	Soap........ 1,000 " .... " pound..			
	10 kegs	Molasses........ 80 gallons........ " gallon..			

(Signed in quadruplicate.)

C. D., *Capt. and C. S.*

FORM 28.—REQUISITION FOR STORES.

Requisition for Subsistence Stores for the use of Troops, etc., at ———, for ——— days, commencing the ——— day of ———, 186 , and ending the ——— day of ———, 186 .

Station.	No. to be supplied.	No. of days.	No. of rations.	Pork.	Bacon.	Ham.	Salt beef.	Flour.	Hard bread.	Beans.	Peas.	Rice.	Hominy.	Coffee, green.	Coffee, roasted and ground.	Tea.	Sugar, brown.	Sugar, white.	Vinegar.	Candles, sperm.	Candles, adamantine.	Soap.	Salt.	Pepper.	Potatoes, fresh.	Molasses.	Desiccated potatoes.	Mixed vegetables.	Whisky.	Remarks.
For issue to troops..																														Fresh beef is obtained at the post by contract.
" citizens.																														
" extra...																														
Sales to officers.....																														
No. of rations needed for use																														
No. of rations on hand......																														
No. of rations to be furnished																														

Examined and approved.

C. D., Col. ———, Reg't of ———, Com'g Post.

A. B., Lieut. ———, Reg't of ———, A. C. S.

ESTIMATE OF FUNDS.

FORM 29.—ESTIMATE OF FUNDS REQUIRED.

Estimate of funds required for purchasing fresh beef, and for contingencies, at ———, in the month of ———, 186 .

Troops.	Number of troops.	Number of days.	Number of rations per day.	Number of pounds per day.	Number of pounds required.	Price per pound.	Amount.		Stationery.	Hospital.	Amount required.		Remarks.
						Cts.	Dolls.	Cts.	Dolls.	Dolls.	Dolls.	Cts.	
Company H, 2d Artillery.... 40th Reg't Pa. Vol. Infantry. 3d Reg't Ohio Cavalry....... Stationery................ Hospital contingencies......													

Amount required for use............................
Probable amount that will be on hand month ending ————, 186 ,............
Amount to be furnished............

Examined and approved.
    C. D., *Col.* —— *Reg't of* ——, *Commanding Post.*
                                        A. B., *Lieut.* —— *Reg't of* ——, *A. C. S.*

CONTRACTOR'S ACCOUNT.   59

FORM 30.—CONTRACTOR'S ACCOUNT FOR COMPLETE RATIONS.

The United States   DR.

To JAMES GORDON, Contractor,

186 .	For rations issued in the month of ——, 186 , to recruits at ——, under command of Lieut. A. B., —— Regiment of ——, Recruiting Officer, as per accompanying Abstract: —— complete rations, at —— cents per ration................................. Due contractor.............................	Dolls.	Cts.

Received, at ——, this —— day of ——, 186 , from the United States (or Lieut. A. B., —— Regiment of ——, Recruiting Officer), —— dollars and —— cents, in full of the above account.

JAMES GORDON, *Contractor.*

(Signed in duplicate.)

FORM 31.—CONTRACTOR'S ABSTRACT OF COMPLETE RATIONS ISSUED.

Abstract of complete rations issued to recruits at ———, under command of Lieut. A. B., ——— Regiment of ———, by James Gordon, Contractor.

No. of return.	No. of men.	No. of days.	Commencing.	Ending.	No. of complete rations.	REMARKS.
186 .						

Number of complete rations furnished ....

I certify that I have carefully compared the above "Abstract" with the original ration returns now in my possession, and find that they amount to ——— complete rations.

A. B, *Lieut.* ——— *Reg't of* ———, A. C. S.

Form 32.

CONTRACT FOR COMPLETE RATIONS.

ARTICLES OF AGREEMENT entered into this —— day of ———, eighteen hundred and ——, between —— ——, an officer in the service of the United States of America, of the one part, and —— ——, of the county of ——, in the State of ——, of the other part.

This agreement witnesseth, that the said —— ——, for and on behalf of the United States of America, and the said —— ——, for himself, his heirs, executors, and administrators (or for themselves, their heirs, executors, and administrators, as the case may be), have mutually agreed, and by these presents do mutually covenant and agree, to and with each other, as follows, viz.:

First. The said —— ——, his (or their) heirs, executors, and administrators, shall supply, or cause to be supplied and issued, at ——, all the rations, to consist of the articles hereinafter specified, that shall be required for the use of the United States recruits stationed at the place aforesaid, commencing on the —— day of ——, eighteen hundred and ——, and ending on the —— of ——, eighteen hundred and ——, or such early day as the Commissary-General of Subsistence may direct, at the price of —— cents and —— mills for each complete ration, in the funds furnished by the United States for public disbursement.

Second. The ration to be furnished by virtue of this contract shall consist of the following articles, at the following prices for each article, viz.: [Here insert the component parts of the ration and the price per pound, quart, etc., for which the articles shall be furnished.]

Third. Fresh beef shall be issued at least twice in each week, and oftener, if required by the commanding officer.

Fourth. The provisions stipulated to be furnished under this contract shall be of the first quality. Should any difficulty arise respecting their quality, then the commanding officer shall appoint a disinterested person to meet one of the same description to be appointed by the contractor. These two thus appointed will have power to decide on the quality of the provisions; but should they disagree, then a third person is to be chosen by the two already appointed, the whole to act under oath, and the opinion of the majority to be final in the case.

Fifth. No member of Congress, officer or agent of the Government, or any person employed in the public service, shall be admitted to any share herein, or to any benefit which may arise herefrom.

In witness whereof, the undersigned have hereunto placed their hands and seals, the day and date first above written.

Witnesses :—

—————— ——————   —————— ——————. [L. S.]

—————— ——————   .   —————— ——————. [L. S.]

Form 88.

FORM OF CONTRACT FOR FRESH BEEF.

ARTICLES OF AGREEMENT entered into this ——— day of ———, eighteen hundred and ———, between ——— ———, an officer in the service of the United States of America, of the one part, and ——— ———, of the county of ———, in the State of ———, of the other part.

This agreement witnesseth, that the said ——— ———, for and on behalf of the United States of America, and the said ——— ———, for himself, his heirs, executors, and administrators (or for themselves, their heirs, executors, and administrators, as the case may be), have mutually agreed, and by these presents do mutually covenant and agree, to and with each other, as follows, viz. :—

First. That the said ——— ——— shall deliver at ———, fresh beef of a good and marketable quality, in equal proportion of fore and hind quarter meat (necks, shanks, and kidney tallow to be excluded), in such quantities as may be from time to time required, and on such days as shall be designated by the commanding officer.

This contract to be in force for ——— months, or such less time as the Commissary-General of Subsistence may direct, commencing on the ——— day of ———, eighteen hundred and ———.

Second. The necks of the cattle slaughtered for beef to be delivered under this agreement shall be cut off at the fourth vertebral joint, and the breast trimmed down. The shanks of fore-quarters shall be cut off from three to four inches above the knee-joint, and of hind-quarters from six to eight inches above the gambrel or hock joint.

Third. The said ——— ——— shall receive ——— cents and ——— mills, per pound, for the fresh beef accepted under this contract.

Fourth. Payment shall be made monthly for the quantity of fresh beef accepted and in the funds furnished by the United States for public disbursement; but in the event of the Commissary who receives the beef being without funds to pay for it, then payment to be made as soon after as funds may be received for that purpose.

Fifth. Whenever the beef to be issued by this contract shall, in the opinion of the commanding officer, be unfit for issue, or of a quality inferior to that required by the contract, a survey shall be held thereon by two officers, to be designated by the commanding officer; and in case of disagreement, a third person shall be chosen by those two officers; the three thus appointed and chosen shall have power to reject such parts (or the whole) of the fresh beef as to them appear unfit for use, or of a quality inferior to that contracted for.

Sixth. In case of failure or deficiency in the quality or quantity of the fresh beef stipulated to be delivered, then the Commissary at ——— shall have power to supply the deficiency by purchase, and the said ——— ——— will be charged with the difference of cost.

Seventh. No member of Congress, officer or agent of the Government, or any person employed in the public service, shall be admitted to any share herein, or to any benefit which may arise herefrom.

In witness whereof, the undersigned have hereunto placed their hands and seals, the day and date first above written.

Witnesses:—

——— ———   ——— ——— [L. S.]
——— ———   ——— ——— [L. S.]

Form 84.

FORM OF BOND.

KNOW ALL MEN BY THESE PRESENTS, That we, ——— ———, of the county of ———, State of ———; ——— ———, of the county of ———, State of ———; and,

FORM OF BOND.

———— ————, of the county of ————, State of ————, are held and firmly bound to the United States of America in the sum of ———— dollars lawful money of the United States; for which payment well and truly to be made, we bind ourselves, and each of us, our and each of our heirs, executors, and administrators, for and in the whole, jointly and severally, firmly by these presents.

Sealed with our seals, dated the ———— day of ————, in the year of our Lord eighteen hundred and ————.

The nature of this obligation is such, That if [here insert name of contractor, or names of contractors, as the case may be] his (or their) heirs, executors, and administrators, or any of them, shall and do in all things well and truly observe, perform, fulfil, accomplish, and keep, all and singular, the covenants, conditions, and agreements whatsoever, which, on the part of the said ———— ————, his (or their) heirs, executors, or administrators, are or ought to be observed, performed, fulfilled, accomplished, and kept, comprised, or mentioned, in certain articles of agreement bearing date the ———— day of ————, eighteen hundred and ————, between ———— ———— and the said ———— ————, concerning the supply of rations at ———— (or of fresh beef at ————), according to the true intent and meaning of said articles of agreement, then the above obligation to be void; otherwise to remain in full force and virtue.

Witnesses:—

———— ————.   ———— ————. [L. S.]
———— ————.   ———— ————. [L. S.]
———— ————.   ———— ————. [L. S.]

July 19.

CLOTHING, CAMP, AND GARRISON EQUIPAGE.

Under this head are comprised all articles of soldier's clothing, tents, canteens, knapsacks, haversacks, blankets, axes, spades, camp kettles, messpans, flags, drums, and regimental and company books.

They are issued by the Quartermaster's Department, to commanders of companies, and others entitled to receive them, on special requisitions approved by the commanding officer of the depot, and are receipted for in triplicate, agreeably to invoices furnished by the Quartermaster at the time of issue.

ISSUES OF CLOTHING.

Clothing is issued to enlisted men, on receipt rolls made agreeably to Form 35, p. 71.

On these rolls erasures and alterations are prohibited, the vacant spaces being filled by cyphers after the issues are entered. Each signature, whether written by the soldier or acknowledged *by mark*, must be witnessed. Regular and extra issues are to be distinguished on the receipt roll.

Mounted men may receive *one* pair of boots and *two* pairs of bootees, instead of *four* pairs of bootees.

EXTRA ISSUES.

Extra issues of clothing are entered on the muster rolls, to be paid for by the soldier when the paymaster makes up the amount due him, as will be more fully described under the head of MUSTER ROLLS.

These issues are generally stated on a separate roll from the regular issues, are acknowledged in the same manner, and the signatures and issues witnessed by a commissioned or non-commissioned officer.

The *total* cost of extra clothing issued to each soldier will be entered against his name on the muster roll; the articles need not be particularized.

ALLOWANCE OF CLOTHING.

A soldier is allowed the uniform clothing stated in the following table, or articles thereof of equal value. When a balance is due him at the end of the year, it is added to his allowance for the next.

	First.	Second.	Third.	Fourth.	Fifth.	Total for 5 years.
Cap, with trimmings complete, light artillery.......	1	1	1	1	1	5
Plume, red horse hair..................................	1	....	1	....	....	2
Cover for artillery cap................................	1	1	1	1	1	5
Hat, with trimmings complete.......................	1	1	1	1	1	5
Forage cap...	1	1	1	1	1	5
Coat or jacket...	2	1	2	1	2	8
Trowsers..	3	2	3	2	3	13
Shirt...	3	3	3	3	3	15
Drawers...	3	2	2	2	2	11
Bootees, pairs of.......................................	4	4	4	4	4	20
Stockings, pairs of.....................................	4	4	4	4	4	20
Leather stock..	1	....	1	....	....	2
Greatcoat...	1	....	....	....	....	1
Stable frock (for mounted men)....................	1	....	1	....	....	2
Fatigue overalls (for engineers and ordnance).......	1	1	1	1	1	5
Blanket, woolen..	1	....	1	....	....	2
Blanket, water-proof, (for foot troops).............	1	1	1	1	1	5
Ponchoes, water-proof, (for mounted troops)	1	1	1	1	1	5
Gaiters (for foot troops)	1	1	1	1	1	5
Flannel sack coat.......................................	2	2	2	2	2	10

One sash is allowed to each company for the first sergeant, and one knapsack with straps, haversack, and canteen with straps, to each enlisted man. These, and the metallic scales, letters, numbers, castles, shells, and flames, and the camp and garrison equipage, will not be returned as issued, but borne on the return while fit for service. They will be charged on the muster roll to the person in whose use they are, when lost or destroyed by his fault.

When these articles become unfit for service, by reason of ordinary wear, the commanding officer of the company will submit them to the examination of a Board of Survey, which will make such report upon the property as will enable the inspector to condemn it, and thus permit the officer responsible to drop it from his return.

Extraordinary losses of this property, and injury thereto, not incident to ordinary service, must be submitted to a Board of Survey, with a certified statement of the officer accountable for the property, and such other certificates and affidavits concerning the circumstances, as will enable the board to report fully in the premises.

COST OF CLOTHING.

CLOTHING.	Engineer Troops.	Hospital Stewards.	Ordnance Sergeants.	Ordnance Mechanics.	Cavalry.	Light Artillery.	Artillery.	Infantry.
Uniform Hat	$1 68	$1 68	$1 68	$1 68	$1 68	$1 68	$1 68	$1 68
" " Feather	15	15	15	15	15	15	15	15
" " Cord & tassel.	14	14	14	14	14	14	14	14
" " Eagle	2	2	2	2	2	2	2	2
" " Castle	10							
" " Shell & flame.			5	5				
" " Cross'd sabres					3			
" " cross'd cann'n						3	3	
" " Bugle								3
" " Letter					1	1	1	1
" " Number					1	1	1	1
" Cap. Light Artil'y						1 06		
" " Tulip						8		
" " Cord and tass'l						75		
" " Plate						4		
" " Rings, pairs of.						8		
" " Pair plume						75		
Forage Cap	56	56	56	56	56	56	56	56
" " cover	18	18	18	18	18	18	18	18
Uniform Coat, Musicians'	7 45						7 45	7 45
" " Privates'	7 21	7 21	7 21	7 21			7 21	7 21
" Jackets, Musici'ns					5 97	5 97		
" " Privates'.					5 55	5 55		
Cheverons, pairs, N. C. S.			1 25		1 25		1 25	1 25
" 1st Sergeants'.	35				35	35	35	85
" Sergeants'	24				24	24	24	24
" Corporals'	20				20	20	20	20
Caduceus		90						
Sh'ld'r sc'les, pairs, N. C. S.		50	50		50		50	5
" " " Ser'gts'	50				50	50	50	50
" " " Privates'.	50			50	50	50	50	50
Trowsers, Sergeants'	3 75	8 75	3 75		4 80	4 80	3 75	3 75
" Corporals'	3 75				4 80	4 80	3 75	3 75
" Privates'	3 55			3 55	4 60	4 60	3 55	3 55
Sash	1 84	1 84	1 84		1 84	1 84	1 84	1 84
Flannel Sack Coat (unlined)	2 40	2 40	2 40	2 40	2 40	2 40	2 40	2 40
" " " (lined	3 14				3 14	3 14	3 14	3 14
Knit Jackets	2 70	2 70	2 70	2 70	2 70	2 70	2 70	2 70
Flannel Shirts	1 46	1 46	1 46	1 46	1 46	1 46	1 46	1 46
Knit "	1 30	1 30	1 30	1 30	1 80	1 30	1 30	1 80
Flannel Drawers	95	95	95	95	95	95	95	95
Knit "	1 00	1 00	1 00	1 00	1 00	1 00	1 00	1 00
Stockings	32	32	32	32	32	32	32	82
Bootees, sewed	2 05	2 05	2 05	2 05	2 05	2 05	2 05	2 05
" " pegged	1 45	1 45	1 48	1 45	1 45	1 45	1 48	1 45
Boots, sewed					3 25	8 25		
" " pegged					2 87	2 87		
Great Coats	9 50	9 50	9 50	9 50	11 50	11 50	9 50	9 50
" " Straps, pairs	14	14	14	14			14	14
Blankets, woolen	3 60	3 60	3 60	3 60	3 60	3·60	3 60	3 60
" painted	1 65	1 65	1 65	1 65			1 65	1 65
" rubber	2 55	2 55	2 55	2 55			2 55	2 55
Leather Stocks	10	10	10	10	10	10	10	10
Leggins, leather								1 25
" linen	-							75
Pouches, painted					2 10	2 10		
" rubber					2 90	2 90		
Overalls	1 58							
Stable Frocks					1 05	1 65		
Talmas					5 00	5 00		

COST OF CAMP AND GARRISON EQUIPAGE.

Item	Cost	Item	Cost
Knapsacks and straps,	$2 14	National colors, (infantry,)	$42 00
Haversacks,	48	Regimental colors, (artillery,)	63 00
Canteens and straps,	44	" " (infantry,	63 00
Bedsacks, (single,)	3 00	Color belt and sling,	4 50
" (double,)	3 15	Trumpets,	3 37
Axes,	83	Bugles, (with extra m'th-piece)	3 00
" helves,	12	Fifes,	50
" slings	53	Drums,	5 50
Hatchets,	32	" head batter,	75
" helve,	3	" " snare,	28
" sling,	35	" slings,	40
Spades,	70	" sticks, (pairs,)	22
Pickaxes,	67	" carriages,	52
" helves,	11	" cords,	30
Camp kettle,	55	" snares,	16
Mess pans,	23	Wall tents, complete,	53 26
Iron pot,	1 15	Sibley " "	63 71
Garrison flag,	43 00	" " stoves,	2 62
" halliards,	3 25	Hospital tents,	123 74
Storm flags,	17 00	Servants' "	22 45
Recruiting flags,	6 50	Regimental books, (set,)	6 26
" halliards,	1 00	Company " "	5 40
Guidons,	12 00	Post " "	2 36
Camp colors,	2 28	Record books for target pract'ce	56
National colors, (artillery,)	42 00	Mosquito bars,	3 15

Clothing and Camp and Garrison Equipage come from the military storekeeper at Philadelphia, who sends direct to the several stations such clothing as is called for by the yearly requisitions of company commanders. Depôt quartermasters are also furnished with their supplies from the same source.

On campaign, the clothing required for troops is furnished by the Depôt quartermaster, on a special requisition made according to Form 36, p. 72. This requisition sets forth the reason for the requirement, and, after approval by the commanding officer of the depôt, is taken to the Quartermaster, who issues the articles, giving duplicate invoices, and receiving duplicate receipts.

Regimental quartermasters sometimes draw clothing and articles of camp and garrison equipage from the depôt-quartermaster on a special requisition, and issue the articles to the commanders of companies, on requisitions approved by the regimental commander, the company commanders giving receipts to the regimental quartermaster, and issuing to their men on the usual receipt rolls.

Hospital tents are procured by the surgeon of the regiment on special requisition, and when the regiment moves, and the hospital tent can not be transported with it, the

the surgeon must turn it over to the depôt-quartermaster, in order to relieve himself from responsibility for it on the books of the accounting officers of the treasury.

In turning over property, DUPLICATE INVOICES must in every case be given, and DUPLICATE RECEIPTS obtained.

Officers responsible for camp and garrison equipage, should never leave it to the charge of others without *receipts*, and never deliver it without giving *invoices* at the same time.

Allowance of camp and garrison equipage.

	In permanent camp.				In camp, garrison, or in the field.						In the field.	
	Wall tents.	Sibley tents.	Common tents.	French tents, O. P.	Spades.	Axes.	Picks.	Hatchets.	Camp kettles.	Mess-pans.	Shelter tents.	Wall tents.
A general officer...............	3	..	..	....	....	1	....	1	....	....	....	..
Field or staff officer above the rank of captain...........	2	..	..	....	....	1	....	1	....	....	....	..
Other staff officers or captains......	1	..	..	....	....	1	....	1	....	....	....	..
Subalterns of company, to every two	1	..	..	....	....	1	....	1	....	....	....	..
To every 15 foot or 13 mounted men	..	..	..	1	2	2	2	2	2	5	....	..
To every 20 foot or 17 mounted men	..	1	..	....	....	....	....	....	....	....	....	..
To every 6 foot or 4 mounted men.	..	..	1	....	....	....	....	....	....	....	....	..
To general commanding corps, division, or brigade............	..	..	..	....	....	....	....	....	....	....	....	1
To every 2 officers of his staff......	..	..	..	....	....	....	....	....	....	....	....	1
Colonel, field and staff of a regiment	..	..	..	....	....	....	....	....	....	....	....	3
To each company officer...........	..	..	..	....	....	....	....	....	....	....	1	..
To every two enlisted men........	..	..	..	....	....	....	....	....	....	....	1	..

Officers receiving clothing, or camp and garrison equipage, will render monthly returns of it to the Quartermaster-General.

Commanders of companies will take the receipts of their men for the clothing issued to them, on a receipt roll, witnessed by an officer, or in the absence of an officer, by a non-commissioned officer; the witness to be witness to the fact of the issue and the acknowledgment and signature of the soldier. The several issues to a soldier to be entered separately on the roll, and all vacant spaces on the roll to be filled with a cipher. This roll is the voucher for the issue to the quarterly return of the company commander. Extra issues will be so noted on the roll.

Each soldier's clothing account is kept by the company commander in a company book. This account sets out only the money value of the clothing which he received at each issue, for which his receipt is entered in the book, and witnessed as in the preceding paragraph.

When a soldier is transferred or detached, the amount due to or by him on account of clothing will be stated on his descriptive list.

When a soldier is discharged, the amount due to or by him for clothing will be stated on the duplicate certificates given for the settlement of his accounts.

Deserters' clothing will be turned into store. The invoice of it, and the Quartermaster's receipt for it, will state its condition and the name of the deserter.

Commanding officers may order necessary issues of clothing to prisoners and convicts, taking deserters' or other damaged clothing when there is such in store.

In all cases of deficiency, or damage of any article of clothing, or camp or garrison equipage, the officer accountable for the property is required by law "to show by one or more depositions, setting forth the circumstances of the case, that the deficiency was by unavoidable accident or loss in actual service, without any fault on his part, and in case of damage, that due care and attention were exerted on his part, and that the damage did not result from neglect."

Officers desiring to obtain any article of clothing can do so, giving the cost price to any soldier who draws the article as an extra issue, and pays for it on his next muster roll.

Bedsacks are not furnished to troops in the field.

Form 37, p. 72a, shows the monthly return of clothing and camp and garrison equipage.

This return must be made to the Quartermaster-General, at the expiration of every month by *every officer who receives and receipts for any article* of clothing and camp and garrison equipage.

In the third column, under "on hand per last return," will be entered the several invoices according to date.

In the lower portion will be entered the several issues according to the date of vouchers. The total of each clothing receipt roll of issues to troops is to be entered.

The total issued, taken from the total received gives the figures for the last line.

The several invoices and receipts, duly numbered, are sent with the return to the Quartermaster-General.

CLOTHING RECEIPT ROLL.

FORM 35.—CLOTHING RECEIPT ROLL.

We, the undersigned Non-commissioned Officers, Artificers, Musicians, and Privates of ———, do hereby acknowledge to have received of ——— the several articles of Clothing set opposite our respective names.

Date of the issue.	Name and designation of the soldier.	Hats, complete.	Caps, forage.	Feathers.	Eagles and rings.	N. C. S.	UNIFORM COATS.				Privates'	UNIFORM JACKETS.				Privates'	Trowsers, pairs.	Flannel shirts.	Drawers, pairs.	Boots, cavalry, pairs.	Bootees, infantry, pairs.	Stockings, pairs.	Leather stocks.	Great-coats.	Fatigue overalls.	Stable frocks.	Blankets.	Signatures.	Witness.
							Sergeants.	Corporals.	Musicians.		Sergeants.	Corporals.	Musicians.															

FORM 36.—SPECIAL REQUISITION.

1861.	For Company A., 3d Regiment Infantry.
June 30.	50 pairs of Trowsers. 2 Wall Tents. 2 " Flies. 2 sets of Poles and Pins.

I certify that the above requisition is correct, and that the articles specified are absolutely requisite for the public service, rendered so by the following circumstances: For a detachment of recruits.

A. B., *Capt. Co. A., 3d Regiment Infantry.*

Major D. H. R., Quartermaster U. S. Army, will issue the articles specified in the above requisition.

E. F., *Commanding.*

Received at Washington, D. C., the 30th of June, 1861, of Major D. H. R., Quartermaster U. S. Army, fifty pairs of Trowsers, and two Wall Tents, with Poles, Flies, and Pins, in full of the above requisition.

A. B., *Capt. 3d Regiment Infantry.*

(Signed Duplicates.)

Monthly Return of Clothing, Camp and Garrison Equipage received and issued at ———, in the month of ————————, 186 , by ————

QUARTERMASTER'S DEPARTMENT.

HORSES.

All horses used for cavalry, artillery, and transportation, are obtained from the Quartermaster's Department; they are issued on special requisitions, (Form 36, p. 72,) approved by the commanding officer.

When receipted for they are to be borne on the officer's return of Quartermaster's property, until they are turned over to another, or are otherwise disposed of.

When a horse becomes unfit for service, he is to be condemned by a *Board of Survey*. Or, if such be impracticable, from the exigencies of the service in the field, the animal may be expended on the officer's certificate. Officers are relieved from responsibility for horses killed in action in the same manner.

Public horses are not to be used for private purposes by any one, commissioned officers being required to furnish their own horses.

In fitting up a vessel for the transportation of horses, care is to be taken that the requisite arrangements are made for conveniently feeding and cleaning them, and to secure them from injury in rough weather by ropes attached to breast-straps and breeching, or by other suitable means; and especially that proper ventilation is provided by openings in the upper deck, wind-sails, etc. The ventilation of steamers may be assisted by using the engine for that purpose.

Horses should not be put on board after severe exercise or when heated. In hoisting them on board, the slings should be made fast to a hook at the end of the fall, or the knot tied by an expert seaman, so that it may be well secured and easily loosened. The horse should be run up quickly, to prevent him from plunging, and should be steadied by guide ropes. A halter is placed on him before he is lifted from the ground.

On board, care is to be taken that the horses are not overfed; bran should form part of their ration. The face, eyes, and nostrils of each horse are to be washed at the usual stable hours, and, occasionally, the mangers should be washed and the nostrils of the horses sponged with vinegar and water.

4

FORAGE.

The forage ration is fourteen pounds of hay and twelve pounds of oats, corn, or barley.

Forage shall be issued to officers only in the month when due, and at their proper stations, and for the horses actually kept by them in service, not exceeding in number as follows: In time of war, Major-General, seven horses; Brigadier-General, five; Colonels who have the cavalry allowance, five; other Colonels, four; Lieutenant-Colonels and Majors who have the cavalry allowance, four; other Lieutenant-Colonels and Majors, three; Captains who have the cavalry allowance, three; all other officers entitled to forage, two; and in time of peace, general and field officers, three horses; officers below the rank of field officers in the regiments of cavalry, two horses; all other officers entitled to forage, one horse.

No officer shall sell forage issued to him. Forage issued to public horses or cattle is public property; what they do not actually consume is to be properly accounted for.

Forage is issued to mounted troops, and for the animals used for transportation by the Quartermaster on requisitions made pursuant to Form 63, p. 122, and for private horses of officers entitled to forage pursuant to Form 64, p. 123.

Mounted detachments frequently have their own Acting Assistant Quartermaster, who obtains forage in bulk from the Depôt Quartermaster, or by purchase; and issues on requisitions, according to forms above mentioned.

Regimental quartermasters obtain forage in bulk, and issue on requisition to the animals of the regiment.

On the arrival of a command at a depôt, it is the duty of the Quartermaster to make a requisition for the necessary forage, have it approved by the commanding officer of the depôt, and then draw the forage of the Depôt Quartermaster.

When a command is detached the Quartermaster will provide forage by purchase, if none can reach him from the depôt.

Officers drawing commutation for forage on their pay accounts, are not allowed to draw forage in kind for their horses.

STRAW.

In barracks, twelve pounds of straw per month for bedding is allowed to each man, servant, and company woman.

The allowance and change of straw for the sick is regulated by the surgeon.

One hundred pounds per month, is allowed for bedding to each horse in public service.

At posts near prairie land owned by the United States, hay is used instead of straw, and provided by the troops.

Straw not actually used as bedding shall be accounted for as other public property.

Straw is drawn by company commanders from the Quartermaster, on requisitions made agreeably to Form 66, p. 126.

STATIONERY.

Stationery for public service is drawn from the Quartermaster. The following is the allowance of officers, to be drawn quarterly:

	Quires of writing paper.	Quires of envelope paper.	Number of quills.	Ounces of wafers.	Ounces of sealing wax.	Papers of ink powder.	Pieces of office tape.
Commander of an army, department, or division (what may be necessary for himself and staff for their public duty).							
Commander of a brigade, for himself and staff....	12	1	50	1	8	2	2
Officer commanding a regiment or post of not less than five companies, for himself and staff...	10	1	40	1	6	2	2
Officer commanding a post of more than two and less than five companies......................	8	½	30	½	5	1	1
Commanding officer of a post of two companies...	6	½	25	½	4	1	1
Commanding officer of a post of one company or less, and commanding officer of a company.....	5	½	20	½	3	1	1
A Lieutenant-Colonel or Major not in command of a regiment or post................................	3	¼	12	¼	2	1	1
Officers of the Inspector-General's, Pay, and Quartermaster's Department (the prescribed blank books and printed forms, and the stationery required for their public duty).							
All officers, including chaplains, not enumerated above, when on duty and not supplied by their respective departments..........................	1½	¼	6	¼	1	½	½

Steel pens, with one holder to twelve pens, may be issued in place of quills, and envelopes in place of envelope paper, at the rate of 100 to the quire.

When an officer is relieved in command, he shall transfer the office stationery to his successor.

To each office table is allowed one inkstand, one stamp, one paper folder, one sand-box, one wafer-box, and as many lead-pencils as may be required, not exceeding four per year.

Necessary stationery for military courts and boards will be furnished on the requisition of the recorder, approved by the presiding officer.

The commander of an army, department, or division, may direct orders to be printed, when the requisite dispatch and the number to be distributed make it necessary. The necessity will be set out in the order for the printing, or certified on the account.

Regimental, company, and post books, and printed blanks for the officers of the quartermaster and pay departments, will be procured by timely requisition on the Quartermaster-General.

Printed matter procured by the Quartermaster-General for use out of Washington may be procured elsewhere, at a cost not to exceed the rates prescribed by Congress for the public printing, increased by the cost of transportation.

Officers draw their stationery on requisitions made out pursuant to Form 69, p. 128, the columns being filled with the amounts of the several articles according to the rank of the officer drawing, as shown by the foregoing table.

The caption of the requisition will set forth the name of the officer, his station, the time drawn for, and the dates of its commencing and ending.

The requisition is made out in duplicate, and a certificate, as indicated, signed by the officer.

Officers making purchases of stationery for office use, must be careful to restrict their purchases to such articles as are authorized. For instance, the purchase of penknives as stationery is not allowed, erasers being the article recognized by the accounting officers of the Treasury as the proper purchase.

The requisite blanks for muster and pay rolls, monthly returns, discharges, descriptive lists, and all returns and reports pertaining to the recruiting service, are obtained from the Adjutant-General's office.

FUEL AND QUARTERS.

The number of rooms and amount of fuel for officers and men are as follows:

	Rooms.			Cords of wood per month.*	
	As quarters.	As kitchen.	As office.	From May 1 to Sept 30.	From Oct. 1 to April 30.
A Major-General.......................................	5	1	..	1	6
A Brigadier-General or Colonel	4	1	..	1	4½
A Lieutenant-Colonel or Major...................	3	1	..	1	3
A Captain or Chaplain...............................	2	1	..	¾	2¼
Lieutenant...	1	1	..	½	2
Military store-keeper	1	1	..	½	2
The General commanding the army..............	..	..	3	...	3
The commanding officer of a division or department, an assistant or deputy Quartermaster-General...	..	..	2	....	2
The commanding officer of a regiment or post, Quartermaster, Assistant-Quartermaster, or Commissary of Subsistence...........................	..	..	1	....	1
An acting Assistant-Quartermaster when approved by the Quartermaster-General	..	..	1	....	1
Wagon and forage master, Serj.-Maj., Ord.-Serj., or Quartermas.-Serj. Med. Cadets, Hosp'l Stew'd or Prin. Musician..	1	..	..	½	1
Each non-commissioned officer, musician, private, officer's servant, and washerwoman	..	..	..	$\frac{1}{12}$	$\frac{1}{6}$
Each necessary fire for the sick in hospital to be regulated by the surgeon and commanding officer, *not exceeding*.......................................	..	..	..	⅓	2
Each guard-fire to be regulated by the commanding officer, *not exceeding*.................................	..	..	..	....	3
A commissary or quartermaster's store-house when necessary, *not exceeding*.......................	..	..	..	...	1
A regiment or post mess...............................	1	..	..	....	1
To every six non-commissioned officers, musicians, and privates, servants and washerwomen, 225 square feet of room north of 38° N., and 256 square feet south of that latitude.					

* Or coal, at the rate of 1500 lbs., anthracite, or 30 bushels bituminous to the cord.

Fuel and quarters are furnished by the Quartermaster. The former on requisitions made out pursuant to Forms 60 and 61, pp. 119 and 120.

The first for a company, and the other for individual

officers, hospitals, guards, and any other requirement for fuel.

When an officer is on such service that fuel and quarters can not be furnished to him by the Quartermaster's Department, he is permitted to commute his allowance and receive of the Quartermaster the cash value thereof.

Form 42, p. 102, shows an officer's account for commutation of fuel and quarters. It must be accompanied by a certificate, showing by whose order the officer was stationed, and the first account must be accompanied by a copy of the order so assigning him.

TRANSPORTATION.

Officers travelling under orders not less than ten miles, are entitled to the means of transportation for themselves and baggage; this the Quartermaster will furnish if he has public means of transport, if not, the officer will commute the allowance at 10 cents a mile for the entire route, measured by the nearest mail route, or if he so elect, the officer may receive the actual cost of the journey. The cash received in lieu of the transportation is paid the officer by the Quartermaster on accounts prepared in conformity with Forms 43 and 44, pp. 103 and 104. The account is to be accompanied by a copy of the order by virtue of which the officer has performed the journey.

This allowance for travelling is only to be paid when the journey is performed.

Form 45, p. 105, shows the account which must be rendered by civilians travelling under orders, and in the service of the army.

In the field, where there are no other means of transportation, the Quartermaster will furnish the officer with a public horse and equipments, taking the officer's receipt therefor.

This property the officer will turn over to the Quartermaster of the post at which his journey terminates, and furnish the requisite return to the Quartermaster-General.

Officers travelling on government transports are furnished with their passage only. The cost of subsistence while on board being a matter of contract with the officers of the vessel. This is the case whether the officer has troops on board or is travelling under orders.

The requisite number of wagons are furnished by the Quartermaster for the transportation of troops in the field, the number depending on the length of the march and the amount of transportation on hand. Under ordinary circumstances, two wagons to a company of infantry is a fair allowance. Where a movement is made by a regiment, the Regimental Quartermaster will receipt for the transportation and take it up on his return.

With a single company, the Captain will be responsible for the means of transportation, or a subaltern acting as Quartermaster.

Where the wagons are to be immediately returned, the Quartermaster furnishing the transportation, may send it in charge of his own wagon-master with his own teamsters, and continue to bear the property on his return. In which case he will be relieved from losses and injury by the certificate of the officer in command of the troops to which the transportation was furnished.

When troops are moved, or officers travel with escorts or stores, the means of transport provided shall be for the whole command. Proper orders in the case, and an exact return of the command, including officers' servants and company women, will be furnished to the Quartermaster who is to provide the transportation.

The baggage to be transported is limited to camp and garrison equipage, and officers' baggage. Officers' baggage shall not exceed (mess-chest and all personal effects included) as follows:

	In the field.	Changing stations.
General officers	125 pounds.	1000 pounds.
Field officers	100 "	800 "
Captains	80 "	700 "
Subalterns	80 "	600 "

These amounts shall be reduced *pro rata* by the commanding officer when necessary, and may be increased by the Quartermaster-General on transports by water, when proper, in special cases.

The regimental and company desk prescribed in army regulations will be transported; also for staff officers, the books, papers, and instruments necessary to their duties; and for medical officers, their medical chest. In doubtful cases under this regulation, and whenever baggage exceeds the regulated allowance, the conductor of the train, or officer in charge of the transportation, will report to the commanding officer, who will order an inspection, and all excess be rejected.

Estimates of the medical director, approved by the commanding officer, for the necessary transportation to be provided for the hospital service, will be furnished to the Quartermaster.

The sick will be transported on the application of the medical officers.

Where officers' horses are to be transported, it must be authorized in the orders for the movement.

The baggage trains, ambulances, and all the means of transport continue in charge of the proper officers of the Quartermaster's Department, under the control of the commanding officers.

In all cases of transportation, whether of troops or stores, an exact return of the amount and kind of transportation employed will be made by the Quartermaster to the Quartermaster-General, accompanied by the orders for the movement, a return of the troops, and an invoice of the stores.

On transports, cabin passage will be provided for officers, and reasonable and proper accommodation for the troops, and, when possible, a separate apartment for the sick.

If the journey be to cash treasury drafts, the necessary and actual cost of transportation only will be allowed; and the account must describe the draft and state its amount, and set out the items of expense, and be supported by a certificate that the journey was necessary to procure specie for the draft at par.

Orders to an officer on leave of absence to rejoin the station or troops he left, will not carry transportation.

In changes of station, an officer entitled to mileage, or actual cost of transportation, shall be entitled to actual cost of transportation of his authorized servants; and in other cases than change of station, an officer entitled to transportation, who, from wounds or disability, requires and takes one servant, shall be entitled to the actual cost of his transportation.

Citizens receiving military appointments join their stations without expense to the public.

But assistant surgeons, approved by an examining board and commissioned, receive transportation in the execution of their first order to duty, and graduates of the Military Academy receive transportation from the academy to their stations.

When officers are permitted to exchange stations, the public will not be put to expense of transportation, which would have been saved if such exchange had not been permitted.

A paymaster's clerk will receive the actual expenses of his transportation, while travelling under orders in the discharge of his duty, upon his affidavit to the account of expenses, and the certificate of the Paymaster that the journey was on duty, as shown by Form 45, page 105.

EXPENSES OF COURTS-MARTIAL.

An officer who attends a general court-martial or court of inquiry, convened by authority competent to order a general court-martial, will be paid, if the court is not held at the station where he is at the time serving, one dollar a day while attending the court and travelling to and from it, if entitled to forage, and one dollar and twenty-five cents a day if not entitled to forage.

The Judge Advocate or Recorder will be paid, besides, a per diem of one dollar and twenty-five cents for every day he is necessarily employed in the duty of the court. When it is necessary to employ a clerk to aid the Judge Advocate, the court may order it; a soldier is to be procured when practicable.

A citizen witness shall be paid his actual transportation or stage fare, and three dollars a day while attending the court, and travelling to and from it, counting the travel at fifty miles a day.

The certificate of the Judge Advocate shall be evidence of the time of attendance on the court, and of the time he was necessarily employed in the duty of the court. Of the time occupied in travelling, each officer will make his own certificate.

These expenses will be paid by the Quartermaster on an account made out according to Form 46, p. 106. The copy of the order to the officer, and of the summons to the witness, will in all cases accompany the account.

The certificate of the Judge Advocate, as to the time of attendance of the officer, will also be furnished the Quartermaster paying the account.

POSTAGE.

The amount paid by officers for postage on account of public service, will be refunded by the Quartermaster on presentation of an account and certificate made out in accordance with Form 47, p. 107

RETURNS OF THE QUARTERMASTER'S DEPARTMENT.

All officers and agents having money and property of the Quartermaster's Department to account for, must make the following monthly returns to the Third Auditor and Quartermaster-General.

RETURNS TO THIRD AUDITOR.

All officers of, or acting in, the Quartermaster's Department, and Regimental Quartermasters must render the following accounts *monthly* to the *Third Auditor of the Treasury*, mailing or forwarding them with the abstracts and vouchers pertaining thereto, within ten days after the expiration of each successive month.

1. Account current on account of the Quartermaster's Department, accompanied by Abstracts A, B, and B b.
2. Accounts current of money received and disbursed under appropriations for contingencies of the army, accompanied by Abstract C.

RETURNS TO QUARTERMASTER-GENERAL.

The following returns must be made monthly to the Quartermaster-General within *ten* days after the expiration of the month.

1. Return of Property, to be accompanied by Abstracts D, E, F, G, H, I, K, L, M, and N, and their respective vouchers.
2. Statement of allowances paid to Officers.
3. Return of Clothing, Camp and Garrison equipage, accompanied by Receipt Roll of Issues.

The following Statements, Reports, and Returns will be

made to the Quartermaster-General monthly, within from five to ten days after the month to which they relate.

Summary statement.—Form 78.
Report of persons and things.—Form 79.
Roll of extra duty men.—Form 80.
Report of stores for transportation.—Form 81.
Return of animals, wagons. harness, etc.--Form 82.
Report of forage.—Form 83.
Report of fuel and quarters commuted.—Form 84.
Report of pay due.—Form 85.
Estimate of funds for the current month.—Form 86.

Abstracts.

These several returns will be accompanied by *abstracts*, in which transactions of a similar nature are collected, previous to the entry of their total on the returns.

Each *abstract* to be supported by the *vouchers* of the respective transactions.

The following are the abstracts, and the character of transactions pertaining to each.

ABSTRACT A.
Form 39, p. 99.

This abstract exhibits all articles *paid for in* the quarter, whether purchased *within or prior to* the quarter, except purchases of clothing, camp, and garrison equipage, and purchases for "*army contingencies.*"

It will be supported by vouchers exhibited by Form 40, p. 100, the certificate on which is made by the officer who *purchased* the property, and the receipt is taken by the officer who *paid* for it.

The total of this abstract is entered at the head of the debtor side of the account current.

ABSTRACT B.
Form 41, p. 101.

This abstract contains all payments except purchases and transfers of funds. In it are entered all payments of mileage for transportation of officers and baggage; payments for attendance on courts-martial, and mileage to and from the court; payments made for actual expenses of transportation; payments of postages, commutation of fuel and quarters, and others too numerous to be particularized; all to be supported by proper vouchers, the principal of which are shown by Forms 42 to 48.

Where no particular Form is given, the officer paying the money, should have the *order* by which the service charged for is performed, the *recipient's certificate* that such service was performed, and the *receipt for the money*.

ABSTRACT Bb.
Form 49, p. 109.

This abstract contains the advances made to officers for disbursements on account of the Quartermaster's Department.

These advances are generally made on the order of the commanding officer, on a special requisition. The fourth column of the abstract states the authority.

This abstract is entered on the debtor side of the account current, under Abstract B.

ABSTRACT C.
Form 51, p. 111.

In this abstract are entered all disbursements on account of contingencies of the army, also necessary purchases made by the Quartermaster of medicines for the hospital, (vouchers, Forms 52 and 53, pp. 112 and 113.)

All payments made for apprending deserters, must be entered in this abstract.

The total of this abstract, is to be entered at the head of the debtor column of the account current for expenditures on account of contingencies of the army.

ABSTRACT D.
Form 55, p. 114.

This abstract pertains exclusively to the PROPERTY RETURN, and is designed to exhibit all the supplies purchased by the Quartermaster, whether paid for or not.

No vouchers of purchases paid for are required with this abstract, as they belong with second division of Abstract A.

Purchases not paid for are accompanied by vouchers shown in Form 56, p. 115, having the officer's certificate of correctness, and the reason specified why payment was not made.

This abstract will be entered in the first division of the quarterly return, shown by Form 54, p. 114*a*.

ABSTRACT E.

Form 57, p. 116.

This abstract is to contain all property received from other officers, whether receipted for or not. It will be supported by invoices shown by Form 58, p. 117; and when no invoice is received, the receiving officer will substitute a list of the stores received, certified by himself. This last will be in the name of the person responsible for the property, when he is known. If not, the property will be taken up, and a statement of the circumstances made on the list.

This abstract is entered in the quarterly return under Abstract D.

ABSTRACT F.

Form 59, p. 119.

This abstract contains all issues of fuel, supported by vouchers, shown by Forms 60 and 61, pp. 119 and 120. Fuel transferred to other officers to be accounted for by them, is to be entered in Abstract M. It is entered at the head of the second division of the quarterly return.

ABSTRACT G.

Form 62, p. 121.

This is the *Abstract of Forage issued* upon returns shown by Forms 63, 64, 65, pp. 122 to 124, which are appended as vouchers. Forage transferred to other officers to be accounted for, does not belong to this abstract, but is to be entered in Abstract M.

Abstract G is entered in the quarterly return under Abstract F.

ABSTRACT H.

Form 66, p. 125.

This abstract comprises all issues of straw made on returns shown by Form 67, p. 126. Straw transferred to officers to be accounted for, will be entered in Abstract M. This abstract is entered in the return under Abstract G.

ABSTRACT I.

Form 68, p. 127.

This is the abstract containing all stationery issued on requisitions shown by Form 69, p. 128, together with all stationery used by the quartermaster in the public service. Transfers of stationery do not belong here, but to Abstract M. The total of this abstract is entered in the return beneath that of Abstract H.

ABSTRACT K.
Form 90, p. 129.

All issues except fuel, forage, straw, and stationery, are entered in this abstract. The vouchers are special requisitions, shown by Form 36, p. 72. It is entered in the return beneath Abstract I.

ABSTRACT L.
Form 71, p. 130.

This abstract shows all articles expended, lost, and destroyed in the public service. It is supported by certificates made pursuant to Forms 72, 73, and 74, pp. 132, 131, and 133, which constitute the officers vouchers for dropping the articles from his return.

This abstract must contain all materials used in the public service which are accounted for in the list of articles expended (Form 72, p. 131). This list is to be examined and approved by the commanding officer, and should be made out monthly, in order that the Quartermaster may be acquainted with the exact state of his supplies.

Public property worn out and unfit for use is condemned by a board of survey, and ordered to be sold. Form 74, p. 133, shows an account of sale pursuant to such order, which will be stated in the Quartermaster's certificate to the account.

The list of the articles lost or destroyed must give a clear statement of the circumstances of such loss, and is to be approved by the commanding officer.

Abstract L is one of the most important abstracts accompanying the return; and great care must be taken in procuring proper vouchers. It is to be entered in the return, under Abstract K.

ABSTRACT M.
Form 75, p. 134.

This abstract contains all transfers of stores to other officers to be accounted for by them. Their receipts are the vouchers. When these are not received in time, the

Quartermaster will substitute his own certified list of the stores sent, and the bill of lading; the receipts he will afterwards transmit when he receives them.

This abstract will be entered in the quarterly return below Abstract L. This concludes the description of the seven abstracts entered in the second branch of the return, comprising all modes of disposing of public property.

ABSTRACT N.
Form 76, p. 135.

This abstract contains all quartermasters' property found at the post not borne on the previous return, all that may come into the Quartermaster's possession without his knowing who may be accountable for it. Articles manufactured in the quarter, material or parts of articles that have been condemned or broken up; fuel and forage issued but not consumed, etc., etc. Separate lists of each class with necessary explanations are to be made out and filed with this abstract.

Abstract N. is to be entered on the first branch of the return, with the articles to be accounted for.

MONTHLY RETURN OF QUARTERMASTER'S STORES.
Form 54, p. 114a.

The property on this return (which does not include clothing, camp and garrison equipage) will be classed as follows:

1. Fuel.
2. Forage.
3. Straw.
4. Stationery.
5. Barrack, hospital, and office furniture.
6. Means of transportation, including harness, etc.
7. Building materials.
8. Veterinary Tools and horse medicines.
9. Blacksmiths' tools.
10. Carpenters' tools.
11. Wheelwrights' tools.
12. Masons' and bricklayers' tools.
13. Miscellaneous tools for fatigue and garrison purposes.
14. Stores for expenditure, such as iron, steel, horseshoes, rope, etc., etc., to be classed alphabetically.

In the first line of the first branch of the return, the articles remaining on hand as shown by the last return, are entered each under its appropriate head. If it be the first return made by the officer, the first line will be left blank, and Abstracts D, E, and N duly entered. *The total to be accounted for* will then be ascertained by adding together the several lines of the first branch of the return.

The total of each of the several abstracts of the second branch will then be duly entered, and their sum will constitute the *total issued and expended;* the difference between which and the *total to be accounted for*, will be the *total remaining on hand*.

The condition of the several articles will be classed under the three heads indicated; the facts relating thereto being of course ascertained by examination.

VOUCHERS TO ABSTRACT D.

The vouchers for Abstract D will be made as shown in Form 56, p. 115. The Quartermaster's certificate stating the reason for the non-payment of the account.

VOUCHERS TO ABSTRACT E.

The vouchers of Abstract E will be the *invoices* of the officers by whom the property is transferred. Form 58, p. 117.

Where no invoice is received, the receiving officer will substitute for this form a list of the stores received, certified by himself. When the person responsible for the property entered without invoice is known, it will be entered in his name.

VOUCHERS TO ABSTRACT K.

The vouchers to Abstract K are to be *special requisitions* shown by Form 36.

VOUCHERS TO ABSTRACT L.

Abstract L is to be supported by vouchers of the Forms 72, 73, 74 according to the nature of the case, as explained in the description of this abstract.

ACCOUNT CURRENT ON ACCOUNT OF THE QUARTERMASTER'S DEPARTMENT.

Form 88, p. 98.

This account must include all moneys received and expended, except that disbursed for clothing, and for the contingencies of the army. On the Dr. side will be entered Abstracts A, B, and Bb; and on the Cr. side the balance *on hand* as per last account, cash received from the U. S. Treasurer, cash received from the sale of public property, and cash received from officers. Where the number of receipts from officers is considerable, they will be consolidated in an abstract, known as Abstract Bbb; but when they are few in number, each transfer will be entered separately in the account.

The same remark applies to Abstract Bb. If the number of transfers be few, each will be entered separately on the Dr. side, the receipts accompanying the account.

The total amount of payments is subtracted from the total receipts and what was on hand at the commencement of the quarter, and the difference is the balance due United States, which must be entered at the foot of the Dr. column.

VOUCHERS TO ABSTRACT A.

The vouchers for Abstract A are shown by Form 39 p. 99, which may be taken as the form for all ordinary vouchers for the payment of money for purchases by any officer.

VOUCHERS TO ABSTRACT B.

The vouchers for Abstract B are shown by Forms 42 to 48, pp. 102 to 108. and for miscellaneous disbursements not specially provided for, will be as shown by Form 87, p. 147.

ACCOUNT CURRENT FOR EXPENDITURES ON ACCOUNT OF CONTINGENCIES OF THE ARMY.

Form 50, p. 110.

The Cr. side of this account will show the money received, and the Dr. side the total of Abstract C, and the balance on hand.

VOUCHERS TO ABSTRACT C.

Vouchers for Abstract C will be of Form 87, p. 147, where the certificate is made by the Quartermaster himself, and according to Form 53, p. 113, where the certificate is by another officer. In which case the requisition on which the purchase may be made must be attached to the bill of purchase, and made to accompany Abstract C. The articles are not to be entered on the Quartermaster's property return.

MONTHLY STATEMENT OF ALLOWANCES PAID TO OFFICERS.
Form 77, p. 136.

This return will be made up from the data furnished by the several abstracts of the quarterly return account current. The form fully explains its nature, and the manner of preparing it.

When officers occupy quarters owned by the public, the number of room only will be reported.

PAPERS CONSISTING OF SEVERAL SHEETS.

In preparing the quarterly returns, if it requires several sheets they will not be pasted together, but will be duly numbered and folded separately.

This remark applies to the monthly papers required of all officers responsible for money and property of the Quartermaster's Department.

MONTHLY SUMMARY STATEMENT.
Form 78, p. 187.

This is simply a statement of receipts and disbursements made during the month. No vouchers accompany it, though advances and transfers may be consolidated in abstracts, if they are numerous.

REPORT OF PERSONS AND ARTICLES.
Form 79, p. 188 and 189.

This report is to contain the names of all persons hired by the Quartermaster during the month, time of service occupation, compensation, and such other information as is fully shown in the Form. Also a full description of all articles hired for the public service, and the amounts paid for them. This report is to be approved by the commanding officer.

ROLL OF EXTRA DUTY MEN.
Form 80, p. 140.

This will give the name, rank, and service of all non-commissioned officers and privates employed by the Quartermaster, together with the rate of compensation, manner of employment, and the order by which each is employed, together with the amount due each.

This roll is certified by the Quartermaster, and examined and approved by the commanding officer.

These extra duty men are paid their extra allowance by the Quartermaster, on receipt rolls similar to that shown in Form 48, p. 108, for hired persons in the Quartermaster's Department.

REPORT OF STORES FOR TRANSPORTATION.
Form 81, p. 141.

This Form gives full instructions concerning this report. The articles appear in no other report.

MONTHLY RETURN OF PUBLIC ANIMALS, WAGONS, HARNESS, ETC.
Form 82, p. 142.

No other articles than those shown in the Form, are to be placed in this return. No vouchers are to be sent with it, it being merely a correct statement of the means of transportation, for which the Quartermaster is responsible.

MONTHLY REPORT OF FORAGE ISSUED.
Form 83, p. 143.

This is a statement of amount of forage issued and to whom. It is sent without vouchers for the information of the Quartermaster-General.

REPORT OF OFFICERS WHOSE FUEL AND QUARTERS ARE COMMUTED.
Form 84, p. 144.

The Form shows the name, rank, and corps of officers drawing commutation, and the order for such payments, together with the amount paid. No vouchers are sent with it, they being entered in Abstract B of the account current.

REPORT OF PERSONS HIRED WHO HAVE DECEASED, DESERTED, OR BEEN DISCHARGED DURING THE MONTH.

Form 85 p. 145.

This report must contain all the information necessary to enable the Department to pay the legal representatives of the deceased persons, to examine into the cases of deserters, and to examine and verify the correctness of payments made, or certificates of discharge.

ESTIMATE FOR FUNDS.

Form 86, p. 146.

The several items of expenditure of the Quartermaster's Department are enumerated in this Form. The officer will of course estimate for funds for such purposes only as he may be obliged to disburse for.

PAY ROLL OF PERSONS EMPLOYED IN THE QUARTERMASTER'S DEPARTMENT.

Form 48, p. 108.

Persons employed by the Quartermaster receive their pay on signing rolls made agreeably to this form, duly witnessed. The amount paid, with the roll as a voucher, is to be entered in Abstract B.

The foregoing are the accounts and returns to be rendered by all officers and persons accountable for quartermaster's funds or property. The extent of the returns will of course be governed by the amount of business transacted; and in many cases, some of the monthly returns will not be required, as the officer's business may not be such as to need them. The officer, in making out his papers, will of course know from the nature of his transactions which of the specified returns he must make.

It should be impressed on all officers that whoever receipts for any article of quartermaster's property, must make the *monthly return*, and *any one* having charge of quartermaster's funds, must make out and transmit the *monthly summary statement*, and the *account current* on account of the Quartermaster's Department.

RETURN OF CLOTHING, CAMP AND GARRISON EQUIPAGE.

Form 37, p. 72a.

The upper branch of this return shows the total to be accounted for during the month, made up of what remained on hand at last return, and the articles received during the month. The names of the parties from whom the articles are received are entered in regular order according to date under "*On hand per last return.*" The invoices being duly numbered and accompanying the return.

In the lower branch of the return are entered all issues made during the month. The vouchers will be special requisitions (Form 36) when turned over to officers, and receipt rolls according to Form 35 when the articles are issued to soldiers by the Quartermaster.

The difference between the total amount to be accounted for, and the total issued, gives the quantity remaining on hand to be inserted in the lower line of the return.

This return is to be made out in *triplicate*, and *two* copies sent to the Quartermaster-General. One copy with vouchers, and the others without vouchers.

CLOTHING RECEIPT ROLL.

Form 35, p. 71.

This roll is to be made out in duplicate. The articles at each issue are to be entered opposite the name of the soldier, and the blank spaces filled by cyphers, at the time of issue. The enlisted man drawing the clothing signs his name under the head of "*Signatures*," and the issue is duly witnessed by a commissioned officer not interested in the issue.

One copy of this roll accompanies the officer's Return of Clothing, Camp and Garrison Equipage, the other is retained with the retained copy of the above return.

SPECIAL REQUISITION.

Form 36, p. 72.

This is the form of requisition upon which transfers of clothing, camp and garrison equipage are made to officers. The requisition first states the requirement, then gives the certificate of the officer as to the necessity of the requirement, and has the approval of the commanding officer of the post, or of some officer appointed by him for that purpose. Below the approval is the receipt of the officer receiving the property.

This requisition is made out in duplicate.

Duplicate invoices of the property transferred are furnished the officer receiving it at the time of transfer.

FORM OF VOUCHER.
Form 87, p. 147.

*This exhibits the form of voucher to be used for miscellaneous disbursements where no definite form is given. It is applicable to either abstracts B or C, according to the nature of the expenditure.

DESCRIPTIVE LIST OF ARTICLES AND PERSONS TRANSFERRED.
Form 88, p. 148.

When persons and articles hired in the Quartermaster's Department are transferred, a descriptive list of this form will be forwarded with them to the Quartermaster to whom they are sent.

DUPLICATE PAPERS.

All of the Returns, Reports and Accounts Current hereinbefore named, together with their accompanying abstracts and the vouchers by which they are supported, are to be made out in *duplicate*, with the exception of the following:

TRIPLICATE PAPERS.

1. The Roll of Non-Commissioned Officers and Privates employed on extra duty (Form 80) is to be made out in *triplicate*. One copy is to be sent to the Quartermaster-General as before stated, and one copy sent to the Third Auditor of the Treasury with the money accounts. The other will be retained.

2. The Return of Property (Form 54) will be made out in *triplicate*, and two copies sent to the Quartermaster-General. One copy with abstracts and vouchers, and the other without them.

3. The Return of Clothing, Camp and Garrison Equipage will be made out in *triplicate*, and two copies sent to the Quartermaster-General. One without vouchers.

RETAINED PAPERS.

One complete set of accounts, returns, vouchers, and all papers pertaining thereto, should be retained by the officer for his own protection, as the originals are frequently lost in transmission, and the duplicates must then be relied on for effecting a settlement.

ACCOUNTS TO BE DULY RENDERED.

Failure to comply with the regulations regarding the rendering of accounts, will cause the delinquent officer to be reported to the President for dismissal from the service.

Whenever an officer ceases, from any reason, to be a disbursing officer, he will immediately render his final accounts, with vouchers, to the Third Auditor.

The Monthly Papers, the Returns of Quartermasters' stores, and the Returns of Clothing, Camp and Garrison Equipage, will each be accompanied by a letter of advice enumerating the papers therein enclosed.

Officers who are not doing duty as Quartermasters, who are not disbursing money, but who are responsible for public property received from the Quartermaster's Department, such as horses, clothing, camp and garrison equipage, etc., will only forward to the Quartermaster-General the monthly returns of the property for which they are accountable, accompanied by vouchers. This includes company commanders, who should hereafter transmit their returns of clothing and other Quartermasters' property to the Quartermaster-General monthly, instead of Quarterly.

All officers doing duty in the Quartermaster's Department are also required to make out and forward to the Quartermaster-General, on the first day of each month, a personal report, giving their post-office address and a statement of the duty upon which they have been employed since their last report.

TELEGRAMS.

Copies of the telegrams must accompany vouchers for their payment when they can be procured. If the copies cannot be procured, the account may be paid by a Quartermaster upon the certificate of the Commanding General of the Department, or the Commanding Officer of the post, showing that the telegrams were on public business, *and that the matter demanded this mode of communication.*

COST OF HORSE EQUIPMENTS.

SADDLE.	Price per set.	Price per piece.	Amount.
Saddle tree, covered with raw hide, with metal mounting attached..........................	$3 87	$3 87	
Saddle flaps with brass screws, each.............	1 18	2 36	
Back straps, with screws, rivets, and D's, each...	52	1 04	
Girth strap, long...............................	36	36	
" " short...............................	23	23	
Cloak straps, each.............................	17	1 02	
Stirrup leathers, each..........................	57	1 14	
Sweat leathers, each...........................	30	60	
Stirrups with hoods, each......................	38	76	
Carbine socket and strap.......................	47	47	
Saddle bags...................................	3 50	3 50	
Crupper......................................	1 01	1 01	
Girth..	66	66	
Surcingle.....................................	1 16	1 16	
Total cost...............................			$18 18
BRIDLE.			
*Bit, No. 1, $3 50........ } average per 100 sets	2 94	2 94	
†Bit, Nos. 2, 3, and 4, $2 80 }			
Brass scutcheon with company letter, each......	5	10	
Reins...	55	55	
Head piece....................................	67	67	
Front...	16	16	
Curb chain with hooks..........................	14	14	
Curb chain safe................................	4	4	
Total cost...............................			4 60
HALTER.			
Head stall, complete...........................	1 55	1 55	
Hitching strap.................................	48	48	
Total cost...............................			2 03
WATERING BRIDLE.			
Snaffle bit, chains, and toggles..................	50	50	
Watering rein.................................	56	56	
Total cost...............................			1 06
Spurs...	20	40	
Spur straps...................................	10	20	
Total cost...............................			60
Currycomb....................................	20	20	
Horse brush...................................	67	67	
Picket pin.....................................	13	13	
Lariat rope....................................	61	61	
Total cost...............................			1 61
Total cost of equipment....................			28 08
Blanket for cavalry service, dark, with orange border, 3 lbs., at 70 cents per lb............	2 10	2 10	
Blanket for artillery, scarlet, with dark blue border, 3 lbs., at 70 cts. per lb.............	2 10	2 10	
Nose bag......................................	1 00	1 00	
Hitching strap.................................	25	25	

* NOTE.—No. 1 is Spanish; Nos. 2, 3, and 4 are American.
† NOTE —For officers scutcheons, gilt, $0 15 each.

COST OF HORSE EQUIPMENTS.

Table showing the prices of malleable iron parts, buckles, D's, rings, etc.

Tabular No. of piece.	Place where used and kind of buckle.	Number required in each set.	Size.	Price.
			Inches.	Cents.
1	Girth, with roller, round..................	1	2	2
2	Stirrup, bar, flattened....................	2	1.375	2
3	Halter, bar, flattened.....................	1	1.125	2
4	Girth and surcingle, roller, round.........	2	1.5	2
5	Bridle, crupper, bar.......................	4	.75	1
6	Throat lash, saddle bags, cloak straps, and carbine socket, bar.....................	12	.625	1
7	Halter, square............................	2	1.6—1.2	2
8	Halter ring...............................	2	1.7	2
9	Ring for crupper and saddle tree...........	5	1.25	1
10	Halter bolt...............................	1	1.10	1
11	Foot staples..............................	6	.9	1
12	D's, back straps, and girths...............	8	1.85	4
13	Saddle bags' stud.........................	1	1—0.4	2

FORM 38.—ACCOUNT CURRENT.

The United States in account current with A. B., Quartermaster United States, on account of the Quartermaster's Department at Camp Scott, in the month of ———— 186 .

Dr.				Cr.
186 . March 31 " 31 " 31 " 31	To amount of purchases, per abstract A... To amount of expenditures, per abstract B.. To amount of transfers to officers, per abstract B *b*.......... To balance due the United States carried to new account.............		186 March 1 " 15 " "	By balance on hand, per last account..... By cash received from Treasurer of the United States, being amount of warrant No. —— By cash received of sundry officers, per abstract B *b b*......... By cash received from sales of public property, as per account herewith........

I certify that the above is a true account of all the moneys that have come into my hands, on account of the Quartermaster's Department, during the month of ————, 186 , and that the disbursements have been faithfully made.

A. B., *Quartermaster.*

ABSTRACT A. 99

FORM 39.—ABSTRACT OF PURCHASES PAID FOR.

Abstract of Purchases paid for at Camp Scott in the month of ———— 186 , by A. B.

Date.	No. of voucher.	Classes.									
		From whom purchased.	Amount.		Fuel				Forage.		Straw.	Stationery.
					Wood.			Coal.				
			Dolls.	Cts.	Cords.	Feet.	Ins.	Lbs.	Corn. Bu.	Oats. Bu.	Hay. Lbs.		

Purchased prior to the month....

Purchased within the month....

Total paid within the month....

FORM 40.—VOUCHER FOR PURCHASES TO ABSTRACT A.

The United States, *To* ——————,   Dr.

Date of purchase.		Dollars.	Cents.
	For—		
June 3, 186.	20 cords of wood, at ——— per cord........		
" 10, "	20,352 pounds of straw, at ——— per 100 lbs...		
" 29, "	100 bushels of coal, ———, per bushel........		
		$	

I certify that the above account is correct and just; the articles are to be (or have been) accounted for on my property return for the ——— quarter ending on the ——— day of ———, 1861.   A. B., *Quartermaster.*

Received at ———, the ——— of ———, 186 , of C. D., Quartermaster U. S. Army, ——— dollars and ——— cents, in full of the above account.   E. F.

(Signed duplicates.)

ABSTRACT B. 101

FORM 41.—ABSTRACT OF EXPENDITURES.

Abstract of Expenditures on account of the Quartermaster's Department, by A. B., at Camp Scott, in the month of ———, 1861.

Date of payment.	No. of voucher.	To whom paid.	On what account.	AMOUNT.	
				Dollars.	Cents.

I certify that the above abstract is correct.

A. B., *Quartermaster.*

FORM 42.—COMMUTATION OF FUEL AND QUARTERS.

The United States,   Dr.

To ———— ————.

Date.		Dollars.	Cents.
	For commutation of quarters at ———, from the ——— of ———, 186 , to the ——— of ———, 186 , inclusive..........		
	For rooms, at ——— dollars each, per month.........		
	For commutation of fuel for the same period:		
	For myself, ——— cords ——— feet ——— inches, at ——— dollars per cord......		
	For my servant, ——— cords ——— feet ——— inches, at ——— dollars per cord......		

I certify, on honor, that there were no quarters owned or hired by the public at the above station which could be assigned to ——— during the above period, and that the fuel is charged at the average market price for the month.

                A. B., *Quartermaster.*

I certify, on honor, that the above account is correct and just; that I have been regularly stationed on duty at ———, by ———, during the period charged for; that I have not been furnished with quarters, rent, or fuel by the public, nor received a commutation of money in lieu thereof.

                C. D.

Received at ———, the ——— of ———, 186 , of ———, Quartermaster of the U. S. Army, ——— dollars and ——— cents, in full of the above account.

                C. D.

(Signed in duplicate.)

FORM 43.—OFFICER'S TRANSPORTATION ACCOUNT.

The United States, Dr.

To ————————.

Date.	From —— of —— to —— of ——		Dollars.	Cents.
	For mileage from —————— to ——————, being —————— miles, at —————— cents per mile............			

I certify, on honor, that the above account is correct and just; that I performed the journey, and under the order hereto annexed, and not returning from leave of absence to the station or troops I had left; that I have not been furnished with public transportation, nor received money in lieu thereof, for any part of the route.

Received, ————, 186 , of ——————, —————— dollars and —————— cents in full of the above account.

(Signed duplicates.)

FORM 44.—ACCOUNT FOR ACTUAL TRANSPORTATION EXPENSES.

The United States, To ――――――.

Dr.

Date.		Dollars.	Cents.
	For expenses incurred for transportation of self and allowance of baggage, and porterage, in travelling from ―― to ――, per annexed statement.................................		

I certify, on honor, that the above account is correct and just; that I have performed the journey, and on urgent public duty, without orders, for the purpose of ――――, and necessarily incurred the expenses as stated; that I have travelled in the customary reasonable manner, and not returning from leave of absence to the station or troops I left; that I have not been furnished with public transportation, or money in lieu thereof, for any part of the route. The approval of the journey by the proper authority is hereto annexed.

Received at ――――, the ―― of ――――, 186 , of ――――, Assistant Quartermaster U. S. Army, ―― dollars and ―― cents, in full of the above account.

Dolls. 100

(Signed in duplicate.)

Certificate in case of journey under orders.

I certify, on honor, that this account is correct and just; that I performed the journey, and under the order hereto annexed, and necessarily incurred the expenses as stated; that I travelled in the customary reasonable manner; that I was not returning from leave of absence to the station or troops I had left; that I have not been furnished with public transportation, nor money in lieu thereof, for any part of the route.

VOUCHER TO ABSTRACT B. 105

FORM 45.—TRANSPORTATION ACCOUNT OF PAYMASTER'S CLERK.

The United States, To ——————. DR.

Date.		Dollars.	Cents.
	For the actual expense of his transportation, while travelling under orders in the discharge of his duty as clerk to Major ————, Paymaster United States Army, from ———— to ————, per annexed statement.		

I certify, on honor, that ———— was, during the time above specified, employed as a clerk in the Pay Department, United States Army, and that the journeys charged for in the above account were performed by him in the discharge of his official duties, under my orders.

———————, *Paymaster of the U.S. Army.*

———— COUNTY, ss.
On this ———— day of ————, one thousand eight hundred and sixty-one, personally appeared before me, the subscriber, a justice of the peace in and for the county aforesaid, ————, and made oath in due form of law, that the above account is correct and just, and exhibits the actual expense of his transportation for and during the journey above specified.

(Subscribed in duplicate.)

———————, *Justice of the Peace.*

Received at ———— the ———— of ————, 1861 of ————, Assistant Quartermaster United States Army, ———— dollars and ———— cents, in full of the above account.
Dollars 1⁄100

(Signed in duplicate.)

Form 46.—ACCOUNT FOR COURT-MARTIAL EXPENSES.

The United States,

To ————

Dr.

Date.		Dollars.	Cents.
	For mileage from ——— to ———, pursuant to annexed copy of Orders No. ———, convening (or annexed summons to attend) a court-martial at ———, distance being ——— miles, at ——— cents per mile. ——— days' attendance on said court-martial, being from the ——— of ——— to the ——— of ———, 186 , inclusive (per annexed certificate), at $———. ——— days' travelling on the ——— of ———, going to, and on the ——— of ———, returning from the court, at $———	$	

I certify, on honor, that the above account is correct and just; that I have actually performed the journeys therein charged for on the days stated, in obedience to the authority hereunto annexed; that I have not been furnished with public transportation, nor received money in lieu thereof, for any part of the route charged for.

Received at ———, the ——— of ———, 186 , of ———, Assistant Quartermaster U. S. Army, ——— dollars and ——— cents, in full of the above account.

(Signed in duplicate.)

VOUCHER TO ABSTRACT B.   107

FORM 47.—ACCOUNT FOR POSTAGE PAID.

The United States,   To ———— ————.   Dr.

Date.		Dollars.	Cents.
	For cash paid for postage on letters and packages on public service, received and sent by him from the ———— of ————, 186 , to the ———— of ————, 186 , inclusive...		
		$	

I certify, on honor, that the foregoing account is correct and just; that the letters and packages on which postage has been paid, as therein stated, were all on public service; that I have actually paid the amount charged.
E. F.

Received at ————, the ———— of ————, 186 , of ————, Assistant Quartermaster U. S. Army, ———— dollars and ———— cents, in full of the above account.   E. F.

(Signed in duplicate.)

FORM 48.—PAY ROLL OF QUARTERMASTER'S MEN.

We, the subscribers, do hereby acknowledge to have received of A. B., Assistant Quartermaster U. S. Army at Camp Scott, Va., the sums opposite to our names respectively, being in full of our pay for the period herein expressed, having signed duplicates thereof.

Date.	No.	Name.	Occupation.	Period of service.			Rate of pay.			Amount of pay.		Am't of stop'ges.		Amount received.		Signers' names.	Witnesses	Remarks.
				From.	To.	Months.	Days.	Dollars.	Cents.	Per month or day.	Dollars.	Cents.	Dollars.	Cents.	Dollars.	Cents.			

I certify, on honor, that the above receipt-roll is correct and just.

A. B., *Quartermaster.*

FORM 49.—ABSTRACT OF ADVANCES TO OFFICERS FOR DISB...

Abstract of Advances made to Officers for disbursement, on account of the Quartermaster's Department, by A. B., in the month of ————, 186 .

Date of the advance.	No. of the receipt or voucher.	To what officer.	By whose order, or for what purpose.	AMOUNT.	
				Dollars.	Cents.

FORM 50.—ACCOUNT CURRENT.

The United States in account current with A. B. for expenditures on account of Contingencies of the army, and of other Departments, in the month of ————, 186 .

DR.   **CR.**

Date.		Dolls.	Cts.	Date.		Dolls.	Cts.
Sept. 30.	To amount of expenditures, per Abstract C...			Sept. 1.	By balance on hand, as per last account.....		
Sept. 30.	To balance due the United States, carried to new account...........			" 3.	By cash received of ————		
		$		" 4.	By cash received from the Treasurer of the United States, being amount of Warrant No. ————		
						$	

I certify, on honor, that the above exhibits a true account of all moneys which have come into my hands on account of contingencies of the army, during the month of ————, 186 , and that the disbursements have been faithfully made.

                                                                    A. B., *Quartermaster.*

ABSTRACT C. 111

FORM 51.—ABSTRACT OF DISBURSEMENTS ON ACCOUNT OF CONTINGENCIES.

Abstract of Disbursements on account of Contingencies of the Army and of other departments, by A. B., in the month of ———, 186 , at Camp Scott, Va.

Date of payment.	No. of Voucher.	To whom paid.	On what account.	Amount.	
				Dollars.	Cents.

A. B., Quartermaster.

VOUCHER TO ABSTRACT C.

FORM 52.—REQUISITION FOR MEDICINE.

Requisition on the Quartermaster's Department for extra Supplies of Medicines and Hospital Stores.

I certify that the medicines and hospital stores above required are necessary for the use of the sick at this post, in consequence [here insert whether from loss, damage, etc.], and that the requisition is agreeable to the supply table.

A. B., *Assistant Surgeon.*

Approved.

C. D., *Commanding Officer.*

Received of ———, on the ——— of ———, 186 , the articles above enumerated.

A. B., *Assistant Surgeon.*

(Signed in duplicate.)

VOUCHER TO ABSTRACT C. 113

FORM 53.—BILL OF MEDICINE.

Bill of Medicine, &c., when purchased by an officer of the Quartermaster's Department.

The United States, To ———, Dr.

Date of purchase.	For		Dollars.	Cents.

I certify, on honor, that the prices of the articles above charged, for the use of the sick at ———, agreeable to the foregoing requisition, are reasonable and just.

A. B., *Surgeon.*

Received, ———, 186 , of ———, ——— dollars ——— cents, in full of the above account.

E. F.

(Signed duplicates.)

ABSTRACT D.

FORM 55.—ABSTRACT OF ARTICLES PURCHASED.

Abstract of Articles purchased at Camp Scott, in the month of —————, 186 , by A. B.

Date.	No. of voucher.	From whom purchased.	Classes........ Amount		Fuel			Forage.	Straw.	Stationery.					
			Dolls.	Cts.	Wood. Cords.	Feet. Ins.	Coal. Bu'ls.								

Articles purchased and paid for ....

Articles purchased and not paid for ....

Total purchased within the month ....

I certify that the above abstract is correct.

A. B., *Quartermaster.*

FORM 54.—MONTHLY RETURN OF QUARTERMASTER'S STORES.

Monthly Return of Quartermaster's Stores received and issued at ———, in the month of ——————, 186 , by ———.

I certify, on honor, that the foregoing return exhibits a true and correct statement of all the property which has come into my hands on account of the Quartermaster's Department, during the quarter ending on the —— of ————, 186 .

A. B., *Quartermaster.*

FORM 56.—BILL OF PURCHASE.

The United States,   Dr.

To ————,

Date of purchase.		Dollars.	Cents.
	For ———— cords of wood, at ———— per cord............		
	For ———— pounds of hay, at ———— per 100 lbs..........		
		$	

I certify, on honor, that the above account is correct and just; that I purchased the articles above enumerated of the said ————, at the prices therein charged, amounting to ———— dollars and ———— cents, and that I have not paid the account. [Here state the cause of non-payment.]
A. B, *Quartermaster.*

ABSTRACT E.

FORM 57.—ABSTRACT OF ARTICLES RECEIVED.

Abstract of Articles received from Officers at Camp Scott, in the month of ————, 186 , by A. B.

Date.	No. of voucher.	Classes........		Fuel				Forage.	Straw.	Stationery.			
			From whom received.	Wood.			Coal.						
				Cords.	Feet.	Inches.	Bushels.						
		Total received......											

I certify that the above abstract is correct.

A. B., *Quartermaster.*

Form 58.—Invoice.

List of Quartermaster's Stores, &c., delivered by C. D. to A. B., at Washington, D. C., on the 10th day of June, 186 .

Number or quantity.		Articles.	Cost when new.	Condition when delivered.	Remarks.
40	Forty	Felling axes	$1 00 each	New	
300	Three hundred pounds	Bar iron, assorted	6 per pound	New	
1,000	One thousand pounds	Cut nails	5 per pound	New	
656	Six hundred and fifty-six bushels	Corn	1 00 per bushel	Good	
30,500	Thirty thousand five hundred pounds	Hay	1 00 per hundred	Good	
10	Ten	Wheelbarrows	4 00 each	Half-worn	
5	Five	Wagons (4-horse)	150 00 each	Half-worn	
5	Five	Wagons do	150 00 each	New	

I certify that I have this day delivered to A. B., Quartermaster United States Army, the articles specified in the foregoing list.

C. D., *Quartermaster.*

NOTE.—When no invoice is received, the receiving officer will substitute for this form of voucher a list of the stores received, certified by himself. When the person responsible for the property entered without invoice is known, it will be entered in his name.

ABSTRACT F.

FORM 59.—ABSTRACT OF FUEL.

Abstract of Fuel issued at Camp Scott, in the quarter ending on the 30th of June, 186 , by A. B.

Date.	No. of Voucher.	To whom issued.	For what period.	Wood.			Coal.		Remarks.
				Cords.	Feet.	Inches.	Pounds.	Bushels.	

Total issued ....

I certify that the above abstract is correct.

A. B., *Quartermaster.*

VOUCHER TO ABSTRACT F. 119

FORM 60.—REQUISITION FOR FUEL.

Requisition for Fuel for ——— Company, ———. Regiment of ———, commanded by ———, for the month of ———, 186—.

Station.	Captains.	Subalterns.	Non-commissioned officers, musicians, and privates.	Laundresses and servants.	Total.	Monthly allowance to each, in cords.	TOTAL ALLOWANCE.					Remarks.
							Wood.			Coal.		
							Cords.	Feet.	Inches.	Bushels.	Pounds.	

Total.............

I certify, on honor, that the above requisition is correct and just, and that fuel has not been drawn for any part of the time above charged.

R. S., *Commanding Company.*

Received, ———, 186—, of ———, Assistant Quartermaster U. S. Army, ——— cords ——— feet ——— inches of wood and ——— of coal, in full of the above requisition.

R. S., *Commanding Company.*

(Signed duplicates.)

FORM 61.—REQUISITION FOR FUEL.

Requisition for Fuel for ———, stationed at ———, for the month of ———, 186 .

Requisition for Fuel for		Wood.			Coal.		Remarks.
		Cords.	Feet.	Inches.	Bushels.	Pounds.	
For myself..............							
For private servant....							
Total..................							

I certify, on honor, that the above requisition is correct and just, and that I have not drawn fuel for any part of the time above charged.

Received, ———, 186 , of ———, Assistant Quartermaster United States Army, ——— cords ——— feet ——— inches of wood and coal, in full of the above requisition.

NOTE.—This form will be used for individual officers, hospitals, guards, &c.

FORM 62.—ABSTRACT OF FORAGE ISSUED.

Abstract of Forage issued at Camp Scott, in the month of ——————, 186 , by A. B.

Date.	No. of voucher.	To whom issued.	For what period.		Number of horses.	Number of mules.	Number of oxen.	Total.	Total allowance.						Remarks.
			From—	To—					Corn.		Oats.		Hay.	Fodder.	
									Bushels. (56 lbs.)	Pounds.	Bushels. (32 lbs.)	Pounds.	Pounds.	Pounds.	
															Public.
															Private.
Total.........															

I certify that the above abstract is correct.

A. B., *Quartermaster.*

FORM 63.—REQUISITION FOR FORAGE.

Requisition for Forage for Public Horses, Mules, and Oxen, in the service of ——— for ——— days, commencing the ——— of ———, 186 , and ending on the ——— of ———, 186 , at ———.

Date of requisition.	Number of horses.	Number of mules.	Number of oxen.	Total number of animals.	Number of days.	Number of rations.	Daily allowance to each animal.					Total allowance.					REMARKS.
							Pounds of corn.	Pounds of barley.	Pounds of oats.	Pounds of hay.	Pounds of fodder.	Corn. Pounds of.	Barley. Pounds of.	Oats. Pounds of.	Hay. Pounds of.	Fodder. Pounds of.	

Required............
On hand, to be deducted............
To be supplied............

I certify, on honor, that the above requisition is correct and just; that I have now in the service the number of animals for which forage is required; and that forage has not been received for any part of the time specified.

Received at ———, on the ——— day of ———, 186 , of ———, Quartermaster United States Army, ——— pounds of corn, ——— pounds of barley, ——— pounds of oats, ——— pounds of hay, ——— pounds of fodder, in full of the above requisition.
(Signed duplicates.)

VOUCHER TO ABSTRACT G.   123

FORM 64.—REQUISITION FOR FORAGE.

Requisition for Forage for ———— Private Horses in the service of ————, U. S. Army, at ————, for ———— days, commencing the ———— of ————, and ending the ———— of ————, 186— .

Date.	Period.		Number of horses.	Daily allowance for each.			Total allowance.					REMARKS.
	From.	To.		Corn. Pounds.	Oats. Pounds.	Hay. Pounds.	Corn. Bushels, (56 lbs.)	Pounds.	Oats. Bushels, (32 lbs.)	Pounds.	Hay. Pounds.	Fodder. Pounds.
Total.......												

I certify, on honor, that the above requisition is correct and just, and that I have not drawn forage for any part of the time above charged.
                                                                                                          A. B.

Received at ————, the ———— of ————, 186 , of ————, Assistant Quartermaster U. S. Army, ——36— bushels corn, —32— bushels oats, ———— pounds hay, ———— pounds fodder, in full of the above requisition.
                                                                                                          A. B.
(Signed duplicates.)

FORM 65.—STATEMENT OF FORAGE.

Statement of Forage issued to and consumed by the Public Animals under my direction at ———, during the month of ———, 186 .

Period.			Number of animals.				Quantity of, consumed.					Remarks.
From—	To—	No. of days.	Horses.	Mules.	Oxen.	Total.	Corn. Pounds.	Oats. Pounds.	Barley. Pounds.	Hay. Pounds.	Fodder. Pounds.	
Total......												

I certify that the above statement is correct; that the forage was issued to the Public Animals as stated, and that the issues were necessary.

Approved: R. S., *Commanding.*   A. B., *Quartermaster.*

ABSTRACT H. 125

FORM 66.—ABSTRACT OF STRAW.

Abstract of Straw issued at Camp Scott, in the month of ————, 186 , by A. B.

Date.	No. of voucher.	To whom issued.	For what period.		Non-commissioned officers, musicians, and privates.	Laundresses.	Servants.	Hospital.	Total allowance.	Remarks.
			From —	To —					Pounds.	
		Total............								

I certify that the above abstract is correct.

A. B., *Quartermaster.*

FORM 67.—REQUISITION FOR STRAW.

Requisition for Straw for —— Company, Regiment of ——, commanded by —— for the month of June, 186 .

Station.	Non-commissioned officers, musicians and privates.	Laundresses.	Servants.	Total drawn for.	Monthly allowance to each.	Total allowance.	Remarks.
					Pounds.	Pounds.	
Fort Adams.	69	4	2	75	12	900	
Total	69	4	2	75	12	900	

I certify, on honor, that the above return is correct and just, and that straw has not been drawn for any part of the time charged.

G. H., *Commanding Company.*

Received at ——, the —— of ——, 1861, of ——, U. S. Army, 900 pounds of straw, in full of the above requisition.
(Signed duplicates.)

G. H., *Commanding Company.*

ABSTRACT I.

FORM 68.—ABSTRACT OF STATIONERY.

Abstract of Stationery issued at Camp Scott in the month of ――――, 186 , by A. B.

Date.	No. of voucher.	To whom issued.	For what period.		Writing paper, quires.	Cartridge paper, sheets.	Quills, number.	Wafers, ounces.	Sealing-wax, ounces.	Ink-powder, papers.	Blank books, number.				Remarks.
			From.	To.											

Total............

I certify that the above abstract is correct.

A. B., *Quartermaster.*

FORM 69.—REQUISITION FOR STATIONERY.

Requisition for Stationery for ————, stationed at Camp Scott, for the month of ————, 186 ,

Quires of letter paper.	Quires of foolscap paper.	Sheets of cartridge paper.	Number of quills.	Ounces of wafers.	Ounces of sealing wax.	Pieces of tape.	Papers of ink-powder.

I certify that the above requisition is correct, and that I have not drawn stationery for any part of the time specified.
A. B.

Received at ————, on the ———— of ———— 186 , or ————, Assistant Quartermaster U. S. Army, ———— quires of letter paper, ———— quires of foolscap paper, ———— quills, ———— ounces of wafers, ———— ounces of sealing-wax, ———— pieces of tape, ———— sheets of cartridge paper, ———— papers of ink-powder.   A. B.
(Signed duplicates.)

Form 70.—Abstract of all Issues except Fuel, Forage, Straw, and Stationery.

Abstract of Articles issued on Special Requisitions at Camp Scott, in the month of ————, 186 , by A. B.

Date.	To whom issued.	Classes.........					Total......

I certify that the above abstract is correct.

A. B., *Quartermaster.*

ABSTRACT L.

FORM 71.—ABSTRACT OF ARTICLES LOST, ETC.

Abstract of Articles Expended, Lost, Destroyed, in the public service, sold, &c., at Camp Scott, under the direction of A. B., in the month of ———, 186 .

Date.	No. of certificate.	By whom made.		Classes
				Total........

I certify that the above abstract is correct.

A. B., *Quartermaster.*

VOUCHER TO ABSTRACT L. 131

FORM 72.—LIST OF ARTICLES LOST, &c.

List of Articles Lost or Destroyed in the public service at Camp Scott, while in the possession and charge of A. B., in the month of January, 186 .

No. or quantity.	Articles.	Circumstances and cause.

I certify that the several articles of Quartermaster's stores, above enumerated, have been unavoidably lost or destroyed while in the public service, as indicated by the remarks annexed to them respectively.

A. B., *Quartermaster.*

Approved: C. D., *Commanding.*

FORM 73.—LIST OF QUARTERMASTER'S STORES EXPENDED.

List of Quartermaster's Stores expended in public service at Camp Scott, under the direction of A. B., Quartermaster, in the month of June, 186 .

No. or quantity.	Articles.	Application.

I certify, on honor, that the several articles of Quartermaster's stores, above enumerated, have been necessarily expended in the public service at this station, as indicated by the marginal remarks annexed to them respectively.

A. B., *Quartermaster.*

(Signed duplicates.)

Approved: R. S., *Commanding.*

FORM 74.—ACCOUNT SALES OF PROPERTY.

Account Sales of articles of public property sold at public auction at ———, under the direction of ———, on the ——— of ———, 186 .

Number or quantity.	Articles.	Purchaser.	AMOUNT.

I certify that the above account sales is accurate and just.

A. B., *Auctioneer.*

I certify that the above enumerated articles were sold at public auction as above stated, pursuant to ——[state the orders or authority.]

C. D., *Quartermaster.*

ABSTRACT M.

FORM 75.—ABSTRACT OF ARTICLES TRANSFERRED.

Abstract of Articles transferred to Officers at Camp Scott, in the month of ———, 186 .
by A. B., Quartermaster.

Date.	No. of voucher.	To whom transferred.				Classes........
						Total........

I certify that the above abstract is correct.

A. B., *Quartermaster.*

Form 76.—Abstract of Articles Received.

Abstract of Articles received from various sources at Camp Scott, during the month of ———, 186 .

Date.	No. of Invoice, &c.	Classes		Fuel.			Forage.			Straw.	Stationery.
		From whence received.		Wood.		Coal.	Corn. Bushels, (56 lbs.)	Oats. Bushels, (82 lbs.)	Hay.		
				Cords.	Feet.	Inches.				Pounds.	Pounds.	
		Found at the post............									
		Manufactured................									
		Parts of articles broken up...									
		Heretofore issued, but not consumed...									
		Captured from the enemy....									
	Total.........										

I certify that the above abstract is correct.

A. B., *Quartermaster.*

FORM 77.—MONTHLY STATEMENT OF ALLOWANCES PAID OFFICERS.

Monthly Statement of Allowances paid to Officers of the Army in money, or furnished in kind, with the money value thereof, by Capt. A. B., Assistant Quartermaster, at Fort Adams, R. I., in the month of ————, 186—.

Officers' names.	Rank and corps.	For Fuel		Quarters					For transportation of baggage.	Per diem on court-martial.	For forage issued in kind.	Straw for servants.	Stationery.	Total amount.	Remarks.
				In money.		In kind.									
		Period.	Amt.	Period.	$ c.	Period.	No. rooms.	Rent.							
			$ c.					$ c.	$ c.	$ c.	$ c.	$ c.	$ c.	$ c.	
W. S.	Maj. Genl.	July, Aug. Sep.	96 00	July, Aug. Sep.	120 00	186.			120 00	40 00			20 00	396 00	B 1, 7, 9—I 9.
J. T.	Brig. Genl.	July	30 00	July, Aug. Sep.	90 00				90 00				15 00	215 00	B 2, 11, 14—I 4.
K. J.	Col. Ajt. Gl.	August	30 00	July, Aug. Sep.	90 00									120 00	B 17
T. M.	Col. Q. M. D.	August	30 00	July, Aug. Sep.	80 00									110 00	B 21
T. L.	Maj. Pay Dt.	July, Aug. Sep.	30 00	Aug., Sep.	80 00	July.	3	30 00	60 00		30 00			230 00	B 4, 20—G 13.
L. B.	Col. Engrs.	July, Aug. Sep.	30 00			July.								130 00	B 19
B. L.	Mj. T. Engrs.					July, Aug.	4	30 00	100 00	40 00	87 50	2 00		110 00	B 26, 27
B. B. M.	Col. Drags.	July, Aug.	20 00			July, Aug.	4	35 00	80 00			1 50		189 50	B 27, 30—G 14.
J. C.	Col. Art.	July, Aug.	12 00			July, Aug.	4		70 00			50		126 50	B 28, 32—H 2.
F. E.	Maj. Infty.	July, Aug.												12 50	F 4—H 6.

I certify that the above is correct.

E. A. O., *Quartermaster.*

MONTHLY SUMMARY STATEMENT.

FORM 78.—MONTHLY SUMMARY STATEMENT.

The United States in account with A. B., at Camp Scott, in the month of June, 186 .

DR.

186 .	To amount of purchases within the month...... To amount of expenditures within the month. To amount of advances made to officers, per abstract........	
	Balance due the United States, carried to next statement........	

CR.

186 .	By balance per last statement........ By cash received from ——— By cash received from Treasurer of the United States, being amount of Warrant No.———	

I certify that the above is a true statement of all the moneys which have come into my hands, on account of the Quartermaster's Department, during the month of ———, 186 , and that the disbursements have been faithfully made. The balance due the United States is deposited in ———.

A. B., *Quartermaster.*

FORM 79.—REPORT OF PERSONS

Report of Persons and Articles employed and hired at New York

Running numbers.	No. of each class.	Names of persons and articles.	Designation and occupation.	Service during the month.			Rate of hire or compensation.		Date of contract, agreement, or entry into service.
				From.	To.	Day.	Amount.	Day, month, or voyage.	
1	1	House, 3 rooms.	Quarters...	1	31	31	$40 00	Month.	July 1, 186 .
2	2	House, 4 rooms.	Store-house	3	31	29	81 00	Month.	Dec. 3, 186 .
3	3	House, 2 rooms	Guard "	1	31	31	10 00	Month.	Dec. 3, 186 .
1	1	Ship Fanny.....	Transport..	1	31	31	2,000 00	Voyage.	May 3, 186 .
2	2	Schr. Heroine...	Transport..	1	31	31	700 00	Month.	June 4, 186 .
1	1	Wagon & team..	....	1	31	31	100 00	Month.	Jan. 1, 186 .
1	1	Chas. James....	Clerk......	1	31	31	75 00	Month.	Dec. 3, 186 .
2	1	Isaac Lowd....	Interpreter	7	10	4	2 00	Day.	Jan. 7, 186 .
3	1	Peter Keene....	Express....	7	12	6	40 00	Month.	Jan. 7, 186 .
4	1	John Peters.....	Blacksmith	22	31	7	2 00	Day.	Jan. 1, 186 .
5	1	Thos. Cross.....	Laborer....	1	31	31	20 00	Month.	May 3, 186 .
		United States Steamer Wave							
1	1	James Corwin..	Captain	1	31	31	150 00	Month.	Dec. 1, 186 .
2	1	Geo. Pratt......	Engineer...	1	31	31	100 00	Month.	Dec. 1, 186 .
3	1	John Paul......	Mate.......	1	31	31	50 00	Month.	Dec. 1, 186 .

Amount of rent and hire during the month............................

I certify, on honor, that the above is a true report of all the persons and articles tions under the head of Remarks, and the statement of amounts due and remaining

Examined.

AND ARTICLES HIRED.

during the month of July, 186 , by E. F., Asst. Quartermaster.

By whom owned.	Amount of rent or pay in the month.	Remarks.	Time and amount due and remaining unpaid.		
			From.	To.	Am't.
A. Byrne...	$40 00	Major 3d. Infantry............	186 . Dec. 1.	186 . Jan. 31.	$80 00
Jas. Black..	29 00	Subsistence Store and Office...	Dec. 3.	Jan. 31.	60 00
Jas. Black..	10 00	Companies I & K, 3d Infantry .	.....	....	......
G. Wilkins..	....	Transp'ting stores to F. Monroe	Voyage	not	completed.
T. Browne..	700 00	Transp'ting stores to Annapolis	186 . Jan. 1..	186 . Jan. 31.	700 00
Jas. Barry..	100 00	Hauling stores to Ft. Schuyler.	Jan. 1..	Jan. 31.	100 00
	75 00	Quartermaster's Office.........	.....	.....	......
	8 00	Employed by Com'ing General	.....	.....	......
	7 74	Express to Annapolis.........	.....	.....	......
	14 00	Shoeing public horses.........	.....	.....	......
	20 00	Helping Blacksmith............	.....	.....	......
	150 00	} Steamship sent to Old Point.............. {	July 1.	July 31	150 00
	100 00		July 1.	July 31	100 00
	50 00		July 1.	July 31	50 00
....	1303 74	Total amount due and remaining unpaid.......			1240 00

employed and hired by me during the month of July, 186 , and that the observa- unpaid, are correct.   E. F., *Asst. Quartermaster.*

C. D., *Commanding.*

FORM 80.—EXTRA DUTY PAY ROLL.

Roll of Non-commissioned Officers and Privates employed on extra duty, as mechanics and laborers, at Camp Scott, during the month of June, 186 , by A. B., Captain and Quartermaster.

No.	Names.	Rank or designation.	Company.	Regiment.	By whose order employed.	Nature of service.	Term of Service.			Rate of pay, or compensation.			How employed.
							From.	To.	No. days.	Per diem.		Dolls. Cts.	REMARKS.
										Cts.			

I certify that the above is a correct roll of non-commissioned officers, musicians, and privates, employed on extra duty, under my direction, during the month of ———, 166 , and that the remarks opposite their names are accurate and just.

Examined. C. D., *Commanding.* A. B., *Quartermaster.*

FORM 81.—REPORT OF STORES FOR TRANSPORTATION.

Report of Stores received for Transportation and Distribution at ———, by ———, in the month of ———, 186— .

Time received.	Marks.	No.	Contents.	From whom received.	By whom received.	Time sent.	To whom sent, and where.	With whom sent.	Intermediate destination.	Ultimate destination.	Remarks.
186 .						186 .					
June 1.	W. S., &c.	1 to 3.	Clothing.	Capt. A. B., Ass't Quartermaster, Boston.	Sloop Sally, Capt. A. W.	June 9.	Capt. C., Ass't. Quar'master St. Louis.	Ship George, Capt. I. B.	......	......	Received in good order.

I certify that the above report is correct.

E. A. O., *Quartermaster.*

FORM 82.—RETURN OF ANIMALS.

Monthly Return of Public Animals, Wagons, Harness, and other means of transportation in the possession of A. B., at Camp Scott, during the month of June, 186 .

Date.	Horses.	Mules.	Oxen.	Wagons.	Ambulances.	Carts.	Wheel harness, single sets of.	Lead harness, single sets of.	Wagon saddles.	Ships.	Schooners.	Sloops.	Steamers.	Boats and barges.	Skiffs and batteaux.	REMARKS.
On hand............																18 horses purchased; average cost $——. Wagons purchased at ——. 6 horses received from ——.
Purchased during the month.....																
Received from officers.........																
Total to be accounted for........																
Transferred...........																Horses transferred to ——. Wagons transferred to ——. 1 horse sold; — horses died on the road to ——.
Sold and worn out.....																
Died and lost.........																
Total issued and expended.......																
Remaining on hand....																

I certify that the above return is correct.

A. B., *Quartermaster.*

REPORT OF FORAGE.

FORM 83.—REPORT OF FORAGE.

Monthly Report of Forage which has been issued to Horses, Mules, and Oxen in the public service at Fort Scott, Va., by A. B., Captain and Ass't. Quartermaster, during the month of August, 186 .

Date.	To whom issued.	Public.			Private.		To-tal. Animals.	Quantity issued.				Average cost of								Remarks.
		Horses.	Mules.	Oxen.	Horses.	Mules.		Corn. Pounds.	Oats. Pounds.	Hay. Pounds.	Fodder. Pounds.	Corn, per bush. (56 lbs.) $	c	Oats, per bush. (32 lbs.) $	c	Hay, per 100 pounds. $	c	Fodder, per 100 pounds. $	c	
186 .																					
Aug. 10.	Field and staff officers....	6	....	....	12	....	16	6,490	....	1,850	....	1	00		50		50	1	00	Hay purchased at — at — per 100 pounds.
" 15.	Company A, 1st Cavalry..	61	....	....	4	....	65	23,400	....	2,340	....									Corn purchased at —, and hauled at — per bush.
" 18.	" B, 2d "	47	....	....	4	....	51	18,360	....	2,100	....									Fodder delivered at the post at — per 100 lbs.
" 25.	" K, 1st Artillery..	45	300	....	6	....	51	18,360	....	....	1,640									
" 31.	Quarterm'r's Departm't..	60	....	80	....	....	440	158,400	....	33,000	....									
	Total.............	219	300	80	26	....	625	225,000	....	38,690	1,640									

I certify that the above report is correct.

A. B., *Quartermaster.*

FORM 84.—REPORT OF FUEL AND QUARTERS COMMUTED.

Report of Officers of the Army stationed at ———, whose Quarters and Fuel are commuted, for the month of August, 186 , by A. B., Captain and A. Q. M.

Names.	Rank.	Corps.	Period.		Quarters.					Fuel.							Under what order.	Remarks.
			From.	To.	Room No.	Rate per month.		Amount.		Wood.			Price per cord.		Amount.			
						Dolls.	Cts.	Dolls.	Cts.	Cords.	Feet.	Ins.	Dolls.	Cts.	Dolls.	Cts.		
																		Paid—
					Amount of Quarters, $								Amount of Fuel, $					

I certify, on honor, that the above report is correct,

A. B., *Quartermaster.*

FORM 85.—REPORT OF PAY DUE.

Report of Persons Hired and Employed in the Quartermaster's Department at Camp Scott, who have deceased, deserted, or have been discharged the service with pay due, during the month of August, 186 , by A. B., Captain and A. Q. M.

No.	Names.	Occupation.	RATE OF PAY OR HIRE.		Per day or month.	TIME FOR, AND AMOUNT REMAINING UNPAID.			REMARKS.
			Dolls.	Cts.		From.	To.	Dolls. Cts.	
11	George Peters	Blacksmith	2	00	Day	1 July, 1861.	31 Aug., 1861.	52 00	Discharged 30th Sept., 186 ; certificates given.
27	John Smith	Teamster	25	00	Month	1 Aug., 1861.	15 Aug., 1861.	12 50	Deserted 16th September,186 .
80	Peter Davis	Laborer	20	00	Month	1 Aug., 1861.	15 Aug., 1861.	10 00	Died 24th September, 186 .
								74 50	

I certify, on honor, that the above is a true report of all persons hired and employed by me in the Quartermaster's Department, who have deceased, deserted, or been discharged the service with pay due, and that the statement of time for, and amount remaining unpaid, and the remarks, are correct and just.

A. B., *Quartermaster.*

FORM 86.—ESTIMATE FOR FUNDS.

Estimate of Funds required for the service of the Quartermaster's Department at ——, by ——, in the month of ——, 186 .

		Dolls.	Cts.
1	For Fuel...		
2	Forage		
3	Straw		
4	Stationery		
5	Materials for building. (State what, and for what purpose)..........................		
6	Hire of mechanics. (State for what work)...		
7	Hire of labourers. (State for what service)...		
8	Hire of teamsters. (State on what service)...		
9	Pay of extra-duty men. (State for what work)		
10	Pay of wagon and forage masters		
11	Hire of clerks, guides, escorts, expenses of courts-martial, of burials, of apprehending deserters, and other incidental expenses		
12	Hire or commutation of officers' quarters.....		
13	Hire of quarters for troops, or ground for encampment or use of military stations		
14	Hire of store-houses, offices, &c. (For what use)		
15	Mileage to officers.........................		
16	Army transportation, viz.:		
	Of troops and their baggage		
	Of Quartermasters', subsistence, ordnance, and hospital stores		
17	Purchase of horses and mules (Q. M. Dept.)...		
18	Purchase of wagons and harness, do. ...		
19	Purchase of horses for mounted troops, viz.:		
	Horses for Company —— Dragoons		
	Horses for Company —— Artillery, &c., &c.		
20	Outstanding Debts		
	Deduct actual or probable balance on hand		

FORM 87.—FORM OF VOUCHER.

The United States,   Dr.
          To ————,

Date.		Dollars.	Cents.

I certify, on honor, that the above account is correct and just; that the services were rendered as stated, and that they were necessary for the public service.
                                                                        A. B, *Quartermaster.*

Received ———, 186 , of ———, ——— dollars and ——— cents, in full of the above account.
                                                                        E. F.
                              (Signed duplicates.)

Form 88.—Descriptive List.

Descriptive List of Persons and Articles employed and hired in the Quartermaster's Department, and transferred by ———, at ———, to ———, Quartermaster, at ———, on the ———, day of ———, 186 .

Number of each class.	Articles and names of persons.	Designation and occupation.	Period for which pay is due.			Rate of hire or compensation.			Amount due		Date of contract, agreement, or entry into service.	By whom owned, and where.	Remarks.
			From—	To—	Month.	Days.	Dollars.	Cents.	Month, day, or voyage.	Dollars.	Cents.			

Total amount due..................

I certify that the above is a true list of persons and articles transferred by me to ———, at ———, on the ——— day of ———, 186 ; and that the periods of service, rates of hire or compensation, and amounts due, are correctly stated.

ORDNANCE.

ARMS AND ACCOUTREMENTS.

The Ordnance Department has charge of the arsenals and armories, and furnishes all ordnance and ordnance stores for the military service.

The general denomination, "Ordnance and Ordnance Stores," comprehends all cannon and artillery carriages and equipments; all apparatus and machines for the service and manœuvres of artillery; all small arms and accoutrements and horse equipments; all ammunition; and all tools and materials for the ordnance service.

The commander of each company or detachment will be accountable for all ordnance or ordnance stores issued to his command. The commander of each post will be accountable for all ordnance and ordnance stores at the post, not issued to the company or detachment commanders, or not in charge of an officer of ordnance or a store-keeper. Ordnance sergeants will account for ordnance property only where there is no commissioned officer of the army or store-keeper.

Commanding officers of the militia in the service of the United States, shall return and account for ordnance and ordnance stores in the use of troops as required in the regular service. And all arms and equipments issued to such militia, shall be charged against the person to whom the issue is made on the muster-roll or pay account, to be accounted for to the mustering and inspecting officer, before receiving pay during service and on his discharge.

When a mustering and inspecting officer relieves such person from charge for loss or damage to his arms or equipments, satisfactory evidence, by affidavit or otherwise, setting out the facts of the loss or damage, and showing that it was not by his fault, shall be annexed to the pay-roll or account.

When charges on account of ordnance stores are made against a soldier, the property return shall give his name and the pay-roll or account in which the charge is made.

Arm chests are to be preserved and accounted for as other ordnance stores.

In the time of peace, ordnance and ordnance stores are issued from the armories only by authority of the ordnance bureau of the War Department. In war, to supply troops in service, they are issued on the order of any general or field officer commanding an army, garrison, or detachment. Though in issues to the militia, they must have been regularly mustered into the service, and the requisition made agreeably to Form 89, p. 161, have been approved by the mustering and inspecting officer of the United States, or a general or a field officer commanding in the regular service.

Requisitions for ordnance and ordnance stores for companies or posts may, in urgent cases, be sent direct to the Adjutant-General's office, a duplicate to be forwarded at the same time to Department headquarters. Requisitions for the Military Academy are to be transmitted to the chief engineer. Requisitions for supplies for arsenals and armories are to be sent direct to the ordnance bureau.

When arms, accoutrements, and equipments need repairs that cannot be made by the troops, the commanding officer may send them to be repaired to the most convenient arsenal.

Ordnance and ordnance stores are issued to States and Territories, on the signing of triplicate receipts by the governor thereof, or the officer or agent appointed by him to receive the stores; one of which, when returned, is to be sent by the issuing officer to the ordnance bureau.

The expenses of issue and delivery of these stores, at any point within the State designated by the governor, if on navigable water or otherwise easily accessible, are paid by the United States from the appropriation for arming and equipping the militia. The officers of the Ordnance Department provide for the transportation and payment of expenses.

SALES OF ARMS TO OFFICERS.

Officers may draw arms and accoutrements from any arsenal, for their own use in the public service, on payment of the regulated prices, and signing duplicate receipts of the following form:

PRICES OF SMALL ARMS.

Received, ——— Arsenal, ———, 18—, of Major ——— ———
    One field officer's sword,
    One pair percussion pistols,
for which I have paid the said Major ——— ——— the cost price,
——— dollars.

                                W. A. N.
                                Major ——— *Artillery.*

(To be made in duplicate.)

PRICES OF SMALL ARMS.

The following table shows the prices of small arms and accoutrements, and the several parts thereof, which will govern officers in making charges on muster rolls for damage and loss:

PARTS.	Musket.	Rifle.	Hall's carbine.	Artillery musketoon.	Cavalry musketoon.	Sapper's musketoon.	Pistol.
Barrel with sight, without breech screw....	$4 10	$4 40	$4 48	$3 50	$3 55	$3 55	$ 2 60
Breech screw................	10	10	....	10	10	10	08
Bayonet or band stud........	01	....	....	01	....	01	....
Tang screw..................	05	05	....	05	05	05	04
Breech sight................	....	06	....	....	....	....	....
Cone.......................	09	09	09	09	09	09	09
Lock plate..................	50	50	50	50	50	50	40
Tumbler....................	27	27	....	27	27	27	25
Tumbler screw..............	03	03	....	03	03	03	03
Bridle.....................	16	16	....	16	16	16	14
Sear	20	20	13	20	20	20	17
Sear spring.................	10	10	13	10	10	10	08
Main spring.................	27	27	20	27	27	27	25
Lock screw, each............	08	03	04	03	03	03	03
Hammer....................	60	60	60	60	60	60	45
Side plate (with band, for pistol)..	07	10	....	07	12	07	40
Side screws, each............	04	04	03	04	04	04	03
Upper band.................	38	45	23	38	38	58	....
Middle band................	28	....	....	....	....	....	....
Lower band.................	15	18	11	21	28	21	....
Upper band spring...........	09	09	05	09	09	09	....
Middle band spring..........	08	....	....	....	....	....	....
Lower band spring...........	08	08	....	08	....	08	....
Guard plate.................	42	50	47	40	50	40	35
Guard plate screw, each......	03	03	03	03	03	03	02
Guard bow without swivels...	30	35	20	20	25	20	20
Guard bow nut, each.........	02	02	02	02	02	02	02
Swivels and rivets, each.....	10	10	....	10	....	10	....
Swivel plate................	....	....	....	10	....	10	....
Swivel plate screw, each.....	....	....	....	03	....	03	....
Trigger.....................	12	12	12	12	12	12	09
Trigger screw...............	02	02	....	02	02	02	02
Butt plate..................	30	53	29	30	50	30	28
Butt plate screw, each.......	08	03	05	03	03	03	02

PRICES OF SMALL ARMS.

PARTS.	Musket.	Rifle.	Hall's carbine.	Artillery musketoon.	Cavalry musketoon.	Sappers' musketoon.	Pistol.
Ramrod	$ 50	$ 50	$ 50	$ 40	$ 50	$ 40	$ 25
Ramrod spring	12	12	12	12	....	12	....
Ramrod wires	01	01	....	01	....	01	....
Ramrod stop	01	01	....	01	....	01	....
Stock	1 45	1 85	2 25	1 86	1 36	1 86	90
Bayonet	1 45	....	....	....	....	....	....
Bayonet clasp	16	....	....	....	....	....	....
Bayonet clasp screw	02	....	....	....	....	....	....
Box plate	....	72	....	....	....	....	....
Box catch	....	05	....	....	....	....	....
Box spring	....	10	....	....	....	....	....
Box spring screw	....	02	....	....	....	....	....
Box screw, each	....	03	....	....	....	....	....
Ramrod swivel and rivet	....	....	....	....	25	....	25
Ramrod swivel and rivet screw	....	....	....	....	03	....	02
Swivel bar	....	....	24	....	24	....	....
Swivel nut	....	....	02	....	02	....	....
Swivel screw	....	....	03	....	03	....	....
Swivel ring	....	....	03	....	03	....	....
Sword bayonet blade	....	....	....	....	....	2 18	....
Sword bayonet hilt, without clasp	....	....	....	....	....	1 60	....
Sword bayonet clasp	....	....	....	....	....	21	....
Sword bayonet clasp screw	....	....	....	....	....	02	....
Guide	....	....	06	....	....	....	....
Bridge	....	....	65	....	....	....	....
Supporters, each	....	....	43	....	....	....	....
Supporter screws, each	....	....	02	....	....	....	....
Chocks, each	....	....	07	....	....	....	....
Chock screws, each	....	....	03	....	....	....	....
Receivers	....	....	2 66	....	....	....	....
Butt piece	....	....	08	....	....	....	....
Butt piece screw	....	....	05	....	....	....	....
Strap	....	....	25	....	....	....	....
Strap screw	....	....	05	....	....	....	....
Set screw	....	....	03	....	....	....	....
Link	....	....	09	....	....	....	....
Link screw	....	....	03	....	....	....	....
Stop	....	....	14	....	....	....	....
Apron	....	....	13	....	....	....	....
Apron screw	....	....	08	....	....	....	....
Catch	....	....	19	....	....	....	....
Catch screw	....	....	03	....	....	....	....
Catch spring	....	....	12	....	....	....	....
Catch spring screw	....	....	04	....	....	....	....
Catch plate	....	....	16	....	....	....	....
Catch plate screw	....	....	03	....	....	....	....
Lever	....	....	20	....	....	....	....
Barrel complete	4 39	4 65	4 57	3 70	3 74	3 75	2 17
Lock complete	2 25	2 25	1 46	2 25	2 25	2 25	1 89
Guard complete	1 06	1 16	....	84	99	84	72
Bayonet complete	1 63	....	....	....	....	....	....
Box plate complete	....	98	....	....	....	....	....
Arm complete	18 00	13 25	17 00	10 37	11 00	10 62*	7 00

* Without sword bayonet.

Appendages. { Screw driver and cone wrench............. 46 cts.
Wiper.. 26 "
Ball screw................................... 12 " } For all arms.
Spring vice................................. 35 "
Bullet mould (rifle calibre)............. 50 "

Prices of Small Arms.

COLT'S REVOLVER.

PARTS.		PARTS.	
Barrel	$7 00	Key screw	$ 02
Sight	01	Lever	1 00
Cylinder	4 00	Rammer	30
Cone	06	Lever screw	02
Base pin	35	Catch spring	01
Lock frame	5 00	Catch on barrel	04
Lock screw	02	Catch on lever	06
Hammer and tumbler	88	Stock strap	50
Bolt	33	Stock strap screw	02
Bolt spring and scar	10	Guard plate	75
Bolt spring screw	02	Guard plate screw	02
Hand	31	Trigger	30
Hand spring	02	Stock	50
Main spring	50	Screw driver & cone wrench	42
Key	31	Ring or spring vice	01
Main spring screw	02	Bullet mould	1 00
Key spring and rivet	10	Pistol and appendages	$24 00

SWORDS AND SABRES.

PARTS.		Cavalry sabre.	Horse artillery sabre.	Artillery sword.	Musketoon sword bayonet.	Non-commissioned officer's sword.	Musician's sword.
Hilt {	Gripe	$ 20	$ 17	$....	$....	$ 24	$ 20
	Head	70	44	87	1 60	50	44
	Guard	1 10	58	....	....	1 20	44
Blade		2 80	1 98	2 13	2 13	2 20	1 92
Scabbard {	Mouth piece	20	10	....	....	....	....
	Body	1 20	1 00	50	62	66	50
	Bands & rings	60	60	....	....	....	....
	Ferrule & stud	15	13	25	40	35	25
	Tip	....	....	25	25	35	25
Arm complete		7 00	5 00	4 00	5 00	5 50	4 00

Prices of Accoutrements.

BLACK LEATHER BELTS.

PARTS.	Infantry.	Artillery.	Cavalry.	Rifle.
Cartridge box........................	$1 10	$....	$....	$ 95
Cartridge box plate...	10	....	10	10
Cartridge box belt.....................	69	....	....	....
Cartridge box belt plate................	10	....	....	....
Bayonet scabbard and frog.............	56	....	....	....
Waist belt, private's...................	25	....	....	37
Waist belt plate.......................	10	....	....	10
Cap pouch and pick..................	40	....	40	40
Gun sling............................	16	....	....	16
Sabre belt............................	....	1 03	1 35	....
Sabre belt plate.......................	....	60	60	....
Sword belt............................	....	1 00	....	....
Sword belt plate......................	....	10	....	....
Sword belt, non-com. officer's & musician's	62	....	....	62
Sword belt plate " "	10	....	....	10
Waist belt " "	37	....	....	37
Waist belt plate " "	60	....	....	60
Carbine cartridge box.................	....	....	87	....
Pistol "	....	....	75	....
Holsters, with soft leather caps	....	....	2 63	....
Carbine sling.........................	....	....	95	....
Carbine swivel........................	....	....	88	....
Sabre knot...........................	....	....	30	....
Bullet pouch..........................	....	....	....	53
Flask and pouch belt..................	....	....	....	40
Powder flask.........................	....	....	....	1 20
Waist belt, sapper's, with frog for sword bayonet, $1.	..			

Artillery.

COMPOSITION AND EQUIPMENT OF A BATTERY FOR WAR.

A field battery usually consists of six pieces. In batteries of eight pieces there are two additional guns, with the material required for their service.

The following is the composition of a battery:

12-POUNDER BATTERY.

4 12-pounder guns, mounted.
2 24-pounder howitzers, mounted.
8 Caissons for guns.
4   "   howitzers.
1 Travelling forge.
1 Battery wagon.

ARTILLERY.

12-POUNDER BATTERY (LIGHT).
6 12-pounder guns mounted, light.
12 Caissons.
1 Travelling forge.
1 Battery wagon.

6-POUNDER BATTERY.
4 6-pounder guns, mounted.
2 12-pounder howitzers, mounted.
4 Caissons for guns.
2 " howitzers.
1 Travelling forge.
1 Battery wagon.

AMMUNITION FOR 12-PDR. BATTERY.
560 Rounds shot.   ⎫
224   "   spherical case.   ⎬ For
112   "   canister.   ⎭ guns
112   "   spherical case.   ⎫
168   "   shell.   ⎬ For Howitzers.
42   "   canister.   ⎭

AMMUNITION FOR 12-POUNDER BATTERY (LIGHT).
504 Rounds shot.
504   "   spherical case.
168   "   shell.
168   "   canister.

AMMUNITION FOR 6-PDR. BATTERY.
400 Rounds shot.   ⎫
320   "   spherical case.   ⎬ For guns.
80   "   canister.   ⎭
160   "   spherical case.   ⎫
120   "   shell.   ⎬ For Howitzers.
32   "   canister.   ⎭

The number of friction primers is fifty per cent. more than the number of rounds furnished the battery.

HARNESS REQUIRED FOR EACH HORSE OF A FIELD BATTERY.

	Wheel.		Lead.	
	Near.	Off.	Near.	Off.
Halter...	1	1	1	1
Bridle...	1	1	1	1
Driver's Saddle.................................	1	...	1	...
Valise saddle and valise......................	...	1	...	1
Collar and harness.............................	1	1	1	1
Pair traces, wheel..............................	1	1	...	...
Pair traces, lead................................	...	...	1	1
Trace loops and belly-band..................	1	1	1	1
Loin straps and trace loops, wheel.........	1	1	...	...
" " " lead................	...	...	1	1
Crupper...	1	1	1	1
Breeching, hip strap, and breast strap	1	1	...	...
Leg guard..	1	...	...	...
Whip...	1	...	1	...
Nose bag...	1	1	1	1
Pole strap..	1	1	...	...

IMPLEMENTS AND EQUIPMENTS FOR FIELD PIECES.
For a Gun-carriage.
2 Sponges and rammers.
2 Sponge covers.
½ Worm and staff.
2 Handspikes.
1 Sponge bucket.
1 Prolonge.
1 Tar bucket.

2 Water buckets, leather.
2 Gunner's haversacks.
2 Tube pouches.
1 Fuse gouge.
1 " wrench.
1 Vent punch.
1 Gunner's pincers.
1 Tow hook.
1 Pendulum hausse.
2 Thumbstalls.
1 Priming wire.
2 Lanyards.
1 Gunner's gimblet.
1 Tarpaulin, large.

For a Caisson.

1 Felling axe.
1 Shovel (long handle).
1 Pick axe.
1 Spare handspike.
1 " pole.
1 " wheel.
1 Fuze gouge.
2 Tow hooks.
1 Tar bucket.
2 Water buckets, leather.
1 Tarpaulin, large.

SMITH'S TOOLS AND STORES REQUIRED FOR A FIELD BATTERY.

In travelling Forges.

300 pounds horse shoes, Nos. 2 & 3.
50 "   "   nails.
30 Washers and nuts, No. 2.
10 "   "   " 3.
4   "   "   " 4.
1 pound nails, No. 1, C.
1   "   "   2, C.
20 Tire bolts.
5 Keys for ammunition chest.
8 Linch washers.
12 "   pins.
2 Ft. chains, Nos. 1 and 2.
50 Cold S links, No. 3.
12 "   "   "   5.
4 Hand cold chisels.
1 Hardie.
12 Files assorted, with handles.
1 Buttress.
2 Hand punches, round & square.
1 Screw wrench.
1 Hand screw driver.
1 Hand vice.

1 Pair smith's callipers.
4 Taps, Nos. 1, 2, 3 and 4.
4 Pairs dies, Nos. 1, 2, 3 and 4.
1 Gross wood screws, 1 in. No. 14.
1 Quart can sperm oil.
1 Fire shovel.
1 Poker.
1 Split broom.
1 Hand hammer.
1 Rivetting "
1 Nailing.   "
1 Sledge.   "
2 chisels for hot iron.
2   "   cold iron.
3 Smith's tongs.
1 Fore punch.
1 Creaser.
1 Fuller.
1 Nail claw.
1 Round punch.
1 Tap wrench.
1 Die stock.
4 Nave bands developed.
2 Tire bands, developed.
1 Shoeing hammer.
1 Pair pincers.
2 Rasps, 12-inch.
1 Shoeing knife.
1 Toe knife.
1 Pritchel
1 Nail punch.
1 Clinching iron.
1 Oil stone.
2 Leather aprons.
1 Iron square.
1 Padlock.
1 Tar bucket.
1 Water bucket, wood.
1 Anvil.
1 Vise.
1 Watering bucket, leather.
250 Pounds bituminous coal.
1 Coal shovel.
1 Padlock.
100 Pounds $\frac{1}{2}$ and $\frac{5}{8}$ in. square iron.
50   "   flat iron, $1\frac{1}{4}$ by $\frac{3}{8}$ inch,
     1 inch by $\frac{1}{2}$ inch, and $1\frac{1}{2}$ inch by $\frac{3}{8}$.
50 Pounds round iron, $\frac{5}{8}$ inch.
5   "   cast steel, $\frac{5}{8}$ inch square.
5   "   English blister steel.
7 Boxes.

ARTILLERY. 157

CARRIAGE-MAKERS' TOOLS.

In Limber-chest of Battery wagon.

2 Hand saws.
1 Tenon saw, 14.
1 Jack plane.
1 Smoothing plane.
1 Brace with 24 bolts.
1 Spoke shave.
1 Gauge.
2 Plane irons.
1 Saw set.
1 Rule (2 feet).
12 Gimlets.
1 Pair compasses.
1 Chalk line.
2 Brad awls.
1 Scriber.
12 Saw files (4¼ inch).
2 Wood files (10 inch).
1 " rasp (10 inch).
1 Trying square (8 inch).
1 Hand screw driver.
1 Oil stove.
1 Broad axe.
1 Hand axe.
1 Claw hatchet.
1 " hammer.
1 Pair pincers (small).
1 Table vise.
2 Framing chisels, 1 in. and 2 in.
2 Firmer chisels, ¾ in. and 1½ in.
2 Framing gouges, 1 in. and 1¼ in.
3 Augers and handles, ½, ⅝, & ¾ in.
1 Screw wrench.
1 Felling axe and handle.
1 Adze handle.
1 Frame saw.
1 Quart can sperm oil.

SADDLER'S TOOLS AND STORES.

Carried in Lumber-chest of Battery wagon.

1 Mallet.
1 Clam.
1 Hammer.
1 Shoe knife.
1 Half round do.
1 Pair shears.
1 Sand stone.
1 Rule (2 feet).
100 Needles.
12 Awls and handles.
2 Punches.
1 Pair pincers.
1 " pliers.
1 Claw tool.
1 Creaser.
4 Thimbles.
1 Strap awl.
2 Pounds beeswax.
3 " black wax.
8 Ounces bristles.
5 Pounds shoe thread.
2 " patent thread.
3 Dozen buckles, assorted.
3 Thousand tacks.
1 Gunner's callipers.
2 Shoe knives.
2 Pair scissors.
1 Padlock.
1 Tar bucket.

STORES.

Carried in Battery Wagon.

1 Gallon linseed oil.
1 " spirits turpentine.
50 Pounds olive paint.
5 " black.
12 Paint brushes.
5 Pounds sperm or wax candles.
4 Rammer heads.
4 Sponge "
12 Sponges.
3 Priming wires.
3 Gunner's gimlets.
4 Lanyards for friction tubes.
6 Cannon spikes.
3 Dark lanterns.
4 Common "
4 Gallons neat's-foot oil.
50 Pounds grease.
20 " nails, assorted.
2 Felling axes.
1 Claw hatchet.
2 Hand bills.
1 Caisson stock.
3 Rammers and sponges.
40 Spokes.
24 Fellies.
1 Grindstone, 14 by 4 inches.
1 Arbour and crank.
3 Screw jacks.

REQUISITION FOR A BATTERY.

10 Wheel traces.	1 Side harness, leather
10 Leading "	1 " bridle "
6 Collars.	1 Prolonge.
16 Girths.	4 Scythes.
16 Whips.	4 Scythe stones.
6 Bridles.	6 Spades.
6 Halters.	2 Pick axes and handles.
12 " chains.	24 Corn sacks.
25 Hame straps.	2 Tarpaulins, 5 feet square.
12 Nose bag, spare.	4 Reaping hooks.
6 Pieces sash cord.	4 Scythe snaths.
50 Yards slow match.	1 Stock for battery wagon, spare.
1 Elevating screw.	1 Padlock.
1 Pole yoke.	1 Watering bucket.

The battery and equipments are obtained from the Ordnance Department, on a special requisition made agreeably to Form 90, p. 162, certified by the officer commanding the company, examined and approved by the commander of the regiment, and the issue ordered by the commander of the department, or general commanding an army in the field.

In filling up this requisition, the strength of the company is stated in the upper branch.

The articles required are inserted in the second branch, under the head of ARTICLES, *in the order in which they appear in the lists above given.*

The first column is to be filled with the total number of each article required for use in the battery. The second column will contain the amount *on hand*, and the third column the *quantity* to be *supplied*, which will be what the requisition calls for.

The first two columns will be used when the requisition is for articles to supply a battery already organized. In fitting out a new battery, the first two columns are to be left blank, and the number of each article, as obtained from the foregoing list, inserted in the third column.

Under the head of remarks it must be stated whether the articles are required to replace articles *lost, defective*, or *consumed in service*. If they be designed to replace like articles received from any State, it must be noted. The calibre of the arms, and whether rifled or smooth bore, must be stated in the column of remarks.

This form of requisition will be used for obtaining small arms and accoutrements; the same rules governing the filling up that have been given for preparing a requisition for a battery.

Duplicate receipts will be given by the officers receiving ordnance and ordnance stores, and duplicate invoices will be furnished by the ordnance officer delivering the property.

The following is the form of a receipt for ordnance:

Received ——— this ——— day of ———, 18—, of Captain ——— ———, commanding ———, the following Ordnance and Ordnance Stores, viz:

4	32 pounder iron cannon.
3	24 " casemate carriages, complete.
3	24 " barbette carriages, complete.
500	muskets, new, brown.

(In duplicate.)   C. D., *Major Commanding.*

When the receipt of the officer to whom the stores are issued, is not received by the issuing officer in time to accompany his property return, his certified invoice and the receipt of the Quartermaster for the packages will be substituted for this voucher.

RETURN OF ORDNANCE AND ORDNANCE STORES.
Form 91, p. 163.

Every officer who is responsible for any article of ordnance or ordnance stores, is required to make, at the expiration of each quarter, a return of *ordnance* and *ordnance stores received, issued, and remaining on hand*, and transmit the same, with his vouchers, to the chief of ordnance, within five days after the expiration of the quarter.

The manner of preparing this return is shown by the form, though varied in every case to suit the articles to be accounted for. The *manner* of accounting will in all cases be like that shown in the form; the upper branch showing in *what manner* the articles have come into possession of the officer, and the lower branch the manner in which they have been disposed of; the difference between what has been issued and expended and the total to be accounted for, giving the amount remaining on hand to be accounted for next quarter.

In the first branch the invoices of articles received are entered, each invoice numbered to accompany the return, and in the second branch every issue is entered, with the receipt duly numbered.

This return, with its vouchers, is to be sent to the *Chief of Ordnance, Washington, D. C.*, accompanied by a letter of transmittal.

Unserviceable arms are to be sent, by the officer responsible for them, to an arsenal for repairs, before accumulating in excess of the surplus arms of the company. By attention to this the arms of the company will always remain in a serviceable condition.

The arms are to be boxed up and delivered to the quartermaster, for transportation to the nearest arsenal. The officer sending will transmit to the commanding officer of the arsenal duplicate invoices of the property.

Companies are not to have property that forms no part of their equipment. Therefore, it is the duty of an officer commanding a company, whose equipment has been changed, to turn into the nearest arsenal all articles belonging to the old equipment.

Officers of artillery whose companies have been serving with batteries, and have been ordered to serve as infantry, will turn in every thing pertaining to the battery, and close the accounts of the property in the next quarterly return.

Officers commanding detachments of recruits who have receipted for arms, must, when the recruits are delivered to their respective companies, furnish invoices of the ordnance property turned over with them to the commanders of the respective companies, who must duly receipt for the property.

These officers must, at the expiration of the quarter, furnish a return of ordnance of the prescribed form (Form 91, p. 163, and close their account with the Department.

All officers must frequently inspect the condition of arms in the hands of their commands, and carefully note all damage, which may be chargeable against the soldier on the next muster roll; the damage to be charged in accordance with the list of prices before given.

FORM 89.—REQUISITION FOR ORDNANCE FOR MILITIA.

Requisition for Ordnance and Ordnance Stores for the use of ———— of militia in the service of the United States.

	6-pdr. brass cannon.	6-pdr. carriages.	Muskets, complete.	Non-com'd officers' swords.	Cartridge boxes.	Cartridge box belts.	Bayonet scabbards.	Waist belt plates.	Gun slings.	6-pdr. shot fixed.	Musket-ball cartridges.	REMARKS.
	2	2	49	9	49	49	49	51	49	120	2500	Company of infantry of 58 non-commissioned officers and privates. Same form for Artillery, Riflemen, and Cavalry.
Total...	2	2	49	9	49	49	49	51	49	120	2500	

I certify that there are ———— non-commissioned officers, musicians, and privates under my command, called into the service of the United States, and that the above requisition is made in conformity thereto. A. B., *Captain of the 5th Regiment of Militia*
(Signed)   *of the State of New Jersey.*
TRENTON, *June 1, 1861.*

The above requisition has been examined in conformity to the Ordnance Regulations, and is approved.
(Signed)   C. D., *Major United States Army.*
TRENTON, *June 5, 1861.*

Form 90.—Requisition for Ordnance.

Special Requisition for Ordnance and Ordnance Stores for the use of Company A, Third Regiment Artillery, Commanded by Captain A. B.

Station.	Number of men.			Remarks.
	Sergeants.	Musicians.	Corporals and privates.	

Number and kind of articles.			Remarks.
Required.	On hand.	To be supplied.	Articles.	

I certify that the above number of men and articles are correct.

A. B., *Commanding Company.*

Examined and found correct.

C. D., *Commanding Regiment.*

The above requisition is approved by me, and immediate issue is necessary.

E. F., *Commanding.*

RETURN OF ORDNANCE. 163

FORM 91.—RETURN OF ORDNANCE.

Return of Ordnance and Ordnance Stores received, issued, and remaining on hand, at ——— Arsenal, Commanded by Major A. B., during the quarter ending ———, 1861.

DATE. 1861.		No. of voucher.	SECOND QUARTER, 1861.	ARMS.			FOR MUSKETS.			FOR RIFLES.	
				Muskets.	Non-commissioned officer's swords.	Infantry cartridge boxes.	Infantry cartridge box plates.	Cartridge box belts.	Wipers.	Ball screws.	Bullet moulds.
April	1		On hand from last quarter.............								
"	15	1	Rec'd from C. D., Military Storekeeper.								
May..	10	2	Do. do. E. F., contractor at ———..								
"	22	3	Do. do. Capt. G. H., —— regiment of artillery........................								
			Total to be accounted for......								
May..	15	7	Condemned and dropped from the return by order of the President of the United States....................								
June..	30	8	Issued to sundry persons, per abstract.								
"	30	9	Expended at the post, per abstract.....								
			Total issued and expended....								
			Remaining on hand to be accounted for next quarter........................								

I certify that the foregoing return exhibits a correct statement of the public property in my charge during the ——— quarter, 1861.

A. B., *Captain Commanding.*

U. S. ARSENAL (ARMORY OR POST),
——— , 1861.

PAY.

TABLE OF PAY, SUBSISTENCE, FORAGE, ETC., OF THE U. S. ARMY.

GRADE.	Pay. Per month.	Subsistence. No. of rations per day.	Forage. No. of horses allowed in time of war.	Forage. No. of horses allowed in time of peace.	No. of servants allowed.
Lieutenant-General...................................	$270 00	40	7	3	4
Major-General......................................	220 00	15	7	3	4
Senior Aid-de-Camp to General-in-Chief............	80 00	4	4	3	2
Aid-de-Camp, in addition to pay, &c., of Lieutenant.	24 00	..	2	1	..
Brigadier-General..................................	124 00	12	5	3	3
Aid-de-Camp to Brigadier, in addition to pay, &c., of Lieutenant..	20 00	..	2	1	..
Adjutant-General	110 00	6	5	3	2
Assistant Adjutant-General, with the rank of Lieutenant-Colonel......................................	95 00	5	4	3	2
Assistant Adjutant-General, with the rank of Major.	80 00	4	4	3	2
Assistant Adjutant-General, with the rank of Captain	70 00	4	3	1	1
Judge Advocate....................................	80 00	4	4	3	2
Inspector-General..................................	110 00	6	5	3	2
Quartermaster-General..............................	124 00	12	5	3	3
Assistant Quartermaster-General....................	110 00	6	5	3	2
Deputy Quartermaster-General	95 00	5	4	3	2
Quartermaster	80 00	4	4	3	2
Assistant Quartermaster............................	70 00	4	3	1	1
Paymaster-General, $2740 per annum.					
Deputy Paymaster-General..........................	95 00	5	4	3	2
Paymaster...	80 00	4	4	3	2
Commissary-General of Subsistence.................	110 00	6	5	3	2
Assistant Commissary-General of Subsistence......	95 80	5	4	3	2
Commissary of Subsistence, with the rank of Major.	80 00	4	4	3	2
Commissary of Subsistence, with the rank of Captain	70 00	4	3	1	1
Assistant Commissary of Subsistence, in addition to pay, &c., of Lieutenant.............................	20 00	..	....	....	..
Surgeon-General, $2740 per annum.					
Surgeon of ten years' service in that grade..........	80 00	8	4	3	2
Surgeon, less than ten years' service	80 00	4	4	3	2
Assistant Surgeon of ten years' service.............	70 00	8	3	1	1
Assistant Surgeon of five years' service............	70 00	4	3	1	1
Assistant Surgeon, less than five years' service......	53 33¼	4	2	1	1
Chaplain...	60 00	4			
Colonel of Engineers................................					
Topographical Engineer					
Ordnance Cavalry..................................	110 00	6	5	3	2
Lieutenant-Colonel of Cavalry......................	95 00	5	4	3	2
Major of Cavalry	80 00	4	4	3	2
Captain of Cavalry.................................	70 00	4	3	2 & 1†	1
Lieutenant (1st and 2d) of Cavalry..................	53 33¼	4	2	2 & 1†	1
Adjutant of Cavalry, in addition to pay, &c., of Lieutenant..	10 00	..	....	....	.
Regimental Quartermaster of ditto..................	10 00	..	....	....	..

PAY.

GRADE.	Pay. Per month.	Subsistence. No. of rations per day.	Forage. No. of horses allowed in time of war.	Forage. No. of horses allowed in time of peace.	No. of servants allowed.
Sergeant-Major of Cavalry..........................	21 00	..	....	....	..
Quartermaster-Sergeant of ditto...................	21 00	..	....	....	..
Chief Bugler of ditto.................................	21 00	..	....	....	..
First Sergeant of ditto...............................	20 00	..	....	....	..
Sergeant of ditto.....................................	17 00	..	....	....	..
Corporal of ditto.....................................	14 00	..	....	....	..
Bugler of ditto..	13 00	..	....	....	..
Farrier and Blacksmith of ditto....................	15 00	..	....	....	..
Private of ditto.......................................	13 00	..	....	....	..
Master Armorer, Master Carriage-maker, or Master Blacksmith of Ordnance.........................	34 00	..	....	....	..
Armorer, Carriage-maker, or Blacksmith of Ordnance	20 00	..	....	....	..
Artificer of Ordnance................................	17 00	..	....	....	..
Laborer of Ordnance.................................	13 00	..	....	....	..
Hospital Steward, appointed by the Secretary of War, and Hospital Steward at posts of more than four companies, pay of Ordnance Sergeant............	22 00	..	....	....	..
Hospital Steward.....................................	20 00	..	....	....	..
Matron..	6 00	..	....	....	..
ARTILLERY AND INFANTRY.					
Colonel..	95 00	6	4	3	2
Lieutenant-Colonel...................................	80 00	5	3	3	2
Major...	70 00	4	3	3	2
Adjutant, in addition to pay, &c., of Lieutenant...	10 00	..	2	1	..
Reg'tal Quarterm'r, in addition to pay, &c., of Lieut.	10 00	..	2	2	..
Captain...	60 00	4	....	....	1
First Lieutenant......................................	50 00	4	....	....	1
Second Lieutenant...................................	45 00	4	....	....	1
Cadet...	24 00	..	....	....	..
Sergeant-Major......................................	21 00	..	....	....	..
Quartermaster-Sergeant............................	21 00	..	....	....	..
Principal Musician of Infantry.....................	21 00	..	....	....	..
First Sergeant.......................................	20 00	..	....	....	..
Ordnance Sergeant, in addition to pay of Sergeant..	5 00	..	....	....	..
Sergeant...	17 00	..	....	....	..
Corporal...	13 00	..	....	....	..
Artificer of Artillery.................................	15 00	..	....	....	..
Musician...	12 00	..	....	....	..
Private...	13 00	..	....	....	..
SAPPERS AND MINERS, PONTONEERS, AND TOPOGRAPHICAL ENGINEER COMPANIES.					
Sergeant...	34 00	..	....	....	..
Corporal...	20 00	..	....	....	..
Musician...	12 00	..	....	....	..
Private of the 1st class.............................	17 00	..	....	...?	..
Private of the 2d class..............................	13 00	..	....	....	..

The commanding officer of a company is entitled to $10 per month for responsibility of arms and clothing.

Officers' subsistence is commuted at thirty cents per ration; forage, $8 per month for each horse actually owned and kept in service.

Officers are entitled to the pay of a private soldier, $2 50 per month for clothing, and one ration per day for each private servant actually employed.

Every commissioned officer below the rank of Brigadier-General is entitled to one additional ration per day for every five years' service.

All enlisted men are entitled to $2 per month additional pay for re-enlisting, and $1 per month for each subsequent period of five years' service, provided they re-enlist within one month.

Paymasters' clerks, $700 per annum, and 75 cents per day when actually on duty.

Only the captains and subalterns of dragoons are entitled to two horses in time of peace.

Commissioned officers are paid upon accounts certified by themselves. Form 93, pp. 174 and 175, shows the manner of preparing them.

A commissioned officer's pay is made up of the following items:

1st. The officer's pay proper.
2d. The pay of his servants, rated at soldiers' pay each.
3d. The commutation allowance of servants' clothing.
4th. The officer's subsistence at thirty cents per ration, for the number of rations to which he may be entitled.
5th. The commutation of servants' rations, one per day for each servant, at thirty cents per ration.

Besides these items, there may be included in the account the charge of ten dollars per month for commanding a company, if such should be the case; the letter of the company and number of the regiment to be stated.

Should the officer have acted as Assistant Commissary of Subsistence, he may make the charge of fourteen dollars per month for such service, but the account must be sent to the Commissary-General of Subsistence for his certificate before it can be paid.

In making up the statement of rations, the number of years' service must be stated, where service rations are charged for.

Double rations for commanding a post will only be charged where the post has been decided to be a "double ration post."

PAYMENT OF DISCHARGED SOLDIERS

Discharged soldiers will be paid upon accounts shown in the form following, furnished them by their company commander at the expiration of their enlistment or time of discharge:

FORM 92.

The United States,

To ———— ————, *discharged from* ———— *Company,* ———— *Regiment of* ————, DR.

	Dolls.	Cts.
For pay from —— of ——, 18—, to —— of ——, 18—, being —— months, —— days, at —— dollars per month....................................		
For retained pay due............................		
For pay for travelling from ————, the place of my discharge, to ————, the place of my residence, —— miles, at twenty miles per day, equal to —— days, at —— dollars per month......................		
For subsistence for travelling as above, —— days, at —— cents per ration or day................		
For clothing not drawn.........................		
Amount......................		
Deduct for Army Asylum..................$ Deduct for clothing overdrawn.............		
Balance due......................		

Received of —— ——, Paymaster U. S. Army, this —— day of ————, 18—, —— dollars and —— cents, in full of the above account.

Pay.............
Subsistence......
Clothing.........

Dollars ...

(*Signed in duplicate.*)

PAYMENT OF SOLDIERS.

The payments, except to officers and discharged soldiers, shall be made on muster and pay rolls; those of companies and detachments, signed by the company or detachment commander; of the hospital, signed by the surgeon; and all muster and pay rolls, signed by the mustering and inspecting officer.

When a company is paraded for payment, the officer in command of it shall attend at the pay-table.

When a receipt on a pay roll or account is not signed by the hand of the party, the payment must be witnessed. The witness to be a commissioned officer when practicable.

Authorized stoppages to reimburse the United States, as for loss or damage to arms, equipments, or other public property; for extra issues of clothing; for the expense of apprehending deserters, or to reimburse individuals (as the paymaster, laundress, etc.); forfeitures for desertion, and fines by sentence of court-martial, will be entered on the roll and paid in the order stated.

The paymaster will deduct from the pay of the soldier the amount of the authorized stoppages entered on the muster roll, descriptive list, or certificate of discharge.

Two dollars each month are retained from the pay of every soldier, which amount will be paid on the discharge of the soldier, unless the same be forfeited by sentence of a court-martial.

The travelling pay is due to a discharged officer or soldier, unless forfeited by sentence of a court-martial, or the discharge is by way of punishment for an offense.

In reckoning the travelling allowance to discharged officers or soldiers, the distance is to be estimated by the shortest mail route; if there is no mail route, by the shortest practicable route. Rations of soldiers, if not drawn in kind, are estimated at the contract price at the place of discharge. The price of the ration shall be stated on the certificate.

Every enlisted man discharged as a minor, or for other cause involving fraud on his part in the enlistment, or discharged by the civil authority, shall forfeit all pay and allowance due at the time of the discharge.

When an officer of the army receives a temporary appointment from the proper authority to a grade in the militia, then in actual service of the United States, higher in rank than that held by him in the army, he shall be entitled to the pay and emoluments of the grade in which he serves. But in no case can an officer receive the compensation of two military commissions, or appointments, at the same time.

When an officer is dismissed from the service, he shall not be entitled to pay beyond the day or which the order announcing his dismissal is received at the post where he may be stationed, unless a particular day beyond the time is mentioned in the order.

No officer shall receive pay for two staff appointments for the same time.

Officers are entitled to pay from the date of the acceptance of their appointments, and from the date of promotion.

No account of a restored officer for time he was out of service can be paid, without order of the War Department.

As far as practicable, officers are to draw their pay from the paymaster of the district where they may be on duty.

No officer shall pass away or transfer his pay account not actually due at the time; and when an officer transfers his pay account he shall give information to the Paymaster-General, and to the Paymaster by whom he expects it to be paid.

Enlisted men are paid every two months if practicable, upon PAY ROLLS (Form 96, p. 202) prepared by the paymaster, from the data given on the MUSTER ROLLS to which they are attached and form a part, full description of which will be given under the head of MUSTER AND PAY ROLLS.

VOLUNTEERS and MILITIA are paid by companies upon pay rolls made agreeably to Form 94, p. 176 and 177, by the paymaster, from the data furnished by the muster rolls; this payment is to be witnessed and certified to by all the officers of the company.

The company officers are paid with the company, upon the roll above mentioned; but the FIELD and STAFF OFFICERS draw their pay from the paymaster upon their individual accounts, in the same manner and according to the same form as is prescribed for officers of the army.

TABLE OF PAY, SUBSISTENCE, ETC., ALLOWED BY LAW TO THE OFFICERS OF THE ARMY.

Rank and Classification of Officers.	Pay. Per month.	Subsist'ce. Number of Rations per day.	Subsist'ce. Monthly Commutation Value.	Servants. Number of Servants allowed.	Servants. Monthly Commutation Value.	Total Monthly Pay.	Forage Furnish'd for Horses. In time of War.	Forage Furnish'd for Horses. In time of Peace.
	$ c.		$ c.		$ c.	$ c.		
General Officers.								
Lieutenant-General.................	270 00	40	360 00	4	90 00	720 00	& for forage	$50
Aides-de-camp and Military Secretary to Lieut.-Gen., each.	80 00	5	45 00	2	45 00	170 00		2
Major-General......................	220 00	15	185 00	4	90 00	445 00		5
Senior Aide-de-camp to General-in-Chief........................	80 00	4	36 00	2	47 00	163 00		2
Aide-de-camp, in addition to pay, etc., of Lieut. or Capt....	24 00	....	......	....	......	24 00		2
Brigadier-General..................	124 00	12	108 00	3	67 50	299 50		4
Aide-de-camp, in addition to pay, etc., of Lieutenant.......	20 00	....	......	....	......	11	✓	2
Adjutant-General's Department.								
Adjutant-General—Brig. Gen.....	124 00	24	216 00	3	67 50	407 50		4
Assistant Adjutant-Gen.—Colonel.	110 00	6	54 00	2	47 00	211 00		2
Assistant Adj't-Gen.—Lieut. Col..	95 00	5	45 00	2	47 00	187 00		2
Assistant Adjutant-Gen.—Major...	80 00	4	36 00	2	47 00	163 00		2
Judge-Advocate-General—Colonel.	110 00	6	54 00	2	47 00	211 00		2
Judge-Advocate—Major...........	80 00	4	36 00	2	47 00	163 00		2
" " (Division)—Major	80 00	4	36 00	2	47 00	163 00		2
Inspector-General's Department.								
Inspector-General—Colonel.......	110 00	6	54 00	2	47 00	211 00		2
Assistant Inspector-Gen.—Major..	80 00	4	36 00	2	47 00	163 00		2
Signal Department.								
Signal Officer—Colonel...........	110 00	6	54 00	2	47 00	211 00		2
Quartermaster's Department.								
Quartermaster-Gen.—Brig. Gen...	124 00	24	216 00	3	67 00	407 50		4
Assistant Quart'master-Gen.—Col.	110 00	6	54 00	2	47 00	211 00		2
Deputy Quart'm'ter-Gen.—Lt. Col.	95 00	5	45 00	2	47 00	187 00		2
Quartermaster—Major............	80 00	4	36 00	2	47 00	163 00		2
Assistant Quartermaster—Captain.	70 00	4	36 00	1	23 50	129 50		2
Subsistence Department.								
Com-Gen. of Subs.—Brig. Gen....	124 00	12	108 00	3	67 00	299 00		4
Assistant Commissary-General of Subsistence—Lieut. Colonel.	95 00	5	45 00	2	47 00	187 00		2
Commiss'ry of Subsistence—Major.	80 00	4	36 00	2	47 00	163 00		2
Commissary of Subsistence—Capt.	70 00	4	36 00	1	23 50	129 50		2
Ass't Commissary of Sub., in addition to pay, etc., of Lieut...	20 00	....	......	....	......	11		....

PAY. 171

Continued.—TABLE OF PAY, SUBSISTENCE, ETC.

Rank and Classification of Officers.	Pay.		Subsist'ce.		Servants.		Total Monthly Pay.		Forage Furnished for Horses.	
	Per month.	Number of Rations per day.	Monthly Commutation Value.		Number of Servants allowed.	Monthly Commutation Value.			In time of War.	In time of Peace.
	$ c.		$ c.			$ c.	$ c.			
Medical Department.									& for	
Surgeon-General—Brig. General...	124 00	12	108 00		3	67 50	299 50		forage	4
Assistant Surgeon-General	110 00	6	54 00		2	47 00	211 00			2
Medical Inspector-General	110 00	6	54 00		2	47 00	211 00			2
Medical Inspectors	95 00	5	45 00		2	47 00	187 00			2
Surgeons of ten years' service.:	80 00	8	72 00		2	47 00	199 00			2
Surgeons of less than ten years' service.	80 00	4	36 00		2	47 00	163 00			2
Ass't Surgeons of 10 years service.	70 00	8	72 00		1	23 50	165 50			2
Ass't Surgeons of 5 years' service.	70 00	4	36 00		1	23 50	129 50			2
Assistant Surgeons of less than five years' service	53 00	4	36 00		1	23 50	112 83			2
Pay Department.										
Paymaster-Gen., $2740 per annum.	....	....	....		....	....	288 83			....
Deputy Paymaster-General	95 00	5	45 00		2	47 00	187 00			2
Paymaster	80 00	4	36 00		2	47 00	163 00			2
Officers of the Corps of Engineers, Corps of Topographical Engineers, and Ordnance Department.										
Chief of Ordnance—Brig. Gen.	124 00	24	216 00		3	67 50	407 50			4
Colonel	110 00	6	54 00		2	47 00	211 00			2
Lieutenant-Colonel	95 00	5	45 00		2	47 00	187 00			2
Major	80 00	4	36 00		2	47 00	163 00			2
Captain	70 00	4	36 00		1	23 50	129 50			2
First Lieutenant	53 33	4	36 00		1	23 50	112 83			2
Second Lieutenant	53 33	4	36 00		1	23 50	112 88			2
Brevet Second Lieutenant	53 33	4	36 00		1	23 50	112 83			2
Officers of Mounted Dragoons, Cavalry, Riflemen, and Light Artillery.										
Colonel	110 00	6	54 00		2	47 00	211 00			2
Lieutenant-Colonel	95 00	5	45 00		2	47 00	187 00			2
Major	80 00	4	36 00		2	47 00	163 00			2
Captain	70 00	4	36 00		1	23 50	129 50			2
First Lieutenant	53 33	4	36 00		1	23 50	112 83			2
Second Lieutenant	53 33	4	36 00		1	23 50	112 83			2
Brevet Second Lieutenant	53 33	4	36 00		1	23 50	112 83			2
Adjutant, Reg'l Quarterm'ster, Reg'l Commissary (in addition to pay of Lieut.)	10 00	....	....		....	....	10 00			....

Continued.—TABLE OF PAY, SUBSISTENCE, ETC.

Rank and Classification of Officers.	Pay.		Subsist'ce.		Servants.		Total Monthly Pay.	Forage Furnished for Horses.	
	Per month.	Number of Rations per day.	Monthly Commutation Value.	Number of Servants allowed.	Monthly Commutation Value.			In time of War.	In time of Peace.
Officers of Artillery and Infantry.	$ c.		$ c.		$ c.		$ c.		
Colonel...........................	95 00	6	54 00	2	45 00		194 00	& for forage	2
Lieutenant-Colonel................	80 00	5	45 00	2	45 00		170 00		2
Major.............................	70 00	4	36 00	2	45 00		151 00		2
Captain...........................	60 00	4	36 00	1	22 50		118 50		....
First Lieutenant..................	50 00	4	36 00	1	22 50		108 50		....
Second Lieutenant.................	45 00	4	36 00	1	22 50		103 50		....
Brevet Second Lieutenant..........	45 00	4	36 00	1	22 50		103 50		....
Adjutant, in addition to pay, etc., of Lieutenant....................	10 00	....	......	....	......		10 00		2
Reg'l Quartermaster, in addition to pay, etc., of Lieutenant........	10 00	....	......	....	......		10 00		2
Military Storekeepers.									
Attached to the Quartermaster's Department; at armories, and at arsenals of construction; the storekeeper at Watertown Arsenal, and storekeepers of ordnance serving in Oregon, California, and New Mexico, $1,490 per annum.	......	....	......	....	......		......		....
At all other arsenals, $1,040 per annum...........................	......	....	......	....	......		......		....
Chaplains.........................	100 00	2	18 00	....	......		118 00		1

Paymaster's clerks, $700 per annum, and one ration (75 cents) per day when on duty.

The officer in command of a company is allowed $10 per month for the responsibility of clothing, arms, and accoutrements.—Act 2 March, 1827, Sec. 2.

Subaltern officers, employed on the *General Staff*, and receiving increased pay therefor, are not entitled to the additional or fourth ration provided by the Act of March 2, 1827, Sec. 2.

Every commissioned officer below the rank of Brigadier-General receives one additional ration per day for every five years' service—Act July 5, 1836, Sec. 12, and July 7, 1838, Sec. 9.

Forage is commuted only when the Government cannot furnish it in kind, and then at $8 per month for each horse actually kept by the officer.

MONTHLY PAY OF NON-COMMISSIONED OFFICERS, PRIVATES, ETC.

CAVALRY.

Sergeant-Major	$21 00	Hospital Steward	$30 00
Quartermaster-Sergeant	21 00	Corporal	14 00
Chief Bugler or Trumpeter	21 00	Bugler or Trumpeter	13 00
First Sergeant	20 00	Farrier and Blacksmith	15 00
Sergeant	17 00	Private	18 00
Saddler Sergeant	21 00	Veterinary Surgeon	75 00
Commissary Sergeant	21 00	African Under Cooks	10 00

ORDNANCE.

Sergeant	$34 00	Saddler	$14 00
Corporal	20 00	Private, first class	17 00
Wagoner	14 00	Private, second class	13 00

ARTILLERY AND INFANTRY.

Sergeant-Major	$21 00	Corporal	$13 00
Quartermaster Sergeant	21 00	Artificer, artillery	15 00
Commissary Sergeant	21 00	Private	13 00
First Sergeant	20 00	Principal Musician	21 00
Sergeant	17 00	Musician	12 00
Hospital Stewards	30 00	African Under Cooks	10 00

SAPPERS, MINERS, AND PONTONIERS.

Sergeant	$34 00	Private, second class	$13 00
Corporal	20 00	Musician	12 00
Private, first class	17 00	African Under Cooks	10 00

BRIGADE BANDS.

Leader	$45 00	Eight of the Band	$17 00
Four of the Band	34 00	Four of the Band	20 00

Medical Cadets	$30 00	Matron	$6 00
Hospital Steward, first class	22 00	Female Nurses, 40 cents per day and one ration.	
" " second class	20 00		

Two dollars per month is to be retained from the pay of each private soldier until the expiration of his term of enlistment, and 12½ cents per month from all enlisted men, for the support of the "Soldier's Home."

All enlisted men are entitled to $2 per month additional pay for re-enlisting, and $1 per month for each subsequent period of five years' service, provided they re-enlist within one month after the expiration of their term.

Volunteers and militia, when called into service of the United States, are entitled to the same pay, allowances, etc., as regulars.

Medical Storekeepers, same as Military Storekeepers, Quartermaster's Department.

FORM 93.—OFFICERS' PAY ACCOUNT.

The United States to A. B., 1st Lieutenant 1st Cavalry.   Dr.

On what account.	Commencement and expiration.		Term of service charged.			Pay per month.		Amount.		Remarks.
	From —	To —	Months.	Days.		Dolls.	Cts.	Dolls.	Cts.	
PAY— For myself........................	1861. Sep. 1.	1861. Sep. 30.	One.			53	33	53	33	
For private servant, not soldier....	"	"	"			13		13	00	
FORAGE— For 2 horses....................	"	"	"					16	00	
CLOTHING— For private servant, not soldier....	"	"	"					2	50	

			No. of days.	No. of rations per day.	Total number of rations.	Post or place where due.	Price of ration.			
							Cts.			
SUBSISTENCE— For myself for 11 years' service.....	"	"	30	6	180	Washington.	30	54	00	
For private servant, not soldier....	"	"	"	1	30	"	30	9	00	
								$147	83	

OFFICERS' PAY ACCOUNT.

I hereby certify that the foregoing account is accurate and just; that I have not been absent without leave during any part of the time charged for; that I have not received pay, nor drawn rations, forage, or clothing in kind, or received money in lieu of any part thereof, for any part of the time therein charged; that I actually owned and kept in service, the horses, and employed the private servants for which I charge, for the whole of the time charged; and that I did not, during the term so charged, or any part thereof, keep or employ a soldier as a waiter or servant; that the annexed is an accurate description of my servant; that, for the whole period charged for my staff appointment, I actually and legally held the appointment, and did duty in the department; that I was the actual and only commanding officer at the double-ration post charged for; and that no officer, within my knowledge, has a right to claim, or does claim, for said services, for any part of the period charged; that for the whole time brevet pay is claimed, I had the command stated; that I was actually in the command of a company for the whole time additional pay is charged; that I have not been in the performance of any staff duty for which I claim, or have received extra compensation during the time an additional ration is charged for; that I have been in the United States Army as a commissioned officer for the number of years stated in the charge for extra rations; that I am not in arrears with the United States on any account whatsoever; and that the last payment I received was from Paymaster ———— and to the ———— day of ————, 18——.

I at the same time acknowledge that I have received of ————, Paymaster, this 30th day of Sep., 1861, the sum of $146 83, being the amount in full of said account.

Pay	$66 33
Subsistence	63 00
Forage	16 00
Clothing	2 50
Amount	$147 83

(*Signed duplicates.*)

DESCRIPTION OF SERVANTS.

Name.	Complexion.	Height.		Eyes.	Hair.
		Feet.	Inches.		
T. Head.	Dark.	5	2	Gray.	Dark.

Form 94.—Pay Roll

We, the subscribers, do hereby acknowledge to have received of ———— the full of our pay and allowances for the period

No.	Names.	Rank.	Period of service.				Pay per month.	Amount of pay.	Clothing.	Subsistence.	Forage.	40 cents per day, use of horse, arms, &c.	25 cents per day for rations and forage, or 12½ cents for either.
			Commencement.	Expiration.	Months.	Days.							

We certify, on honor, that we actually employed the servants and owned and kept charged, and did not, during any part of the time, employ a soldier as a servant: the commissioned officers and privates of the company to which we belong, who are service for the time paid for, although, in some cases, they may not have been valued.

OF MILITIA.

————, *Paymaster, the sums annexed to our names respectively, being herein expressed, having signed duplicates thereof.*

Pay.	Subsistence.	Travelling allowances.	Total amount.	Stoppages.	Balances paid.	Signature.	Witness.	REMARKS.

in service the horses for which we have received payment, for the whole of the time names and description of our servants are below. We also certify that the non-made up for pay, &c., as having horses and arms, actually owned and had them in We also certify that we witnessed the payment of the whole company.

———— ————, *Captain,* servant named ———— ————.
———— ————, *1st Lieut.,* do. ———— ————.
———— ————, *2d Lieut.,* do. ———— ————.
———— ————, *Ensign,* do. ———— ————.

ROLLS, RETURNS AND REPORTS.

All commanding officers of troops are required to make out and transmit certain ROLLS, RETURNS and REPORTS, showing the strength and condition of their respective commands, and the changes that may have taken place since the previous report or return. Also, returns for the public property for which they may be responsible, showing the quantity on hand, and its condition, and the loss or damage that has occurred to arms, accoutrements, and other public property, and to whom chargeable.

Rolls, Returns, and Reports Required from Company Commanders.

The following returns, rolls and reports are to be made by company commanders:

MUSTER ROLLS.
Form 95, p. 201.

Muster rolls are made out every two months, by the commanding officer of each company, and must embrace all matter that serves to give a correct statement of the condition of the company, and all data necessary to ensure justice to the soldier, and guide the paymaster in making the payments.

The number of such rolls to be made out are one MUSTER ROLL, as shown by Form 95, p. 201, to be sent by the mustering officer to the Adjutant-General's office within three days after each regular muster; and three MUSTER AND PAY ROLLS; one to be retained in the archives of the company, and two for the paymaster. These must be carefully compared with each other, to ensure their perfect correspondence.

In making out the roll, the names of the commissioned and non-commissioned officers are placed at the head of the column of names in the order of their rank; and the privates below them in alphabetical order.

In the third column, the rank of each individual will be placed after his name.

Under the head of "enlisted," will be entered the facts as to *when*, and *where*, and *by whom* enlisted, and for what period. This data is obtained from the *descriptive roll* received with the man when he enters the company.

By whom and *to what time* paid is learned from the previous roll. This will also give the facts to be entered under the head of *bounty*.

The next column, under the head of NAMES, is to contain the names of all who have responded to the roll-call at muster, such being those who are present.

All officers and soldiers are to be taken up, on the rolls, so soon as ASSIGNED to the company by COMPETENT AUTHORITY, whether they have yet JOINED or not, and to be dropped when similarly transferred from it. The fact of an officer or soldier belonging to the company not being dependent on his actual presence with it.

Under the head of REMARKS, the *date* when any assignment *takes effect*, the *No.. date*, etc., of *order* therefor; the *date* of any officer or soldier's *joining*, whether *originally*, or from *any absence;* the *date* of an officer's *assuming*, or being *relieved*, from any *command*, or *special duty;* the *description* of any *special, extra,* or *daily* duty, on which the officers or soldiers may be; all changes of rank, by *promotion, appointment*, or *reduction*, with *date of* same, and *No., date,* etc., of order; all *authorized stoppages, fines, sentences*, with *No., date*, etc., of order, etc.; in case of ABSENCE, the *nature* and *commencement* of, *No., date,* etc., of order, and *period* assigned for, same (to be *repeated on every roll, while it lasts*); if *wounded* in battle, or *injured on duty,*—if *sick*, or *confined*, a remark to that effect; etc., etc.—must be *carefully stated* opposite to the name of the person concerned, *with everything else necessary, either to account fully* for *every individual of the company,—to guide the paymaster,—or ensure justice to the soldier, and to the United States.*

In noting STOPPAGES to be made for *loss*, or *damage* to public property, the *gross amount* due for *Ordnance*, for *Horse equipments*, for *Clothing*, etc., will be *separately* stated under the head of Remarks. These items will be obtained from lists kept by the first sergeant. The amounts to be charged will be found by reference to the tables containing the prices of the several articles in another part of this book.

The damage to and loss of public property in the charge of a soldier will, in all cases, be entered on the muster roll against him, unless such loss and damage was unavoidable from the exigencies of the service; in which case a *board of survey* will relieve the officer from the responsibility.

The clothing entered on the *muster roll* comprises all *extra issues* for which the soldier has to pay.

When men are entitled to the benefits of the 2d section of the act of August 4th, 1854, the following remarks will be made: "$2 pr. mo. for former services."

The expression "former services" being used to designate the *whole period of the soldier's former service prior to the date of the act.*

If he be entitled to $1 additional for re-enlisting subsequent to its date, the remark will be "$2 pr. mo. for former services, and $1 for re-enlisting;" for a second re-enlistment "$2 pr. mo. for former services, and $2 for re-enlistment," etc.

For soldiers coming under the head of *Entitled to a certificate of merit* under the 3d and 4th sections of act of August 4th, 1854, the remark will be "$2 pr. mo. for former services, and $2 for certificate of merit, and $1 for re-enlisting," etc., according to the facts of the case.

All forfeitures of pay by sentence of court-martial must be entered in the remarks, stating amount forfeited per month, and for how many months with No. and date of order approving of the sentence.

The remark "*discharge and final statements given*" will be made opposite to the name of every discharged soldier to whom such papers have actually been given. But the blank spaces, under the head of *Last Paid*, are to be filled as usual by the name of the paymaster, and time he was paid with the company.

In all cases of "*re-enlistment*" prior to the expiration of the term of service, the *discharge* on the old enlistment will be given at the time the soldier "re-enlists," from and on which day his pay on the new enlistment will commence.

As the amount of pay due the soldier is computed from the *remarks* by the paymaster, great care must be taken by the commander of a company that there are no errors in the rolls.

In the column of names immediately after the roll of those *belonging to the company*, will follow the names of the officers and soldiers who, since last muster, *have ceased to belong to it*. These will be classed in the following order, viz: *discharged, transferred, died, deserted*, and the *utmost particularity* will be observed in the remarks concerning them. DATE and PLACE will in every case be given; and the *number, date,* etc. of *orders* or *description* of *authority* be always carefully specified. Soldiers discharged and *re-enlisted*, or who have deserted *and been retaken* since last muster, have their places in both of the rolls, appearing first as belonging to the company, and then under the appropriate head to show the change, as, *discharged* or *deserted*.

The bounties granted for re-enlistment by the acts approved July, 1838, and June, 1850, having been repealed by the act approved August 3d, 1861, in future no such bounties will be paid; and after the payment of all sums due soldiers on such account, the column relating to these bounties will have no place on the rolls.

MUSTER AND PAY ROLLS.
Form 96, p. 202.

These are the same as the simple muster roll, with the addition of the pay-roll, as shown in Form 96, p. 202.

The commander of the company has nothing to do with the filling up of the columns of the pay roll. This is done by the paymaster from the data given him by the muster-roll and its remarks.

At the foot of the muster roll there will be noted the actions in which the company, or any part of it, has been engaged, *scouts, marches, changes of station*, and everything of interest relating to the *discipline, efficiency* or *service* of the company, with *date, place, distances marched,* etc.

There will also be prepared a recapitulation of the company, to agree with the facts of the muster roll. This is shown on pages 144 and 145, and sets forth the number of officers and enlisted men present for duty, the number absent on extra duty, sick, or in arrest. The number died, deserted and transferred from the company. The number joined, and where from, whether as recruits, from desertion, &c.

The books of instruction received from the Adjutant-General's office will each be accounted for, as also the number of blanks on hand furnished from the same office.

RECAPITULATION

RECAPITULATION.			Captain.	1st Lieutenants.	2d Lieutenants.	Bvt. 2d Lieuts.	Sergeants.	Corporals.	Buglers.	Musicians.	Farriers and blacksmiths.	Artificers.	Privates.	Total commissioned.
PRESENT.		For duty............												
		On extra, or daily duty.												
		Sick..................												
		In arrest, or confinem't.												
ABSENT.		On detached service.....												
		With leave...........												
		Without leave........												
		Sick.................												
		In arrest, or confinem't..												
STRENGTH—Present and Absent.														
ALTERATIONS SINCE LAST MUSTER.	JOINED.	Recruits from depots...												
		Enlisted in company....												
		By re-enlistment......												
		By transfer, or app't....												
		From desertion........												
		Resigned												
	DISCHARGED.	Expiration of service...												
		For disability.........												
		By sent. of G. C. Mart'l.												
		By civil authority......												
		By order.............												
		Transferred...........												
	DIED.	Killed in action........												
		Of wounds............												
		From disease, &c.......												
		Deserted.............												

OF MUSTER ROLL.

Total enlisted.	AGGREGATE.	AGGREGATE LAST MUSTER.	MEMORANDA.				BOOKS AND BLANKS—TO BE ACCOUNTED FOR BY THE COMPANY COMMANDER.							
			Number of recruits required.	Wounded in action.	Serviceable horses.	Unserviceable horses.	General Regulations, (No. of copies.)	Artillery Tactics, (No. of copies.)	Cavalry Tactics, (No. of copies.)	Infantry Tactics, (No. of copies.)	Rifle and Light Infantry Tactics.	Military Laws.	Macomb's Practice of Courts Martial.	Ordnance Manual.	Ordnance Regulations.

BOOKS AND BLANKS—(Continued.)							
Blank Muster Rolls.	Blank Muster and Pay Rolls.	Blank Company Monthly Returns.	Blank Certificates of Disability.	Blank Enlistments.	Blank Re-enlistments.	Blank Recruiting Accounts Current.	Blank Monthly Recruiting Returns.	Blank Discharges.	Descriptive Lists.

The roll, when complete, will be certified to in the following manner by the commanding officer of the company:

I CERTIFY, on honor, that this Muster Roll is made out in the manner required by the *printed notes;* that it exhibits the true state of Captain A. B.'s Company A, of the Third Regiment of Artillery, for the period herein mentioned; that the "Remarks" set opposite the name of each officer and soldier are accurate and just; and that the "Recapitulation" exhibits in every particular the true state of the company, as required by Regulations and the Rules and Articles of War.

STATION: Washington, D. C.
DATE: June 30th, 1861.

A. B.,
Capt. 3d Artillery, Commanding the Company.

The mustering officer will make the following certificate, with appropriate remarks touching *discipline, instruction,* etc., according to the facts exhibited in the course of his inspection, together with such other remarks as may be necessary or useful for the information of the War Department:

I CERTIFY, on honor, that I have carefully examined this Muster Roll; and that I have mustered and minutely inspected the company, the condition of which is found to be as expressed in my remarks hereunto annexed:

DISCIPLINE:

INSTRUCTION:

MILITARY APPEARANCE:

ARMS:

ACCOUTREMENTS:

CLOTHING:

M. N.,
Inspector and Mustering Officer.

MUSTER AND PAY ROLLS OF DETACHMENTS.

These will be made out as prescribed for a company, according to Forms 95 and 96, pp. 201 and 202; the only difference being that the Captain will specify *Detachment of ordnance men,* or whatever the command may be. And this will be substituted wherever the designation *company* occurs on company rolls.

This mustering of detachments does not apply to detachments belonging to a regular company. These are accounted for on the company rolls, as *absent on detached service*. But all detachments of troops, *unattached*, will have muster rolls prepared by their commanding officer.

Hospital attendants, and others belonging to a hospital will be mustered on rolls made out in the same manner as the company rolls, except that the caption will indicate that it is the *muster roll of the steward, wardmaster, cooks, nurses, matrons, and detached soldiers, sick*.

The certificates of the surgeon and mustering officer will be as follows:

I CERTIFY, on honor, that this Muster Roll is made out in the manner required by the printed notes; that it exhibits the true state of the Hospital Department for the period herein mentioned; that the "Remarks" set opposite each name are accurate and just; and that the "Recapitulation" exhibits in every particular the true state of the hospital, as required by the Regulations and the Rules and Articles of War.

STATION:
DATE:
P. Q.,
Surgeon, in charge of Hospital.

I CERTIFY, on honor, that I have carefully examined this Muster Roll; that I have mustered and minutely inspected the hospital attendants; and that the police and general condition of the Hospital Department is found to be as follows:

R. S.,
Inspector and Mustering Officer.

The *Surgeon* and *Assistant Surgeon* are not mustered with the occupants of the hospital, but with the Field, Staff, and Band of the command.

MUSTER ROLLS OF THE FIELD, STAFF AND BAND.

These are made out in a similar manner to what has been prescribed for the company, and contain the names of the *Field Officers* of the regiment, and staff officers, together with the non-commissioned staff, and members of the band.

The roll will be signed by the commanding officer of the regiment, and certified by the mustering officer, as before set forth for company rolls.

The Adjutant-General furnishes blanks for all rolls.

INVENTORY OF EFFECTS OF DECEASED SOLDIERS.

This return is to be made out and forwarded to the Adjutant-General and Regimental Adjutant, by the company commander, *immediately* after the death of the soldier. If the soldier should die possessed of no effects, this fact will be so stated in the inventory.

FINAL STATEMENT OF DECEASED SOLDIERS.

This is to be made out agreeably to the form for discharged soldiers, and transmitted to the Adjutant-General and Regimental Adjutant, immediately after the death of the soldier. Should there be no effects, the fact will be stated.

RETURN OF DECEASED SOLDIERS.

This return is to be made by the company commander at the end of every quarter, and transmitted to the Regimental Adjutant, the first day of the subsequent month. It will contain the *name* and *rank* of the soldier, and the *time, cause,* and *place* of his death; together with a statement of the pay due the soldier, and his indebtedness to the United States. Also the amount due the *Laundress*, and the date of forwarding the inventory and final statement to the Adjutant-General.

This return is to be forwarded even though there be no deaths to report. In such cases blank forms will be forwarded, properly headed and signed, with a black or red ink line drawn obliquely across the body of the return, from left to right.

RETURN OF CLOTHING, CAMP AND GARRISON EQUIPAGE.

This return is to be made out in duplicate, by every company commander, at the end of every month, and sent to the Quartermaster-General within the first *ten days* of the ensuing month.

One of the returns is to be supported by vouchers, and the other without. The form of this return is shown by Form 37, p. 72a, and the manner of preparing described under the head of *Clothing*.

RETURN OF ORDNANCE AND ORDNANCE STORES.

This return is to be made by every commander of a company, and commander of detachment, at the end of every quarter, and transmitted to the *Chief of Ordnance* within twenty days thereafter. It will be prepared according to Form 91, p. 163, and as prescribed under the head of *Arms*.

CERTIFICATE OF INVENTORY ON RETURN OF ORDNANCE AND ORDNANCE STORES.

This certificate is to be made yearly on the return for quarter ending June 30th. It will certify that the balance on hand, shown by the return, has been verified by an inventory.

REPORT OF DAMAGED ARMS.

This is to be made at the end of every two months, and forwarded to the Chief of Ordnance on the first day of the subsequent month. It will contain all damages to arms, equipments, and implements belonging to the officer's command, noting those occasioned by negligence or abuse, and naming the officer or soldier by whose negligence or abuse the damages were occasioned. This report is to be made by every officer commanding a regiment, corps, garrison, or detachment, at the end of February, April, June, August, October, and December.

DESCRIPTIVE LIST OF MEN JOINED.

This return is made at the *end of every quarter*, to the Adjutant of the regiment, by every commander of a company, and will be made out agreeably to Form 106, p. 207. It will be transmitted the first day of the subsequent month.

The men joining will, in the column of names, be classed in the following order, viz.:

1. Recruits from depôts.
2. Enlisted in the regiment.

3. Re-enlisted.
4. By transfer.
5. From missing in action.
6. From desertion.

The list will be filled up from the description rolls of the several soldiers, and be signed by the first sergeant and the commander of the company.

COMPANY RETURN.

This will be made by commanders of companies at the end of every month, and transmitted to the Regimental Adjutant, on the first day of the subsequent month. It will contain the state of the company *present* and *absent*, and will be made out as shown by Form 97, p. 202*a*.

If in the field, the return will contain an account of actions in which the company, or any part of it, has been engaged; *scouts, marches, changes of station*, and every thing of interest relating to the discipline, efficiency, or service of the company will be minutely and carefully noted, with *date, place, distance, march, etc.*

The name and rank of officers and soldiers killed in action, or wounded, with date and place, will also be accurately noted in this report.

Commissioned officers present will be accounted for by name on the back of the return, giving the *date* (with number, date, etc., of order) at which an officer is *assigned* or *transferred* to, *joins* or *re-joins* the company, *assumes* or is *relieved from* command of it, or from any special duty. The names of absent officers will be entered below those present, and against them in Remarks, will be entered the *number* and *date* of order, the *reasons* for and commencement of absence, and the period assigned for the same. To be repeated on every return while it lasts.

After the list of absent officers will follow the record of those *resigned, died,* or transferred from the company, with No., date of order, *date, place,* and in case of death, its *cause*.

On the back of the return the alterations made since the last return, among the *enlisted men*, will be noted, accounting for every man by name who shall have been *transferred* to or from the company, with particulars of order. All *apprehensions, discharges, furloughs, deaths, desertions,* etc., will be accurately noted; also the *places* of discharge, death, desertion, etc. In fact, all information concerning the state of the company will be entered on the *company return*.

One copy of the monthly return is to be forwarded to the *Post Adjutant* on the first day of the subsequent month, which copy will afterwards be returned to the company commander for file in the archives of the company.

TRANSCRIPT OF ORDERS MAKING TEMPORARY APPOINTMENTS OF NON-COMMISSIONED OFFICERS, AND REDUCING NON-COMMISSIONED OFFICERS.

This return is to be made to the regimental adjutant, *immediately* after the issue of the company order, appointing non-commissioned officers temporarily, or reducing non-commissioned officers.

MORNING REPORT OF COMPANY.

Form 93, p. 202b.

This will be made to the Post-Adjutant every morning before eight o'clock A. M. The number of commissioned officers and enlisted men *for duty*, will be first entered under their appropriate heads. Then *commissioned officers* on special duty, and *enlisted men* on extra or daily duty. Then the *sick*, to be followed by those *in arrest*. Then the *total* commissioned officers *present*, and total enlisted men *present*. Next will follow the report of commissioned officers, and enlisted men *absent*, under the appropriate heads, to be followed by the *total absent* of each. Then will follow the total commissioned officers *present and absent*, and the same for enlisted men, and in the next space will be the *aggregate*, comprising the sum of the total commissioned officers and enlisted men present and absent, or the number making up the company.

If it be a *mounted* company, the report of *horses* will be made under the appropriate heads.

After the *aggregate* will follow the alterations since last report, under the several heads shown by the former.

In the column of remarks, the *names* of all who appear under the head of alterations, are entered with such particulars as may be necessary to note the event.

Regimental and battalion staff officers, when belonging

to companies, will be reported in such companies as "on detached service," and be accounted for in field and staff of the consolidated regimental return, to be described hereafter.

RETURN OF COMPANY FUND.

This return is to be made by the company commander at the end of every four months, and transmitted to the Post Adjutant on the first of the subsequent month. It will give a full statement of the amount received on account of the company fund, and of the amounts disbursed, showing the balance on hand, certified by the commander of the company.

The same returns, as specified for commanding officers of companies, will be made by officers commanding bands and small detachments of troops.

Rolls, Returns and Reports required of Regimental Commanders.

RETURN OF THE REGIMENT.

Form 99, p. 202c.

This return is to be made to the *Adjutant-General* at the end of every month, and is to be made up as soon as the several company returns are received, and forwarded as soon as completed.

This return will contain the same information as the company returns, it being made up by consolidating the returns of the several companies composing the regiment, together with the field and staff and band. The first column will contain the stations of the companies, the second the names of the captains, and the third the letter of the company.

The report of *present* and *absent* will be made up from the company returns, the figures of each being placed after their respective letters.

The column *where*, under ABSENT, is to be filled up only when the regiment is serving with, and returned for, as part of a division or brigade in the field.

Under the head of memoranda, the number of recruits required to fill up the regiment is noted. Care must be taken to deduct those men of the band who do not form a part of the legal organization, from the total required for the companies.

The enlisted men on extra or daily duty will be accounted for by name, as in the company return, as also the absent enlisted men.

Upon the back of the return the commissioned officers of the regiment will be entered by name, with the memoranda of the company returns concerning them, and such other as the commander of the regiment may deem necessary.

The alterations since last return among the *enlisted men* will be duly entered, with such memoranda as is specified under that head in the *company returns*.

This return will be signed by the adjutant of the regiment and the commanding officer.

If the station of any company be so distant, that its return cannot be received at regimental headquarters within ten days after the end of the month, the regimental return will be made out without the return of this company, a blank being left for its insertion at the Adjutant-General's office, to which a copy of the company return must be sent direct by the captain of the company.

RECRUITING RETURN OF THE REGIMENT.
Form 121, p. 238.

This return is to be made to the Adjutant-General of the Army by the regimental commander, monthly, as soon as returns are received from all the recruiting parties. When no recruits are obtained during the month, the return will, nevertheless, be forwarded, properly headed and signed, with a red ink line drawn across the body of the return from left to right.

The return will be composed of returns of recruiting parties for the same month, and will contain in the column of remarks the date a rendezvous (except at a garrisoned post) is opened or closed.

All changes since the last return will be entered by name at the foot of the return. All *transfers* (except to companies of the regiment, or to other stations) will also be noted, together with all *discharges, deaths, desertions, apprehensions,* etc. The real and assumed names, company and regiment of recognized deserters will also be noticed.

MUSTER ROLL OF THE FIELD STAFF AND BAND.

This will be made by the commanding officer of the regiment every two months, and sent to the Adjutant-General within *three* days thereafter by the *mustering officer.*

There will be one muster roll and three muster and pay rolls, one to be kept in the archives of the regiment, and two for the paymaster.

The manner of preparing these rolls is prescribed in the description of *Company Muster Rolls.*

QUARTERLY RETURN OF DECEASED SOLDIERS.
Form 100, p. 204 and 205.

This return will be forwarded quarterly by commanders of regiments to the Adjutant-General, as soon as the company quarterly returns of deceased soldiers are received, and a duplicate sent at the same time to the *Second Auditor.*

The return will show the name, rank and company of the soldier, where he died, when he died, and the cause of his death; also, a full statement of his account, as shown by the form. It will be signed by the Regimental Adjutant and the commanding officer.

ANNUAL RETURN OF CASUALTIES.
Form 101, p. 202d.

This return is to be made at the end of every year, (December,) and when completed, is to be sent by the commander of the regiment to the Adjutant-General.

It will contain all *gain* and *loss* occurring in the regiment, under appropriate heads, and such memoranda as is shown in the form. Under the head of remarks, the colonel will record such other facts, and add such general information relative to the *movements, service* and *discipline* of the regiment as may be necessary or useful for the records of Adjutant-General's office; such as all changes made in the headquarters of the regiment, or of any company, within the year, etc.

The name and rank of every officer and enlisted man, who may be *killed* or *wounded* in action, or *die* of *wounds* received therein, with the *time* and *place* of action, will be reported under the head of remarks.

REGIMENTAL AND COMPANY FUNDS. 193

When soldiers are confined by civil authority, it must be stated whether they were discharged without trial, and if tried, whether they were acquitted or convicted.

All commissioned officers borne on the face of the return are to be accounted for, by name, on the back of the return, and will be classed and reported in the same order as on the face of the return.

REPORT BY LETTER OF APPOINTMENT OR CHANGE OF STAFF OFFICERS.

Every commanding officer of a regiment will report, by letter, to the *Adjutant-General*, all appointments and changes of staff officers *immediately* after making such appointment or change.

ACKNOWLEDGEMENT OF BOOKS AND BLANKS.

The receipt of books and blanks by regimental commanders are to be acknowledged by them, by letter, to the *Adjutant-General*, immediately after the reception of the articles.

REPORT OF PRIZEMEN OF TARGET PRACTICE.

The commander of the regiment shall, at the end of every year, make to the *headquarters of the army*, a report of the *name*, *company* and *record* of firing of the prizeman of the regiment, as obtained from the company reports of target practice.

ACCOUNTS OF REGIMENTAL AND COMPANY FUNDS.

Every regimental commander will make to Department Headquarters, *when in the field*, accounts of regimental and company funds. These accounts are to be prepared every four months, and transmitted immediately after preparation. They will show from what source the money has been received, and the manner in which it has been expended. The account is to be prepared by the Treasurer, who has the disbursing of the funds. · Further particulars concerning these funds will be found under their appropriate heads.

REPORT OF DAMAGE TO ARMS.

This will be made every two months by the regimental commander to the Chief of Ordnance.

MORNING REPORT.
Form 102, p. 203.

This will be made out by the Regimental Adjutant every morning before 9 o'clock, from the data given by the company morning reports. It will be signed by the Adjutant and commanding officer, and sent to brigade headquarters at such time as may be directed.

Regimental and battalion staff-officers, when belonging to companies, will be reported in such companies, as "on detached service," and be accounted for in "Field and Staff." They will, however, be dropped from aggregate of *present and absent*, and be accounted for in the aggregate of their respective companies.

The form shows the first columns of the report, which differ from the company report; the remainder of the report is the same as the company report, shown by Form 98, p. 202*b*.

Returns, Rolls and Reports, required from Post Commanders.

POST RETURN.
Form 103, p. 206*a*.

This return is to be made out at the end of every month, and sent by the post commander on the first day of the subsequent month to the following persons and places, viz: one copy to the *Adjutant-General* of the Army, one copy to *Headquarters of the Army*, and one copy to the *Headquarters of the Department*. It will embrace a full return of all commissioned officers and enlisted men at the post, and such other persons as will be hereinafter mentioned.

Enlisted men, "casually at the post," will be accounted for by name. A record of important events connected with the post during the month will be given, together with a record of official communications received during the month, and the purport thereof.

When a post or station is garrisoned by *different regiments*, or parts of different regiments, the troops will be reported on separate lines by *regiments;* but if of the same regiment, the troops will be reported *by companies.*

All the *absent* are to be accounted for under the head of "*How*," and *again* under the head of "*Where.*"

Whenever a post is *evacuated,* or its command *relieved,* an *exact return* of the withdrawn *garrison,* on the *day* of its *departure,* is to be left among the records of the post.

The DATE and PLACE of *death, desertion, apprehension,* or *discharge* of every soldier not mustered in any company of the garrison, will be reported by the *commanding officer of the post* to the commanding officer of the *company* or detachment to which the soldier belongs, pursuant to articles 17 and 18 of the Regulations. *A duplicate of the above report will, moreover, in every case, be forwarded* to the commanding officer of the *regiment* to which the man belongs.

Whenever the garrison is *re-inforced* (by recruits as well as soldiers), *reduced,* or *relieved,* or a post is *established, evacuated,* or *re-occupied,* the commanding officer will immediately report the fact to the Adjutant-General and to General and Department Headquarters, and *note the same* on the *first subsequent post return.* Such report and record, *in the case of a new post, must indicate its position,* which should be identified with some known object, as 25 miles west from —— river, or town, post-office, etc.; and in all cases the *best means of communicating* with the new post by mail must be stated, pursuant to paragraph 458 of Regulations. *All* commissioned officers borne on the face of the return, in figures, must be accounted for, *by name,* on the back of the return; and they are to be classed and reported in the following order: 1st. "PRESENT;" 2d. "ABSENT," in the order here given, viz: "*On detached service,*" "*With leave,*" "*Without leave,*" "*Sick,*" "*In arrest;*" 3d. "ALTERATIONS SINCE LAST MONTHLY RETURN;" which will embrace "*Resigned,*" "*Transferred,*" "*Died,*" etc.

The *day* on which an officer *joins* or *leaves* his *post, assumes* or is relieved from any *command* or *special duty,* will, with the nature of such duty, be specified opposite his name, under the head of Remarks.

The *Chaplain,* and *Schoolmaster,* and citizen *Physician* employed, if any, will be reported at *the foot of the list of officers present,* but are not to be embraced in the strength of the command.

The *nature* and *commencement* of an officer's absence, with number, date, etc., of *order*, and the *period* assigned for the same, are, so long as he is reported absent, to be repeated on every return.

The *name* and *rank* of every *officer and enlisted man*, who may be *killed* or *wounded*, in *action*, or *die* of *wounds* received therein, with the *time* and *place* of action must be reported.

The *number*, but not the *names*, of *civilians*, employed at the post during the month, will be noted on the *monthly* return, with the amount of compensation allowed, and the staff department in which employed.

The pasting of pieces of paper is to be avoided whenever it is possible to do so, by means of finer writing, closer ruling, or using blank spaces in other parts of the return.

In accounting for the commissioned officers by name the *brevet* rank, as well as that by ordinary commission, is to be given.

REPORT OF ARRIVAL AND DEPARTURE OF TROOPS.

This report will be made to the Adjutant-General of the Army, to the Headquarters of the Army, and to the Headquarters of the Department, by all commanding officers of posts immediately after the event.

REPORT OF CHANGE OF OFFICERS ACTING IN STAFF DEPARTMENTS.

This report will be made to the Adjutant-General by post commanders, immediately after any such change.

ACKNOWLEDGEMENT OF BLANKS AND BOOKS.

All books and blanks received from the Adjutant-General's office, will be acknowledged immediately by commanders of posts.

QUARTERMASTER'S REPORT OF CONDITION OF BUILDINGS.

This report will be transmitted to the Quartermaster-General, by post commanders, on the 30th of June every year.

RETURN OF ORDNANCE.

Form 91, p. 163.

This return will be made out by post commanders at the end of every quarter. One copy, without vouchers, will be sent to the Headquarters of the Department, and one copy, with vouchers, to the Chief of Ordnance. The June return sent to the Chief of Ordnance, will be accompanied with a certificate of having taken an inventory, to be made on the return.

These returns must be transmitted within twenty days after the expiration of the quarter to which they relate.

RETURNS OF COMPANY AND POST FUNDS.

Every four months, the commander of the post must make to Department Headquarters, a return of these funds. These returns are the accounts current of the Post Treasurer, made agreeably to Form 104, p. 206, signed by the Treasurer, and approved by the commanding officer of the post.

In order that the making out of these accounts may be understood, a statement of the manner in which these funds are raised and disbursed, must be given.

Post Fund.

This fund is raised at each post by a tax of not more than ten cents a month for every officer and soldier of the command, according to the average in each month; and from the saving of the flour ration, ordinarily thirty-three per cent., by baking the soldier's bread at the post bakery.

This fund pays the expenses of the bake-house, and the expenses of the soldier's children at the post school.

The officer in charge of the fund, is the Post Treasurer, designated by the commanding officer. He keeps the fund and disburses it on the warrants of the commanding officer, drawn in pursuance of specific resolves of the Council of Administration.

At each settlement of the treasurer's account, the council distributes the unexpended balance of the post fund to the several companies and other troops, in the ratio of their average force during the period; and if a company leaves the post, it then receives its distributive share of the accrued fund.

In the field, the regulations regarding the post fund, are, as far as practicable, applied to a regimental fund, raised, administered, expended and distributed in the same manner as the post fund, by the regimental commander and a regimental council.

Company Fund.

The *company fund* is formed from the savings of the company ration, paid for by the commissary, and the distribution of the post or regimental fund. It is disbursed by the captain for the benefit of the enlisted men of the company, pursuant to the resolves of the majority of the company officers present. This constitutes the *company council*, to be convened by the captain every two months, or oftener if necessary.

Every four months, and whenever the company leaves the post, or another officer takes command of the company, the company fund account is made up, and submitted with a duplicate to the post commander, who, after examination, forwards the duplicate to department headquarters.

In the field, all that is stated here for the post commander, devolves on the regimental commander.

The form given for the account of the post treasurer, is the same as that to be made out for the company fund, making the proper alterations in the heading. Form 104, p. 206.

Directions for Regimental Fund Accounts.

1. All receipts and expenditures during the period for which the account is made, and none but those, will be entered.

2. The per centage allowed for disbursing will be charged in each account upon the expenditures exhibited therein.

3. Amounts received from post treasurers will be entered separately, according to the months for which they were appropriated, those from each post being specified.

4. The amounts of particular items will be entered in the first column of dollars and cents, and the gross amounts under each head will alone be carried to the second column.

Directions for Post Fund Accounts.

1. The receipts will be entered in the following order: 1st. "Balance on hand last account," or "Balance received from ———, Post Treasu-

rer;" 2d. "Received from sales of bread, flour, etc.;" 3d. "Sutler's Tax;" 4th. "Received from companies" (the letter of company, the name of commander and regiment, and the date of receipt to be given); 5th. "Received from other sources" (the sources and the amounts to be specified).

2. The expenditures will be entered in the following order: 1st. "Expenses of bakehouses (the items enumerated), pay of bakers, etc.;" 2d. "Other appropriations of the council," (except for the regimental fund), named separately; 3d. "Two and a half per cent. on the amount expended;" 4th. "Transferred to companies" (the letter of company, name of commander and regiment, and the date of transfer, to be given); 5th. "Appropriations for regimental fund and for the military asylum."

3. Amounts set aside for regimental funds will be entered separately, according to the months for which they were appropriated, those for each regiment being specified.

4. The amounts of particular items will be entered in the first column of dollars and cents, and the gross amounts under each head will alone be carried to the second column.

5. All receipts, expenditures, and transfers, during the period for which the account is made, and none but those, will be entered.

6. The percentage allowed for disbursing will be charged in each account, upon the expenditures exhibited therein.

Monthly Return of Departments, Army Corps, Divisions, and Brigades.

Form 105, p. 206*b*.

This return shows in the first line, the condition of the department, division, or brigade staff, as the case may be. Under which follows the return of each garrison, regiment, or corps, according to the character of the return.

The command will be accounted for under the heads of *present*, *absent*, and *present and absent;* and the alterations since the last return shown.

On the back of the return, the *officers of the staff*, present and absent, will be accounted for by name; the brevet rank of the officers, as well as that by ordinary commission, being given.

In department returns, only those officers are to be accounted for, under the head of *department staff*, who are not already accounted for as *staff* officers in the post returns.

The date at which an officer joins his station, *assumes*, or is *relieved* from any command or duty, is to be stated against his name; against that of an *absent* officer will be stated the *No.*, and *date of order*, the *reasons for*, and *commencement of* absence.

The *date* of all *transfers*, to or from the department staff, will be accurately noted, together with the *No.* and *date* of the order making such change. As likewise of resignations and dismissals, together with *date* and *place of death*, or other casualty.

Transfers *from*, resignations, dismissals, death, and other separations, will be recorded at the *foot* of the list of officers.

Any change of department headquarters, all *re-inforcements* or *reductions* of the command, and the establishment or abandonment of posts, will be noted. The department returns, corresponding to the *record of events*, in the post returns, should contain *a brief summary of the military operations* during the month.

The name and rank of every officer included in the *department staff*, who may be killed or wounded in action, with the *time* and *place* of action, must be reported.

The foregoing instructions for department returns, applies to division or brigade staff, in division or brigade returns.

The return is to be signed by the *Assistant Adjutant-General*, and the commander of the department, division or brigade.

FORM 95.

Muster Roll of Captain A. F's., Company A., of the Third Regiment of Artillery, Army of the United States, Colonel William Gates, from the 30th day of April, 1861, when last mustered, to the 30th day of June, 1861.

NAMES.	RANK.	ENLISTED.				LAST PAID.		BOUNTY.		NAMES.	REMARKS.
No. Present and Absent.		When.	Where	By whom	Period.	By Paymaster.	To what Time.	Paid.	Due.	Present.	
	Captain....							$	$		
	1st Lieut....										
	"										
	2d Lieut....										
	Bvt. 2d Lt..										
	1st Serg't..										
	Sergeant ...										
	"										
	"										
	Corporal...										
	"										
	"										
	"										
	Private....										
	"										
	"										

FORM 96.—MUSTER AND PAY ROLL.

Muster and Pay Roll of Capt. A. B.'s Company (A) of the Third Regiment of Artillery, Army of the United States, Colonel W. G., from the 30th day of April, 1861, when last mustered, to the 30th day of June, 1861.

No.	Names present and absent.	Rank.	ENLISTED.				LAST PAID.		BOUNTY.		Names present.	Remarks.	PERIOD PAID FOR.		PAY PER MONTH.	AMOUNT OF PAY.		RETAIN'D PAY.		BOUNTY.			TOTAL DUE.		AMOUNT OF STOP'GES.		BALANCE PAID.		RECEIVED PAYMENT OF.	WITNESS.
			When.	Where.	By whom.	Period.	By Paym.	To what.	Pd.	Due			M's.	D's.		$	c.	$	c.	Pd.	Due	c.	$	c.	$	c.		

Report of a Company.

...giment of Artillery, commanded by Captain E. K. S.

PRESENT AND ABSENT.				ALTERATIONS SINCE LAST REPORT.																		
				GAIN.									LOSS.									
				COM'D OFIC'RS	ENLISTED MEN.						COMMIS'D OFFICERS.				ENLISTED MEN.							
													DIED.	DISCHARGED.							DIED.	
COMMISSIONED OFFICERS.	TOTAL ENLISTED.	AGGREGATE.	AGGREGATE LAST REPORT.	TOTAL OF HORSES.	By promotion or appointment.	By transfer.	Recruits from depôts.	Enlisted in the regiment.	Re-enlisted.	By transfer.	From missing in action.	From desertion.	Resigned or disbanded.	Dismissed.	Transferred.	Missing in action.	In action, or of wounds received there.	Of disease, &c.	Expiration of service.	For disability.	By sentence G. Court-Martial.	By order.	By civil authority.	Transferred.	In action, or of wounds received there.	Of disease, &c.

Return of Captain E. N. S.'s Company (H), of the 3d Regiment of Artillery, Army of the United States, (Colonel W. G.), for the month of January, 1868.

Present		Absent			Present and absent				Alterations since last monthly return		Memoranda
Commissioned officers	Enlisted men	Commissioned officers	Enlisted men	Whole (Within the Dept. / Without the Dept.)	Com'd officers	Enlisted men	Total enlisted	Aggregate	Aggregate last monthly return	Gain / Loss	
[illegible]	[illegible]	[illegible]	[illegible]	[illegible]	[illegible]	[illegible]	[illegible]	[illegible]	[illegible]	[illegible]	[illegible]

Enlisted Men on "Extra or Daily Duty," accounted for by name.

(The specific kind of such duty to be carefully stated.)

Sergeants.	Corporals.	Musicians.	Artificers, Saddlers, &c.	Privates.	
....	....	....	....	1	J. Jones—on duty in Commissary Store.
1	....	....	....	....	A. Brown—Acting Commissary Sergeant.
....	1	....	....	....	E. Burk—on duty in Quartermaster's Department.
....	....	....	....	1	A. Jukes—
1	1	....	....	2	

Absent Enlisted Men, accounted for by name.

(The nature, commencement, period, and place, of absence to be invariably stated.)

Sergeants.	Corporals.	Musicians.	Artificers, Saddlers, &c.	Privates.	
....	....	....	....	1	A. McKay—absent in Florida, from June 15, 1861, to extend until July 15, for the purpose of settling his father's estate.
....	....	....	....	1	

FORM 96.—MORNING REPORT OF A COMPANY.

Morning Report of Company " A," 3d Regiment of Artillery, commanded by Captain E. K. S.

E. K. S., *Commanding the Company.*

				MEMORANDA.	REMARKS.
Missing in action.	Deserted.	Wounded in action.	No. of recruits required.	No. of horses required.	

E. K. S., *Commanding the Company.*

RETURN OF ALTERATIONS AND CASUALTIES.

1861, *in the 3d Regiment of Artillery, commanded by Colo*

ENLISTED MEN.			DEATHS.						WOUND'D				BY MILITARY AUTH			
By civil authority.	Transferred to other regiments or corps.	Turned over to civil authority.	Ordinary.	Killed in action.	Died of wounds received in action.	Accidental.	Missing in action.	Deserted.	AGGREGATE.	In action.	Accidental.	Number tried for desertion.	Number convicted of desertion.	Number restored to duty, without trial, (for desertion).	Number pardoned, (after sentence for desertion).	Number tried by General Court-Martial.	Number tried by Regimental

HEADQUARTERS THIRD REGIMENT OF ARTILLERY.
STATION: San Francisco, Cal.
DATE: *December* 30, 1861.

FORM 90.—REGIMENTAL MONTHLY RETURN.

Return of the 1st Regiment of Artillery, Army of the United States, (Colonel J. C.), for the month of January, 1862.

C. D., *Adjutant.*

HEADQUARTERS OF THE ——— REGIMENT OF ———
STATION:
DATE:

J. C., *Commanding the Regiment.*

FORM 101.—ANNUAL REGIMENTAL RETURN OF ALTERATIONS AND CASUALTIES.

Annual Return of Alterations and Casualties, for the year 1861, in the 3d Regiment of Artillery, commanded by Colonel W. G.

nel W. G.

			RANDA.						REMARKS.
Missing in action.	Deserted.	Wounded in action Court-Martial.	ORITY.		BY CIVIL AUTHORITY.				
			Number tried by Garrison Court-Martial.	Aggregate number tried by General, Regimental, and Garrison Courts-Martial.	* Nature of offence to be specified; and, if tried, give the name and State, and whether acquitted or not.				
					Number arrested.	Number returned to service.	Number tried.	Number acquitted	Number convicted

W. G., *Commanding the Regiment.*

FORM 102.—MORNING REPORT OF A REGIMENT.

Consolidated Morning Report of the 3d Regiment of Artillery.

Date.	Companies.	Field officers.	Assistant surgeon.	Regimental staff officers.	Battalion staff officers.	Captains.	First lieutenants.	Second lieutenants.	Regimental non-commissioned staff.	Battalion non-commissioned staff.	Hospital stewards.	First sergeants.	Company quartermaster sergeants.	Sergeants.	Corporals.	Saddlers.	Wagoners.	Field music.	Artificers and blacksmiths.	Privates.	Recruits.
									PRESENT. FOR DUTY.												
1861.	Field, Staff, and Band.																				
	A.																				
	B.																				
	C.																				
	D.																				
	E.																				
	F.																				
	G.																				
	H.																				
	I.																				
	K.																				
	Unassigned.																				
	Total.....																				

C. D., *Adjutant.*

FORM 100.—RETURN OF

Quarterly Return of Deceased Soldiers of the 3d Regiment of

No.	Name.	Rank.	Company.	DIED.			DUE THE SOLDIER.							
							P. P.		R. P.		E. P.		R. B.	
				When.	Where.	Cause.	M	D	$	c.	$	c.	$	c.

C. C. C., *Adjutant.*

DECEASED SOLDIERS.

Artillery, for the quarter ending the 30th day of June, 1861.

Cl'g.	DUE THE U. S.			DUE THE LAUN-DRESS.		DATE OF FORWARDING INVENTORY.		REMARKS.
Cl'th	A'ms	Cl'th	O. S.					
$ c.	$ c.	$ c.	$ c.	Name.	$ c.	Inventory	Final statement.	

Headquarters of the 3d Regiment of Artillery.
Station: Fort Adams.
Date: *June* 30, 1861. W. G., *Commanding the Regiment.*

FORM 104.—POST TREASURER'S ACCOUNT CURRENT.

C. E. S., 2d Lieut. 3d Artillery, Post Treasurer, in account current with the Post, during the months of January, February, March, and April, 1861.

Date.	From what source received.	Dollars.	Cents.	Dollars.	Cents.	Date.	How expended.	Dollars.	Cents.	Dollars.	Cents.
1861. Jan. 1.	To balance on hand last account............ " received sales of flour. " sutler's tax.......... " received from companies..............										

The above account is correct and just.

C. E. S., *2d Lieutenant 3d Artillery, Treasurer.*

The above payments have been made pursuant to appropriations of the council of administration, and on warrants drawn by the commanding officer.

Station: Fort Adams.
Date: *April 30, 1861.*

W. G., *Commanding Officer.*

. DEPARTMENT, DIVISION OR BRIGADE.

ed by Brigadier-General J. K. F. M., for the month of J

		PRESENT AND ABSENT.		
HE T.		COMMISSIONED OFFICERS.		ENLISTED MEN.
	General officers. / Aides-de-camp. / Adjutant General's Department. / Inspectors General. / Judge Advocate. / Quartermaster's Department. / Subsistence Department. / Medical Department. / Pay Department. / Engineers. / Topographical Engineers. / Ordnance. / Military storekeepers. / Regimental field officers. / Regimental staff officers. / Captains. / Subalterns. / TOTAL COMMISSIONED.		Non-commissioned staff of reg'ts. / Ordnance sergeants. / Hospital Stewards. / Sergeants. / Corporals. / Musicians. / Artificers, Farriers, & Bl'ksmiths. / Privates. / TOTAL ENLISTED.	

HEADQUARTERS OF THE DEPARTMENT (
STATION: Washington, D. C.
DATE: *July* 31, 1861.

FORM 103.—POST RETURN.

Post Return of Fort Monroe, Va., commanded by Colonel J. D., for the month of January, 186 .

STATION:
DATE:

J. D., *Commanding Post.*

FORM 105.—RETURN FOR A DEPARTMENT, DIVISION OR BRIGADE.

Return of the Department of Washington, commanded by Brigadier-General J. K. F. M., for the month of July, 1861.

HEADQUARTERS OF THE DEPARTMENT OF WASHINGTON.
STATION: Washington, D. C.

uly, 1861.

AGGREGATE.	AGGREGATE, LAST MONTHLY RETURN.	ALTERATIONS SINCE LAST MONTHLY RETURN.						MEMORANDA.								
		GAIN.			LOSS.			No of recruits required.	Recruits received from general depot.	Recruits enlisted or re-enlisted in reg'ts.	Aggregate killed or missing in action.	Aggregate wounded in action.	HORSES.		PIECES OF ARTILLERY		
		Commissioned officers.	Enlisted men.	AGGREGATE.	Commissioned officers.	Enlisted men.	AGGREGATE.						Serviceable.	Unserviceable.	Heavy.	Field.	Mountain.	No. blank returns on hand.

)F WASHINGTON.

J. K. F. M., *Commanding the Department*.

FORM 106.—RETURN OF MEN JOINED.

Return of Men Joined Company A, Third Regiment of Artillery, during the quarter ending the 30th day of June, 1861.

No.	Name.	Rank.	Age.	Eyes.	Hair.	Complexion.	Feet.	Inches.	Town.	State or kingdom.	Occupation.	When.	Where.	By whom.	Period.	No. of enl'st.	When last discharged.	Add pay.	REMARKS.
				DESCRIPTION.					WHERE BORN.			ENLISTMENT.				RE-ENLISTMENT.			

Station, Fort Adams.
Date, June 30th, 1861.

C. D., Capt. 3d Artillery, Commanding the Company.
A. B., 1st Sergeant.

RECRUITING SERVICE.

This comprehends the duty by which the ranks of the army are filled. It is conducted by the Adjutant-General, through *superintendents* of recruiting service and recruiting parties.

Recruiting is made for both general and regimental service. In the latter case the colonel of the regiment is the superintendent.

A *recruiting party* generally consists of one lieutenant, one non-commissioned officer, two privates, and a drummer and fifer.

The superintendent is supplied with clothing, arms, accoutrements and equipage, by requisitions on the proper departments, sent through the Adjutant-General, and with funds, on an estimate of the amount required sent to the Adjutant-General.

RECRUITING PARTIES.

Recruiting parties are supplied with funds, clothing, equipage, and arms from the superintendent, the officer in charge of the party receipting therefor.

Recruiting officers may purchase such articles of furniture as are *absolutely* necessary for the service, on special authority of the superintendent; but such purchases should be made with great caution, as there is much difficulty in getting such accounts allowed.

Necessary stationery will be purchased monthly or quarterly, not to exceed per quarter at each station six quires of paper, twenty-four quills, or twenty-four steel pens and two holders, half an ounce of wafers, one paper of ink-powder, one bottle of red ink, four ounces of sealing-wax, one quire of cartridge paper or one hundred envelopes, one-fourth quire of blotting paper, and one piece of tape. If necessary, an additional supply of one-fourth of these rates will be allowed to the recruiting officer having charge of one or more auxiliary rendezvous distant from his permanent station. At the principal depôts the allowance is fixed by the wants of the public service.

To each office table is allowed one inkstand, one wafer-stamp, one wafer-box, one paper-folder, one ruler, and as many lead pencils as may be required, not exceeding four per annum.

Such blank books as may be necessary are allowed to the general superintendent and at permanent recruiting depôts; also one descriptive book for the register of recruits at each permanent station. Blank books will be purchased by recruiting officers, under instructions from the superintendent.

When a recruiting officer is relieved, the blank books and unexpended stationery, with all the other public property at the station, will be transferred to his successor, who will receipt for the same.

Officers in command of parties will send recruits to the depôt every ten days, provided the number of disposable recruits exceeds three. The recruits should be sent in charge of a non-commissioned officer.

RECRUITS.

To become a recruit, it is necessary that the person offering be over five feet three inches high, free from physical defect, and with sufficient knowledge of the English language to understand when spoken to, and be not less than eighteen nor more than thirty-five years of age.

This restriction as to age does not apply to musicians, nor to soldiers who may re enlist after serving a previous enlistment in the army. Nor is it to be rigidly enforced in time of war, provided the applicant have the requisite physical qualifications.

Minors cannot be enlisted without the written consent of their parents, guardians, or masters, if they have any. This consent will be appended to their enlistment, and will be in the following form:

Consent in case of Minor.

I, C—— D——, Do CERTIFY, That I am the father of A—— B——; that the said A—— B—— is twenty years of age; and I do hereby freely give my CONSENT to his enlisting as a SOLDIER in the ARMY OF THE UNITED STATES for the period of THREE YEARS.

GIVEN at New York, the 16th day of August, 1861.
WITNESS: E—— F——. C—— D——.

Permanent parties at depôts, and *recruiting* parties, are to be mustered and paid in the same manner as other soldiers. Recruits are to be paid at the depôts only, and one half of their pay is to be retained until they join their regiments.

Commanders of recruiting parties will issue to recruits only such articles of clothing as are indispensable. Their equipment will not be made complete until after they have passed the inspection, subsequent on their arrival at the depôt. This inspection will take place within two days after the arrival of the recruit, and should he be found unfit for service, a Board of Inspectors shall be convened by the superintendent to examine into the case.

Applicants for enlistment will be examined by the medical officer in the presence of the recruiting officer.

The room in which this examination is conducted should be well lighted, and large enough to admit of the men being walked about freely, that every organ concerned in locomotion may be subjected to inspection.

The person of the applicant should be *washed clean* before inspection, as it is impossible for the medical officer to ascertain the existence of certain *disqualifying defects*, when concealed as they sometimes are under incrustations of filth.

Certain defects can only be ascertained from the man himself; it is necessary, therefore, to avoid all subsequent evasions, that his answers to questions should be recorded on the spot upon blanks of the following form, which will be furnished from the Adjutant-General's office:

FORM FOR EXAMINING A RECRUIT.

RECRUIT A—— B——, age 22 years, occupation cooper, born in Elmira, New York, presented by C—— D——.

1. Have you ever been sick?
   When, and of what diseases?
2. Have you any disease now, and what?
3. Have you ever had fits?
4. Have you ever received an injury or wound upon the head?
5. Have you ever had a fracture, a dislocation, or a sprain?
6. Are you in the habit of drinking?
   Or have you ever had the "horrors?"
7. Are you subject to the piles?
8. Have you any difficulty in urinating?
9. Have you been vaccinated, or had the small pox?
   Head.
   Ears.

Face.
Eyes and Appendages.
Nose.
Organs of Mastication and Voice.
Neck.
Chest
Abdomen.
Genital and Urinary Organs.
Vertebral Column.
Superior Extremities.
Inferior Extremities.

Remarks.

DATE: E. F.,
RENDEZVOUS: *Inspecting Surgeon.*

The answers to the questions will be entered opposite to them, and the result of the examination of the several parts and organs duly entered in the same manner. Under the head of remarks the approval or rejection of the recruit will be noted. To be followed with the date and rendezvous, and signature of the inspecting surgeon.

Should an interpreter be required during the inspection, the fact will be noted.

If *absolute disqualification* be discovered at any stage of the inspection, the proceedings will be stopped, and the recruit rejected.

This form, when filled up, is to be sent to the depôt with the recruit, and thence transmitted to the regiment to which he may be assigned.

Defects discovered at the depôt, upon re-inspection, are to be endorsed on this form, and signed by the surgeon, and in case of rejection, the document thus completed, is to be sent with the proceedings of the Board of Inspection to the Headquarters of the Army.

Accounts, Returns and Rolls to be Rendered by Officers on Recruiting Service.

RECRUITING ACCOUNTS CURRENT.

Form 109, p. 225.

These are to be rendered *quarterly*, to the Adjutant-General. They will be in the usual form of accounts current, and will be accompanied with an abstract of disbursements as shown by Form 107, p. 212, supported by vouchers, according to Form 108, p. 213, and one set of enlistments. This account is to be rendered by every officer who receives funds, whether he makes any expenditures or not, during the quarter. A copy of the quarterly abstract of expenditures is to be sent to the superintendent of recruiting service, to which the party belongs, within three days after the expiration of the quarter.

FORM 107.

Abstract of Disbursements on Account of Contingencies of the Recruiting Service, by 1st Lieutenant A. B., in the Quarter ending June 30, 1861, at Rochester, New York.

No. of Voucher.	Date of Payment.	To whom paid.	On whose account.	Amount.	
				$	Cts.

A. B.,
Recruiting Officer.

FORM 108.

The United States,
　　　　　　　　To A. B.,　　　　　　　　　　Dr.

Date.		$	Cts.
1861. Sept. 2.	For office rent for month of August,	30	00
		30	00

I certify that the above account is correct.

　　　　　　　　　　　　　　　　　　　　C. D.,
　　　　　　　　　　　　　　　　　　Recruiting Officer.

Received, New York, this 2d day of September, 1861, of C. D., recruiting officer, thirty dollars and ———— cents, in full of the above account.　　　　　　　　　　　　　　　　　　A. B.

$30.00

(Duplicate.)

QUARTERLY RETURN OF PROPERTY.

This will be made out at the end of every quarter, and transmitted to the Adjutant-General. It will comprise books, fuel, stationery, and other property that may have been purchased with the recruiting fund. Its form is shown by No. 110, p. 226.

MONTHLY SUMMARY STATEMENT.

This report will be made out on the last day of the month, and transmitted to the Adjutant-General. It will be prepared as shown by Form 111, p. 227. No vouchers will accompany this return.

TRI-MONTHLY REPORT.
Form 112, p. 228.

This report will be made out, and forwarded directly to the Adjutant-General, without letter of transmittal, on the 10th, 20th, and last day of every month. It will contain a statement of the operations of the station during the ten days.

The date on which the rendezvous is established will be stated on the first subsequent tri-monthly report; when broken up, on a report made at that date.

MUSTER ROLL.

This roll will be made out every two months, and will embrace all enlisted men at the rendezvous, including the names of all who may have joined, died, deserted, been transferred or discharged during the period embraced in the muster roll. This roll will be made out according to the directions previously given for muster rolls of companies and detachments, and will be sent direct to the Adjutant-General's office.

Duplicate *muster rolls for pay* of the permanent recruiting party, will be sent to the Superintendent of recruiting service. Though when authorized by the Superintendent, these rolls may be sent direct to the nearest paymaster. A triplicate of this roll being retained at the station.

MONTHLY RETURN OF RECRUITS.

This return, in form similar to Form 113, p. 229, will be made to the Superintendent at the end of every month. It will comprise both the recruiting party and the recruits, and will be accompanied with one copy of the enlistment of every recruit enlisted within the month.

RETURN OF CLOTHING, CAMP AND GARRISON EQUIPAGE, AND QUARTERMASTER'S PROPERTY.
Form 114, p. 230.

This return will be made at the expiration of every quarter, by the commanding officer of every recruiting party, to the *Quartermaster-General*. It will be made out in the same form as prescribed for commanders of companies, on blanks furnished by the Quartermaster-General.

RETURN OF ARMS AND ACCOUTREMENTS.
Form 115, p. 281.

This will be made to the Chief of Ordnance at the end of every quarter, in the same manner as prescribed for commanders of companies. It will include all arms and accoutrements, and such other ordnance stores as the officer may have received.

ESTIMATES FOR FUNDS, ETC.

These will be made quarterly to the Superintendent of Recruiting Service, and will embrace estimates of clothing and arms for one year, six months, or such other period as the officer may deem necessary.

MUSTER AND DESCRIPTIVE ROLLS OF RECRUITS SENT TO DEPÔT OR TO REGIMENTS.
Form 116, pp. 232 and 233.

These rolls will be made out by the recruiting officer, and sent to the Superintendent with every detachment of recruits sent to the general depôt, and also when recruits are sent direct to regiments. They will also be prepared by the Superintendent and sent with every detachment forwarded to a regiment from the general depôt.

The last column of names will be filled up by the officer in command of the detachment, or by the commanding officer of the post, when no commissioned officer accompanies it; and will only include the names of those *present* on the day of arrival at the post.

In the remarks, the command exercised by any officer accompanying the detachment, with the date of assuming or being relieved therefrom, and the names of the officers relieved will be stated.

Also, the date and place of all deaths, transfers, discharges, desertions, and apprehensions, are to be noted; also any other information that may be necessary or useful for the records of the Adjutant-General's office.

This roll will be made out in a manner similar to other muster rolls. The names of the commissioned officers accompanying the detachment at the head of the roll, and the privates following in *alphabetical order.*

The roll, when furnished the officer commanding the detachment, will be signed by the Superintendent, and will be certified to by the commanding officer of the detachment when the recruits are turned over; he completing the roll to show the condition of the detachment when turned over.

The commanding officer of the post at which the recruits are delivered, will, after the inspection of the recruits by himself and the Surgeon of the post, make the certificate shown in the form. He will also, after stating the result of the inspection, and referring to the report of the Board of Inspectors (should it be found necessary to organize such board), add to his certificate such general remarks relative to the appearance, quality, etc., of the recruits, as, in his judgment, the facts may justify. He will retain a correct copy of the muster and descriptive roll for the information of company commanders, and forward the original roll to the Adjutant-General's office without delay.

ACCOUNT OF CLOTHING.
Form 117, p. 234.

This will accompany the muster roll of every detachment of recruits sent to the depôt, or from the depôt to regiments.

It will be given to the commanding officer of the post where the recruits are turned over, and furnishes the data from which the soldier's account of clothing is opened when assigned to a company.

Letters addressed to the Adjutant-General "*on recruiting service,*" will be so endorsed on the envelopes, under the words "official business."

On all vouchers for premiums for bringing recruits, and fees for oaths of enlistment, the names of the recruits for whom the expenditure is made must be given. The vouchers may be made in form of consolidated receipt-rolls, authenticated by the officer's certificate that they are correct.

The fee usually allowed for administering the oath of enlistment being twenty-five cents for each recruit, when a greater amount is paid, the officer must certify on the voucher that it is the rate allowed by law of the State or Territory.

To each voucher for notices inserted in newspapers, a copy of the notice will be appended.

Enlistments must be filled up in a fair and legible hand. The *real* name of the recruit must be ascertained, correctly spelled, and written in the same way wherever it occurs; the *Christian* name must not be abbreviated. Numbers must be written, and not expressed by figures. Each enlistment must be endorsed as follows:

No. —.
A——— B———,
enlisted at
————————,
' January —, 186–,
By Lt. C——— D———,
— Regiment of ———.

Enlistments are to be filled up as shown below, and signed in triplicate.

The following Declaration will be appended to the enlistment:

I, ——— desiring to enlist in the Army of the United States for the period of three years, do declare that I am ——— years and ——— months of age; that I have neither wife nor child; that I have never been discharged from the United States service on account of disability, or by sentence of a court-martial, or by order before the expiration of a term of enlistment; and I know of no impediment to my serving honestly and faithfully as a soldier for five years.

Witness:

FORM OF ENLISTMENT.

State of New York. — Town of New York.

I, A. B., born in Rochester, in the State of New York, aged twenty-four years, and by occupation a Carpenter, DO HEREBY ACKNOWLEDGE to have voluntarily enlisted this 16th day of August, 1861, as a SOLDIER in the ARMY OF THE UNITED STATES OF AMERICA, for the period of THREE YEARS, unless sooner discharged by proper authority: Do also agree to accept such bounty, pay, rations, and clothing, as are, or may be, established by law. And I, A. B., do solemnly swear, that I will bear true faith and allegiance to the UNITED STATES OF AMERICA, and that I will serve them honestly and faithfully against all their enemies or opposers whomsoever; and that I will observe and obey the orders of the President of the United States, and the orders of the officers appointed over me, according to the Rules and Articles of War.

Sworn and subscribed to, at New York, }
This 16th day of August, 1861, }   A. B.
BEFORE me, G. H., *Justice of the Peace.* }

I CERTIFY, on honor, that I have carefully examined the above-named Recruit, agreeably to the Regulations of the Army, and that in my opinion he is free from all bodily defects and mental infirmity, which would, in any way, disqualify him from performing the duties of a soldier.

C. D., Examining Surgeon.

I CERTIFY, on honor, that I have minutely inspected the Recruit, A. B., previously to his enlistment, and that he was entirely sober when enlisted; that, to the best of my judgment and belief, he is of lawful age; and that, in accepting him as duly qualified to perform the duties of an able-bodied soldier, I have strictly observed the Regulations which govern the recruiting service. This soldier has *dark eyes, dark hair, dark complexion,* is *five feet six inches* high.

E. F., Recruiting Officer.

Transportation.

The transportation of recruits to depôts, and from one recruiting station to another, will be paid from the recruiting funds; transportation of officers and enlisted men on the recruiting service will be paid in the same manner, except when first proceeding to join that service, or returning to their regiments after having been relieved.

No expenses of transportation of officers will be admitted that do not arise from orders emanating from the Adjutant-General's office, except that they be required to visit branch or auxiliary rendezvous under their charge, when they will be allowed the stage, steamboat, or railroad fare, porterage included.

Whenever an officer is relieved or withdrawn from the recruiting service, he will forward to the Adjutant-General the evidence of the disposition he may make of the funds, according to regulations and the special orders he may have received, and report the fact to the Superintendent, or to his colonel if on regimental recruiting service.

The rent of the recruiting rendezvous is paid from the recruiting funds. The terms of the contract will be immediately reported to the Adjutant-General.

BLANKS.

Officers on recruiting service will make timely requisitions for printed blanks, direct, as follows:

To the Adjutant-General.—For enlistments; re-enlistments; muster rolls; muster and descriptive rolls; monthly returns; tri-monthly reports; recruiting accounts current; accounts of clothing issued; posters or hand-bills; forms of declaration, and consent for minors.

To the Quartermaster-General.—For estimates of clothing, camp and garrison equipage; clothing receipt rolls; quarterly returns of clothing, camp and garrison equipage.

No blanks of the above kinds will be used except the printed forms furnished. Blanks of other kinds, when required, must be ruled.

Blanks for the regimental recruiting service are furnished to the company commanders.

Boards of Inspection.

When a recruit is received at a post with such defects as to disqualify him for the duties of a soldier, a Board of Inspectors will be assembled to examine into and report on the case.

Boards of Inspectors for the examination of recruits will be composed of the three senior regimental officers present on duty with the troops, including the commanding officer and the senior medical officer of the army present.

In all cases of *rejection*, the reasons therefor will be stated at large in a special *report* by the board; which, together with the surgeon's certificate of disability for service, will be forwarded by the superintendent or commandant of the post direct to the Adjutant-General. If the recommendation of the board for the discharge of the recruit be approved, the authority will be endorsed on the certificate, which will be sent back to be filled up and signed by the commanding officer, who will return the same to the Adjutant-General's office.

The Board will state in the report whether the disability, or other cause of rejection, existed before his enlistment, and whether, with *proper care and examination*, it might have been then discovered.

Returns from Officers commanding Recruits.

An officer intrusted with the command of recruits ordered to regiments, will, on arriving at the place of destination, forward the following papers:

1. To the *Adjutant-General* and the *Superintendent*, each, a descriptive roll and an account of clothing of such men as may have deserted, died, or been left on the route from any cause whatever; with a special report of the date of his arrival at the post, the strength and condition of the detachment when turned over to the commanding officer, and all circumstances worthy of remark which may have occurred on the march.

2. To the *Commanding Officer* of the regiment or post, the muster and descriptive roll furnished him at the time of setting out, properly signed and completed by recording the names of the recruits *present*, and by noting in the column for remarks, opposite the appropriate spaces, the time and place of death, desertion, apprehension, or other casualty that may have occurred on the route.

3. To the *Quartermaster-General*, a return of clothing, camp and garrison equipage (form 37, p. 72a), and return of Quartermaster's property (form 54, p. 114a), if he shall have had such articles in charge.

4. To the *Chief of Ordnance*, a return of ordnance and ordnance stores if the detachment was armed.

5. To the *Commissary-General of Subsistence*, returns of provisions received and issued; and of Commissary property, as prescribed under the head of subsistence; provided no other officer accompanied the detachment as *Acting Assistant Commissary of Subsistence*, in which case these returns will be made by the A. A. C. S.

Should an officer be relieved in charge of a detachment *en route*, before it reaches its destination, the date and place, and name of the officer by whom he is relieved, must be recorded on the detachment roll. Without the evidence of such record, no charge for extra pay for clothing accountability of a detachment equal to a company will be allowed.

The "original muster and descriptive roll" of every detachment will, after completion, be sent to the Adjutant-General by the commanding officer of the post where the recruits are delivered.

DESCRIPTIVE LIST.
Form 118, p. 235.

This list is furnished every detachment of men transferred from one company to another, and to individual soldiers in any way detached from their commands. It gives a full history of the soldier and his description. To it is appended a clothing account, showing the quantity of clothing received by the soldier, from which a full statement of his account may be prepared wherever he may be.

In the field, when men are left in a hospital, their descriptive lists and clothing accounts must be left with the surgeon.

The *Descriptive List* is prepared from the data furnished by the *Muster Roll*. Particular attention must be paid to the following considerations in making it out:

The amount of additional pay, if any, *for former services* under the act of *August* 4, 1854, must be carefully noted in the exact words used on the *Muster Roll*.

Likewise, the amount due the soldier for a *certificate of merit*, or in lieu of a *commission*, under sec. 4, *act of August* 4, 1854, in the exact words used on the *Muster Roll*.

So, also, of any other *extra* pay, for which he may be mustered, *ex. gr.* as *Acting Hospital Steward*, as *Saddler*, etc., and which may be *still due* him.

In the column headed "BOUNTY PAID," must be entered the *whole* amount *hitherto paid* him; in that of "BOUNTY DUE," the *whole* amount *yet due*, on account of the bounty provided by sec. 3, *act of June* 17, 1850.

The amount of RETAINED PAY due, at *date*, will be carefully stated.

Stoppages for *loss* or *damage* done to *arms*, or other *public property* must be noted, and the *articles*, and *particular damage* to each specified.

When stoppages are due, under sentence of a Court-martial, *a transcript of the same* must be entered here; and the amount *already stopped*, must be *carefully* stated.

In *every* case of *desertion*, the *date*, and that of *delivery*, or *apprehension*, must be given, together with a correct transcript of the order of *sentence*, or *pardon*.

A careful settlement of the man's CLOTHING ACCOUNT *must be made, to date, and the amount* DUE TO, *or* FROM *him must be precisely stated*.

Should the man have been engaged in any *action*, or *skirmish*, it must be mentioned, together with *date* and *place*.

A *full and particular mention* will be made of any *wounds* he may have received in *action*, or, *other injury*, whilst in the *line of his duty*.

Regimental Recruiting Service.

This is under the direction of the commanding officer of the regiment as superintendent, subalterns of the regiment being detailed at the several posts garrisoned by the regiment, as recruiting officers.

The same regulations established for the *general recruiting service* govern the regimental recruiting service.

The regimental recruiting officer will make the following returns, together with those prescribed for recruiting officers:

Monthly return of recruiting party.
Quarterly return of recruits enlisted.
Quarterly account current.

MONTHLY RETURN OF REGIMENTAL RECRUITING PARTY.
Form 119, p 236.

This return is to be made to the commander of the regiment, at the end of each month. It will contain the strength of the party and recruits, *present* and *absent*, and the alterations since the last return. It will also give the names of enlisted men, required in explanation of the alterations, with the particulars of their enlistment as shown in the form.

The date a rendezvous (except at a garrisoned post) is opened or closed, will be stated.

The date and place of all transfers (except to the regiment or other stations), all discharges, deaths, etc., the real and assumed name, company, and regiment, of recognized deserters, will also be noted on this return.

QUARTERLY RETURN OF RECRUITS.
Form 120, p. 237.

This return will be made to the Adjutant-General at the expiration of every quarter. It will give the names of men enlisted in alphabetical order, by months, and the other particulars shown by the form.

ACCOUNT CURRENT.
Form 109, p. 225.

The Dr. side of this account will show the several items of expenditure made by the recruiting officer, during the quarter. Each payment supported by its voucher, which will accompany the account.

The Cr. side will show the amount of money received by the officer.

This account will be sent to the Adjutant-General, at the expiration of every quarter.

In every respect, the regimental recruiting service is to be governed and conducted according to the same rules, and under the same regulations as the general service, except that the recruiting officer must obtain the approbation of the commanding officer of the station to enlist a recruit.

When leaving a post, the regimental recruiting officer will turn over the funds in his hands to the senior company officer present, unless some other be appointed to receive them.

Recruiting of Volunteers.

Volunteers for the army of the United States are recruited by their own officers, at their own expense or that of the state to which they belong, under ordinary circumstances. But, when by act of Congress a special appropriation is made for collecting, drilling, and organizing volunteers, certain expenses of recruiting then become chargeable to the United States.

The following are the expenses which, under such appropriations, are to be paid by the mustering officer:

1st. Rent of rendezvous or office for recruiting.

2d. Commutation of fuel and quarters for officers already mustered into service when detached on recruiting duty.

3d. Subsistence of volunteers prior to their muster into service. After such muster, subsistence will be provided by the Subsistence Department. If possible, subsistence will be issued in kind, as recognized in the regular service; or if other articles are substituted, the cost of the whole must not exceed the regular supplies, and will be paid for at rates not exceeding the current prices at the place of purchase. If subsistence cannot be furnished in kind, and board be necessary, it will be furnished at a rate not to exceed forty cents per diem.

4th. Necessary transportation of volunteers prior to completion of company organization, and muster into service as a company. After completion of such organization and muster, transportation will be paid by the Quartermaster's Department. Transportation will be at the rate of two cents per mile for railroad travel, and at the current rates for stage and steamboat fare.

5th. Rent of grounds and buildings for camping purposes, cost of erection of quarters, of cooking stoves when absolutely necessary, of clerk and office hire, when authorized by the Adjutant-General, and of all expenses incidental to camps of rendezvous.

6th. Knives, forks, tin cups, and tin plates for volunteers.

7th. Necessary medicines and medical attendance prior to organization of regiments, or the mustering in of the regimental surgeons.

8th. Actual railroad, stage, or steamboat fare, necessarily incurred by authorized agents in raising or recruiting volunteers.

9th. Advertising. Officers recruiting will be authorized in not to exceed two newspapers for each rendezvous under their charge.

10th. Fuel and straw, previous to company organization, according to the allowance for the regular army.

11th. All other expenses allowed for recruiting in the regular service, not herein mentioned, and incurred for volunteers previous to their muster into the United States service.

Payment will only be made on account of troops, officers, and men that have been or may be mustered and received into, or actually employed in the service of the United States. Organizations raised, or attempted to be made, but not mustered and received into service, are not to be recognized.

Personal expenses of commissioned officers in recruiting their companies, prior to their being mustered into service, will not be paid; but commissioned officers will be paid the same rates for subsistence and quarters (board and lodging) as privates, from the date of enrolment until mustered into service. The necessary and actual travelling expenses of officers, when accompanied by bills of particulars and receipts for payments, properly authenticated, will be allowed.

Bills of particulars, with dates and rates of charges, and the receipt of the party to whom payment was made, must in all cases be furnished. In short, original vouchers for expenditures of every description must be furnished. The accounts must also designate the particular regiment and company, and name of the commanding officer who authorized the expenditure.

When expenses have been incurred for "board," or "board and lodging," the amount must be reasonable, and in accordance with the usual rate of the neighborhood; the bills must also specify the regiment or company to which the troops so subsisted or quartered belonged.

FORM 109.—RECRUITING ACCOUNT CURRENT.

The United States in account current with A. B., 1st Lieut. 3d Artillery.

DR.						CR.
Date.		Dollars.	Cents.	Date.	Dollars.	Cents.
1861 June 30.	For amount of disbursements during the quarter, as per abstract......... For balance on hand due U. S.......	370 130	00 00	1861. May 20. By amount received from Major C. D., Superintendent of Recruiting Service............	500	00
		$500	00		$500	00

I certify, on honor, that the above statement is correct; that the expenditures have been faithfully made for the objects expressed in vouchers, and that the balance of one hundred and thirty dollars and —— cents is due to the U. S.

Date: *June* 30, 1861.
Station: Rochester, N. Y.

A. B., *Recruiting Officer.*

FORM 110.—QUARTERLY RETURN OF PROPERTY OF RECRUITING DEPOT.

Return of Property received, expended, and remaining on hand in the quarter ending September 30, 1861, *by Lieut. G. P., on general recruiting service at Rochester, N. Y.*

Date. 1861.	CLASSES	WOOD.		STATIONERY.				FURNITURE.	
		Cords.	Feet.	Cap paper.	Letter paper.	Envelopes.	Blank books.	Officers' desks.	Stoves.
		No.	No.	Qrs.	Qrs.	No.	No.	No.	No.
	On hand last return.........								
	Total to be accounted for...............								
	To A. B..................... Expended...................								
	Total issued and expended.............								
	Total on hand...								
Condition, 1.. " 2.. " 3..	In good order................ Unfit for service, but repairable Worn out....................								

FORM 111.—MONTHLY SUMMARY STATEMENT OF A RECRUITING OFFICER.

The United States in account with A. B., 1st Lieut. 1st Infantry, on general recruiting service at Rochester, New York, in the month of September, 1861.

Dr.			Cr.
1861.	To amount of disbursements within the month............	1861.	By balance from last statement.........
	Balance due the United States, carried to next statement...........		By cash received from Major C. D., Superintendent of Recruiting Service.....

FORM 112.—TRI-MONTHLY RECRUITING REPORT.

Tri-Monthly Report of the state of the Recruiting Service at Rochester, New York, from the 10th day of June to the 20th day of June, 1861.

Number enlisted last ten days.	Recruits detached since last report.	Number disposable.	Minors.	Under size.	Over age.	Moral disability.	Appearance of intemperance.	Mal-formation.	Unsound constitution.	Mental disability.	Impaired vision.	Deafness.	Rupture.	Varicose veins.	Brand of letter D.	Extreme ignorance.	Married.					TOTAL NUMBER REFUSED.	REMARKS.

Number of applicants REFUSED, and specification of cause.

Date: *June* 20, 1861.
Station: Rochester, N. Y.

1st Lieut. 3d Artillery, and Recruiting Officer.

FORM 113.—MONTHLY RETURN OF RECRUITS AND RECRUITING PARTY.

Return of the Recruiting Party stationed at Philadelphia, Pa., under the command of 1st Lieut. C. E., of the 3d Regiment of Artillery, for the month of July, 1861.

PERMANENT AND PARTY RECRUITS.				ALTERATIONS SINCE LAST RETURN.				REMARKS.
PRESENT.				**JOINED.**				
Captains			..	Enlisted this month			12	
Subalterns			1	Re-enlisted this month			..	
Sergeants			1	From recruit'g stations			..	
Corporals			..	From principal depot			..	
Musicians			2	From civil authority			..	
Boys learning music			..	From desertion			..	
Privates			8	**TRANSFERRED.**				
Disposable recruits			8	To recruiting stations			..	
Recognised as deserters from regiments			..	To principal depot			11	
ABSENT.				To regiments			..	
With leave	Com'd Officers		..	To civil authority			..	
With leave	Enlisted men		9	**DISCHARGED.**				
Without	Com'd Officers		..	Expiration of service			..	
Without	Enlisted men		..	For disability			..	
P. AND A.				By civil authority			..	
Commiss'd Officers			1	Rejected recruits			..	
Enlisted men			9	Died			..	
Aggregate			10	Deserted			..	
Aggregate l'st ret'n			9					

NAMES OF ENLISTED MEN, REQUIRED IN EXPLANATION OF THE "ALTERATIONS SINCE LAST RETURN," &c.

No.	Name.	ENLISTED.				DATE OF JOINING.		Date of transfer.	Date of discharge.	Date of death.	Date of desertion.	Date of R. as D's from R.s.
		When.	Where.	By whom.	Period.	From civil auth'ty.	From desertion.					

C. E.   *1st Lieut. 3d Artillery, Recruiting Officer.*

FORM 114.—RETURN OF CLOTHING.

Return of Clothing received and issued at Rochester, N.Y., by Lieut. G. P., on general recruiting service, during the quarter ending the 30th day of September, 1861.

When received.	No. of invoices.	Of whom received.	CLOTHING.													
			Sergeants' wool jackets.	Privates' wool jackets.	Sergeants' wool overalls.	Privates' wool overalls.	Sergeants' cotton jackets.	Privates' cotton jackets.	Sergeants' Cotton overalls.	Privates' cotton overalls.	Sergeants' cotton shirts.	Privates' cotton shirts.	Flannel shirts.	Flannel drawers.	Boots, pairs of.	Stockings, pairs of.	Leather stocks.	Great coats.	Blankets.
1861.		On hand per last return............																	
		Total to be accounted for.......																	

When issued.	No. of roll.	To whom issued.																	
		Total issued..................																	
		On hand to be accounted for....																	

G. P., *Lieut. 3d Artillery.*

FORM 115.—ORDNANCE RETURN OF A RECRUITING OFFICER.

Return of Ordnance and Ordnance Stores received and issued by Lieut. G. P., 3d Regiment of Infantry, on general recruiting service at Rochester, N. Y., during the quarter ending September 30, 1861.

Date. 1861.	No. of voucher.	THIRD QUARTER, 1861.	ARMS.		FOR MUSKETS.			FOR RIFLES.		
			Muskets.	Non-commissioned officers' swords.	Cartridge boxes.	Cartridge box plates.	Cartridge box belts.	Wipers.	Ball screws.	Bullet moulds.
		On hand from last quarter.........								
		Total to be accounted for......								
		Total issued and expended....								
		Remaining on hand to be accounted for next quarter................								

I certify that the foregoing return exhibits a correct statement of ordnance and ordnance stores in my charge during the third quarter, 1861.

G. P., *Lieut. 3d Infantry, Recruiting Officer.*

Rochester, N. Y.
September 30, 1861.

Form 116.—Muster and Descriptive Roll of

Muster and Descriptive Roll of a Detachment of United States panies of the 1st Regiment of Infantry, stationed at Fort Monroe,

No.	Names.	Rank.	DESCRIPTION.							
			Where born.		Age.	Occupation.	Enlisted.			Period
			Town, County or Province.	State, Empire, or Kingdom.			When.	Where. (Town and State.)	By whom.	

RECAPITULATION.

To be filled up by the Commander of the Detachment after the arrival of the recruits at the post.

	Commissioned officers.	Sergeants.	Corporals.	Musicians.	Recruits.	TOTAL COMMISSIONED.	TOTAL ENLISTED.	AGGREGATE.
PRESENT. { For duty............ Sick................. In arrest or confinem't.								
ABSENT... { Left sick on the march. In arrest or confinem't.								
STRENGTH—PRESENT AND ABSENT.								
ALTERATIONS ON THE MARCH. { Discharged........ ...... Transferred............ Died................. Deserted............ Apprehended............				•				

I certify, on honor, that this "Recapitulation," and the "Remarks" set opposite the names of this Detachment of Recruits by me, are correct.

Station: Fort Monroe, Va.
Date: *July* 10, 1861.

A. B., *Commanding the Detachment.*

RECORD OF EVENTS WHICH MAY BE USEFUL FOR REFERENCE AT THE ADJUTANT GENERAL'S OFFICE.

A Detachment of United States Recruits.

Recruits, forwarded by the General Superintendent for the Com- Va., pursuant to Special Orders No. 66, dated June 30th, 1861.

Eyes.	Hair.	Complexion.	Height.		By Paymaster.	To what time.	Bounty.		Date of first muster.	Names.	Letters of companies to which assigned	Remarks.
			Feet.	Inches.	By Paymaster.	To what time.	P'd. Dollars.	Due Dollars.				

I certify, on honor, that this Muster and Descriptive Roll is correct, and that it exhibits the true statement of this detachment of recruits.

Station: Fort Columbus, N. Y.
Date: *July* 4, 1861.   C. D., *Superintendent.*

This detachment of recruits has been minutely inspected this tenth day of July, 1861, by the undersigned, and the Surgeon of the Post, agreeably to regulations; and the recruits are found to be

Station: Fort Monroe, Va.
Date: *July* 10th, 1861.   E. F., *Commanding the Post.*

FORM 117.—ACCOUNT OF CLOTHING ISSUED TO RECRUITS.

Account of Clothing issued to Recruits, whose names are hereunto annexed, forwarded by the General Superintendent, for the Companies of the 4th Regiment of Artillery, stationed at Fort Monroe, pursuant to Order No. 25, dated July 10, 1861.

No.	Names.	Cap complete.	Coat complete.	Woollen overalls, pairs of.	Cotton overalls, pairs of.	Woollen jackets.	Cotton jackets.	Cotton shirts.	Flannel shirts.	Boots, pairs of.	Stockings, pairs of.	Blanket.	Forage cap.	Great coat.	Leather stock.	Drawers, pairs of.	Haversack.	Knapsack.	Remarks.
1	A. W......			1		1		2		1	2	1	1		1	2	1	1	
2	B. C......			1		1		2		1	2	1	1		1	2	1	1	
3	B. M......			1		1		2		1	2	1	1		1	2	1	1	
4	C. R......			1		1		2		1	2	1	1		1	2	1	1	

I certify that the articles of clothing set opposite the above named recruits have been issued to each respectively.

G'ven this ⸺ day of ⸺, 1861, at ⸺.

⸺⸺⸺, Commanding.

FORM 118.—DESCRIPTIVE LIST AND ACCOUNT OF PAY AND CLOTHING OF ABSOLAM BURNS.

No.	NAMES.	RANK.	DESCRIPTION.						WHERE BORN.		OCCUPA-TION.	ENLISTED.				LAST PAID.		BOUNTY. (Act of June 17, 1850.)
			Yrs. age	Eyes.	Hair.	Complexion.	Feet.	Inches.	State or kingdom.	Town or county.		When.	Where. (Town & State)	By whom.	Period.	By paymaster.	To what time.	
1	A. B.	Private.	26	Dark.	Black.	Dark.	5	4	England	London.	Carpenter	Jan. 1, '61.	N. Y.	Lt. E. F.	5 Yrs.			Paid $ (See note 4.)
2	C. D.	"	23	Light.	Brown.	Fair.	5	6	N. York	Buffalo.	Miller.	"	"	"	"			Due $ (See note 4.)

REMARKS.

I certify that the above is a correct transcript from the records of
STATION:
DATE:

RETURN OF RECRUITING PARTY.

FORM 119.—MONTHLY RETURN OF REGIMENTAL RECRUITING PARTY.

Return of the Regimental Recruiting Party at Fort Adams, under charge of Lieut. C. C. C., of the 3d Regiment of Artillery, for the month of July, 1861.

RECRUITING PARTY AND RECRUITS.					ALTERATIONS SINCE LAST RETURN.				REMARKS.
PRESENT.		ABSENT.		P. AND A.	JOINED.	TRANSF'D.	DISCHARGED.		
		With leave.	Without.					Died.	
Captains.									
Subalterns.									
Sergeants.									
Corporals.									
Musicians.									
Privates.									
Recruits.									
Recognised as deserters from regiments.									
		Com'iss'd Officers.			Enlisted this month.	To other stations.	Expiration of service.	Deserted.	
		Enlisted men.			Re-enlisted this month.	Recruits sent to comp's	For disability.		
		Com'd Officers.			From other stations.	To civil authority.	By civil authority.		
		Enlisted men.			From civil authority.		Rejected recruits.		
		Com'iss'd Officers.			From desertion.				
		Enlisted men.							
				AGGREGATE.					
				AGGREGATE L'ST RET'N.					

NAMES OF ENLISTED MEN, REQUIRED IN EXPLANATION OF THE "ALTERATIONS SINCE LAST RETURN," &c.

Name.	ENLISTED.			REMARKS.
	When.	Where.	By whom.	Period.

C. C. C., *Commanding Recruiting Party.*

Form 120.—Return of Regimental Recruiting Service.

Recruits enlisted by Lieut. C. C. C. C., of the 3d Regiment of Artillery, stationed at Fort Adams, R. I., for the quarter ending June 30, 1861.

No.	Names.	Rank.	Date of enlistment.	Regiment.	RE-ENLISTED SOLDIERS.			"THREE MONTHS' EXTRA PAY," (to re-enlisted soldiers).		Remarks.
					Letter of company in which last mustered.	Date of expiration of prior enlistment.	Letter of company in which re-enlisted.	Due.	Paid.	
1	A. I........	Private..	May 30, 1861..	3d Art'y	D........	May 29, 1861.	D........	$33		
2	B. D........	"	June 2, "							

FORM 121—MONTHLY RETURN OF REGIMENTAL RECRUITING SERVICE.

Recruiting Return of the 3d Regiment of Artillery, for the month of July, 1861.

Rank.	Names.	Regiment.	Stations.	RECRUITING PARTIES AND RECRUITS.											ALTERATIONS SINCE LAST RETURN.									Remarks.
				PRESENT.							ABSENT.				JOINED.				TRANSF'D.		DISCHARGED.			
				Field officers.	Captains.	Subalterns.	Sergeants.	Corporals.	Musicians.	Privates.	Recruits.	Recognised as deserters from regiments.	Comiss'd Officers.	Enlisted men.	With leave.		Without.		Comiss'd Officers.	Enlisted men.	AGGREGATE.	AGGREGATE L'ST RET'N.	Enlisted this month.	Re-enlisted this month.	From other stations.	From civil authority.	From desertion.	To other stations.	Recruits sent to comp's	To civil authority.	Expiration of service.	For disability.	By civil authority.	Rejected recruits.	Died.	Deserted.	
																Comm'd Officers.	Enlisted men.	Comm'd Officers.	Enlisted men.																		
	Disposable rec'ts in Depôt.																																				
	AGGREGATE.																																				

NAMES OF ENLISTED MEN, REQUIRED IN EXPLANATION OF THE "ALTERATIONS SINCE LAST RETURN," &c.

No.	Name.	ENLISTED.				DATE OF JOINING.		Date of transfer.	Date of discharge.	Date of death.	Date of desertion.	Date of R. as D's from R'e.
		When.	Where.	By whom.	Period.	From desertion.	From civil auth'ty.					

Headquarters of the —— Regiment of ———.
STATION :
DATE :

A. B., *Commanding the Regiment.*

MUSTER-IN ROLL.

FORM 122.—MUSTER-IN ROLL.

Muster-in Roll of Capt. John Bing's Company, in the 16th Regiment (3d Brigade,) of New York Volunteers, commanded by Colonel Hart, called into the service of the United States by ———— ————, from the 30th day of June, 1861 (date of this muster), for the term of three years, unless sooner Discharged.

No.	NAMES. Present and Absent.	Rank.	Age	JOINED FOR DUTY AND ENROLLED.					TRAVELLING.		VALUE IN DOLLARS OF—		REMARKS.
				When.	Where.	By whom.	Period.	To place of rendezvous, No. of miles.	From place of discharge home, No. of miles.	Horses.	Horses equipments.	
1	Bings, John......	Captain..	45	May 1, '61.	N. York.	John Bings	3 Years.					
1	Williams, James..	1st Lieut.	36	" "	"	"	"					
2	Clay, Warren......	2d Lieut.	28	" "	"	"	"					
1	Corroll, Michael...	1st Sergt.	31	" "	"	"	"					
2	McConnell, Wm...	Sergt.....	36	" "	"	"	"					
3	Moseley, Robert...	"	29	" "	"	"	"					
1	Jackman, William.	Corporal.	26	" "	"	"	"					
2	Gillespie, Hugh...	"	23	" "	"	"	"					
3	Maxwell, Thomas.	"	32	" 16	"	"	"					
4	Hunter, Henry....	"	39	" 19	"	"	"					
				" 1								
1	Arnion, Lewis.....	Private...	31	" 20	"	"	"					
2	Bogel, Martin.....	"	25	" 19	"	"	"					

Form 123. —Muster-

Muster-out Roll of Capt. Charles Cabell's Company (A,) in the 10th Grace, called into the service of the United States by the President, the 30th day of April, 1861, to serve for the term of three months day of April, 1861 (when mustered), to the 30th day of July, 1861. in the month of April, 1861, and marched thence to Elmira, where

No. of each grade.	NAMES. Present and absent.	Rank.	Age.	JOINED FOR SERVICE AND ENROLLED AT GENERAL RENDEZVOUS—COMMENCEMENT OF FIRST PAYMENT BY TIME.				MUSTERED	
				When.	Where.	By whom.	Period.	When.	
1	Cabell, Chas.	Captain...	49	Apl. 10, '61.		Capt. C. Cabell	3 M's	Apl. 30, '61.	
1	Debits, W..	1st Lieut.	28	" "		" "	"	"	
2	Wesson, T..	2d Lieut..	31	"		" "	"	"	
1	Dougherty, J	1st Sergt..	36	" 13,		Lt. T. Wesson.	"	"	
2	Weddel, W..	Sergt.....	32	" "		" "	"	"	
3	Burns, Jas..	"	26	" 19,		" "	"	"	
1	Douill, Thos.	Corporal..	24	" 20,		Capt. C. Cabell	"	"	
2	Wilson, P'r.	"	28	"		" "	"	"	
3	Weymiss, J.	"	29	"		" "	"	"	
4	Jones, John.	"	32	"		Lt. W. Debits.	"	"	
1	Armour, P'r	Private...	22	" 22,		Capt. C. Cabell	"	"	
2	Bensil, John	"	27	" 21,		" "	"	"	
3	Crandell, J.	"	23	"		" "	"	"	

OUT ROLL.

Regiment of New York Volunteers, commanded by Colonel John of the U. S., at Elmira (the place of General Rendezvous), on from the date of enrollment, unless sooner discharged, from the 30th The Company was organized by Capt. Charles Cabell at Bloomsburg, it arrived the 30th of April, a distance of forty miles.

INTO SERVICE.		LAST PAID.		TRAVELLING				Subsist'ce and forage		Amount for clothing in kind, or in money advanced.		Value of arms, &c., received from U.S. to be paid for if lost.		Valuation in dollars of—		REMARKS.
Where.	By whom.	By paymaster.	To what time.	To rendezvous, miles.	Home, No. of miles.	Days.	Days.	S.	F.	$	c.	$	c.	Horses.	Horses' equip'ts	
Elmira,N.Y.	Mj.J.Gibson	Pay due	Fm enl'mt	40	40											
"	"	"	"	40	40											
"	"	"	"	40	40											
"	"	"	"	40	40											
"	"	"	"	40	40											
"	"	"	"	40	40											
"	"	"	"	40	40											
"	"	"	"	40	40											
"	"	"	"	40	40											
"	"	"	"	40	40											
"	"	"	"	40	40											
"	"	"	"	40	40											
"	"	"	"	40	40											

MILITIA IN THE SERVICE OF THE UNITED STATES.

Whenever volunteers or drafted militia are called into the service of the United States, by any officer authorized to make such call, the requisition is made on the Governor of the State or Territory in which the militia are to be raised, and the number of officers, non-commissioned officers and privates stated in the requisition, according to the organization prescribed by law of the United States.

Before militia are received in the service of the United States, they are mustered by an Inspector-General or some other officer of the regular army, specially designated to muster them.

It is the duty of the officer designated to muster and inspect militia, to forward muster rolls of each company, and of the field and staff of each regiment, *direct* to the Adjutant-General of the Army, Washington; and he will also immediately forward a consolidated return, by regiments and corps, of the force received into service, for the information of the War Department.

MUSTER-IN ROLLS.
Form 122, p. 239.

This roll, under the head of *Names*, will contain a list of the entire company; the officers being placed first, according to rank. The privates will be placed in alphabetical order, the surnames first, and the christian names written in full.

The date of *enrolment* of each will be placed under the head of *when*. It is important to the recruit that this date be correctly inserted, as it governs the commencement of his pay.

Every man whose name appears on this roll *must be accounted for* on the next muster roll. If the company be mounted, and furnish their own horses, all exchange of horses by the men, *after muster*, is strictly forbidden.

After the muster of the company, the Captain will sign the following certificate at the foot of the roll:

I CERTIFY, on honor, that this Muster Roll exhibits the true state of Captain JOHN BING's Company of the Sixteenth Regiment of New York Volunteers, for the period herein mentioned; that each man answers to his own proper name in person; and that the remarks set opposite the name of each officer and soldier are accurate and just.

JOHN BINGS,
Commanding the Company.

DATE: June 30th, 1861.
STATION: New York, N. Y.

The authorized private horses of the command will be valued, together with their equipments, by three appraisers, to be sworn by the mustering officer. They will subscribe to an oath of the following form upon the muster roll:

WE CERTIFY, on oath, that the figures opposite the names on this roll, for valuation of horses and horse equipments, represent and show the true cash value of the horses and equipments of the men, respectively, at the place of enrollment, according to our honest, impartial judgment.

C. D.,
E. F., } *Appraisers.*
G. H.

Sworn to and subscribed before

A. B.,
Mustering Officer.

DATE: June 30th, 1861.
STATION: New York, N. Y.

The appraised value of each horse and equipments will be inserted in the proper column of the roll.

The mustering officer will sign the following certificate at the foot of the roll:

I CERTIFY, on honor, that I have carefully examined the men whose names are borne on this Roll, their horses, and equipments, and have accepted them into the service of the United States, for the term of three years, from this thirtieth day of June, 1861.

A. B.,
Mustering Officer.

DATE: June 30th, 1861.
STATION: New York, N. Y.

In the caption of the roll, reference will be made to the

particular act or acts of Congress, under which the militia are called into service. If there be no such act, then to the act May 8, 1792, amended by the acts April 18, 1814, and April 20, 1816. Mustering officers will not muster into service a greater number of officers, or of higher rank than the law prescribes. No officer of the general staff will be mustered or received into service, except such general officers, with their aids-de-camp, as may be required to complete the organization of brigades or divisions.

When a regiment is mustered into service, the field officers, staff officers and band, will be mustered upon a separate roll.

There will be prepared for each company, and for the field and staff, three rolls; one to be sent immediately to the Adjutant-General, by the mustering officer, and two for the company archives.

MUSTER-OUT ROLL.
Form 123, p. 240.

The rolls for mustering volunteers and militia out of service, must be compared with those of the first muster. All persons on the first rolls, and absent at the final muster, must be accounted for — whether dead, captured, discharged, or otherwise absent; and if the mustering officer, in any particular case, shall have cause to doubt the report made to be entered on the rolls, he shall demand the oath of one or more persons, to prove the fact to his satisfaction; further, he shall take care that not more persons of the several ranks be mustered out of service than were mustered in, if there be an excess over the requisition or beyond the law, nor recognize additions or substitutes, without full satisfaction that the additions or substitutions were regularly made, and at the time reported on the rolls.

Officers charged with the duty of mustering militia, should take care that the muster rolls contain all the information that may in any way affect their pay; the distance from the places of residence to the place of rendezvous or organization, and the date of arrival, must be stated in each case; the date and place of discharge, and the distance thence to the place of residence; all stoppages for articles received by the Government, must be noted on the rolls; and in case of absence at the time of discharge of the company, the cause of absence must be stated. When the necessary information can not be obtained, the mustering officer will state the reason.

The roll will contain the names of the command arranged in the order explained for the muster-in roll. It will state for each man the *time, place*, and *by whom* enrolled; the period of enlistment; the *time, place*, and *by whom* mustered into service; when last paid, and by whom.

Under the head of *Travelling*, will be inserted the number of miles from the place of enrollment to the place of rendezvous.

The number of days' subsistence and forage, furnished by the men, will be inserted under the proper heads.

The amount of clothing in kind, or money advanced, will be stated against each name.

The value of equipments, arms, and other public property received from the United States that has been lost or destroyed, will be charged against each name, in order that it may be deducted by the paymaster in making up the pay roll.

The valuation of horses and equipments, as shown by the muster-in roll, will be inserted opposite each name.

The list of those *still* belonging to the company will be immediately followed by that of *all* the officers and soldiers who, since the first muster into service, have *ceased to belong to it*. These will be classed in the following order, viz: *discharged, transferred, died, deserted;* and the *utmost particularity* will be observed in the *remarks* concerning them. *Date* and *place* will, in every case, be given; and *No., date*, etc., of *orders*, or *description of authority*, by which these changes have occurred, must always be carefully specified, since this roll is to contain a correct history of all who were originally mustered into the service of the United States.

It will be observed that soldiers who have *deserted*, and *been retaken*, since last muster, will have their places in *both* lists; being first mentioned as present, and then again as deserted.

Actions in which the company has been engaged, *scouts, marches, changes of station*, and everything of interest relating to the discipline, *efficiency*, or *service* of the company, will be carefully noted in the column of remarks, with *date*, *place*, and other particulars of the several events.

At the foot of the roll will appear a recapitulation of the state of the company, in form as shown under the head of *muster rolls*, p. 182.

The following certificates will be made by the commanding officer of the company, and the mustering officer at the foot of the roll:

I CERTIFY, on honor, that this Muster Roll exhibits the true state of Captain CHARLES CABELL's company of the Tenth Regiment New York Volunteers, for the period herein mentioned; that each man answers to his own proper name in person; that the remarks set opposite the name of each officer and soldier are accurate and just, and that the valuation of all horses and horse equipments since the muster into service, was made by disinterested and good judges, and at fair and just rates.

C. CABELL,
Commanding the Company.

DATE: July 30th, 1861.
STATION: Elmira, N. Y.

I CERTIFY, on honor, that I have at Elmira, N. Y., on this thirtieth day of July, 1861, carefully examined this Roll, as far as practicable, caused the allowances, stoppages, and remarks to be justly and properly stated; and mustered the company for discharge; and it is hereby *honorably* discharged from the service of the United States.

J. G.,
Major First Infantry, Mustering Officer.

DATE: July 30th, 1861.
STATION: Elmira, N. Y.

If, as has sometimes happened, militia, at the end of a term of service, shall, from the want of a mustering officer, disperse or return home without being regularly mustered out; and if, with a view to a payment, a muster shall afterward be ordered by competent authority, the officer sent for the purpose shall carefully verify all the facts affecting pay, by the oath of one or more of the officers belonging to such militia, in order that full justice may be done.

In all cases of *muster for payment*, whether final or otherwise, the mustering officer will give his particular attention to the state and condition of the public property; such as quarters, camp equipage, means of transportation, arms, accoutrements, ammunition, etc., which have been in the use or possession of the militia to be paid; and if any such public property shall appear to be damaged, or lost, beyond ordinary wear or unavoidable accident, such loss or damage shall be noted on the muster rolls, in order that the injury or loss sustained by the United States may be stopped from the pay that would otherwise be due to the individual or detachment mustered for payment. This provision shall be read to all detachments of militia on being mustered into service, and as much oftener as may be deemed necessary.

Payments will, in all cases, be made by the Paymasters of the regular army.

In cases of *muster for pay*, the rolls will be of the same form as above described for muster-out rolls, the word *out* being erased in the caption.

The payments will be made on rolls prepared by the paymaster.

There will be four muster-out rolls prepared for each company, and for the field and staff, one of which is sent to the Adjutant-General's office, two to the paymaster, and one retained in the archives of the company.

ALLOWANCES TO VOLUNTEERS.

Officers, non-commissioned officers and privates of the volunteer organization of the United States, are placed on the same footing in respect to pay and allowances as similar corps of the regular army.

The allowance to be paid non-commissioned officers and privates for clothing, when not furnished in kind, is three dollars and fifty cents per month, and each company officer, non-commissioned officer, private, musician, and artificer of cavalry shall furnish his own horse and horse equipments, and shall receive forty cents per day for their use and risk, except that in case the horse shall become disabled, or shall die, the allowance shall cease until the disability be removed or another horse be supplied. Every volunteer non-commissioned officer, private, musician and artificer, who enters the service of the United States, shall be paid at the rate of fifty cents in lieu of subsistence, and if a cavalry volunteer, twenty-five cents additional, in lieu of forage, for every twenty miles of travel from his place of enrollment to the place of muster—the distance to be measured by the shortest usually travelled route; and when honorably discharged an allowance at the same rate, from the place of his discharge to his place of enrollment; and, in addition thereto, if he shall have served for a period of two years, or during the war, if sooner ended, the sum of one hundred dollars. Such companies of cavalry as may require it, may be furnished with horses and horse equipments in the same manner as in the United States army.

Any volunteer who may be received into the service of the United States, and who may be wounded or otherwise disabled in the service, shall be entitled to the benefits which have been or may be conferred on persons disabled in the regular service; and the widow, if there be one, and if not, the legal heirs of such as die, or may be killed in service, in addition to all arrears of pay and allowances, shall receive the sum of one hundred dollars.

The bands of the regiments of infantry and of the regiments of cavalry are paid as follows: one-fourth of each shall receive the pay and allowances of sergeants of engineer soldiers; one-fourth those of corporals of engineer soldiers; and the remaining half those of privates of engineer soldiers of the first class; and the leaders of the band shall receive the same pay and emoluments as second lieutenants of infantry.

Wagoners and saddlers receive the pay and allowances of corporals of cavalry. The regimental commissary sergeant receives the pay and allowances of regimental sergeant-major; and regimental quartermaster sergeants receive the pay and allowance of sergeants of cavalry. The pay of each of these grades will be seen in the table of pay, page 173.

RETIRED LIST.

HOW FILLED.

Any commissioned officer of the army, or marine corps, who has become incapable of performing the duties of his office, shall be placed upon the *retired list*, and withdrawn from active service and command, and from the line of promotion.

Any commissioned officer of the army, or of the marine corps, who shall have served as such for forty consecutive years, may, upon his own application to the President of the United States, be placed upon the retired list.

There must not however be upon this list at any one time, more than seven per centum of the whole number of officers of the army as fixed by law.

PAY OF OFFICERS ON THE RETIRED LIST.

Officers on the retired list will receive the pay proper of the highest rank held at the time of retiring, whether by staff or regimental commission, and four rations a day, and no other pay and emoluments.

The only exceptions to this is, that in case of the retirement of the Brevet Lieutenant-General, it shall be without reduction of his current pay, subsistence, or allowance.

Officers thus retired are entitled to wear the uniform of their respective grades, and will be borne upon the army or navy register, as the case may be, and will be subject to the rules and articles of war, and to trial by general court-martial, for any breach of the said articles.

MANNER OF RETIRING OFFICERS.

The Secretary of War, or the Secretary of the Navy, as the case may be, under the direction and approval of the President, will, as occasion may require, assemble a board of not more than nine, nor less than five commissioned officers, two-fifths of whom shall be of the medical staff;

the board, except those taken from the medical staff, to be composed, as far as may be, of seniors in rank to those officers who may be brought before it.

This board will determine the facts as to the nature and occasion of the disability of such officers as appear disabled to perform military service. The board being invested with the powers of a court of inquiry and court-martial, and their decision being subject to like revisions as that of such courts, by the President of the United States.

The board, whenever it finds an officer incapacitated for active service, will report whether, in its judgment, this incapacity results from long and faithful service, from wounds or injury received in the line of duty, from sickness or exposure therein, or from any other incident of service. If so, and the President approve such judgment, the disabled officer shall thereupon be placed upon the list of retired officers.

If the disability results from other causes, and the President concur in opinion with the Board, the officer will be retired, either with his pay proper alone, or with his service rations alone, at the discretion of the President. Or, he shall be wholly retired from the service, with one year's pay and allowances; and in this last case his name shall be thenceforward omitted from the register.

The members of the Board are in every case to be sworn to an honest and impartial discharge of their duties. And no officer of the army shall be retired, either partially or wholly from the service, without having had a fair and full hearing before the Board, if upon due summons he shall demand it.

PROMOTIONS CONSEQUENT ON THE RETIRING OF AN OFFICER.

Upon the retirement of an officer, the officer next in rank is to be promoted in the place of the retired officer, according to the established rules of the service. And the same rule of promotion shall be applied successively to the vacancies consequent upon the retirement of an officer.

DISCHARGE OF SOLDIERS.

Enlisted men are not to be discharged prior to the expiration of their enlistment without authority of the War Department, except by sentence of a general court-martial, or by the commander of a Department or of an army in the field, on certificate of disability, or on application of the soldier after twenty years' service.

When an enlisted man is discharged, his company commander furnishes him with certificates of his account, as shown under the head of pay, Form 92, p. 167, and his discharge duly filled up and signed, as shown by Form 124, p. 252.

The following oath of identity will be taken by the soldier upon the back of the discharge, in order that the paymaster may be certain of the individual when the account is presented:

OATH OF IDENTITY.

District of Columbia, county of Washington.

On this 25th day of June, in the year one thousand eight hundred and sixty-one, personally appeared before me, the undersigned, a Justice of the Peace for the county above mentioned, A. B., who, being duly sworn according to law, declares that he is the identical A. B., who was a private in the company commanded by Captain C. D., in the regiment of Infantry commanded by Colonel E. F.; that he enlisted on the 25th day of June, 1856, for the term of five years, and was discharged at Washington, D. C., on the 25th day of June, 1861, by reason of the expiration of his enlistment. A. B.

Sworn and subscribed before me the day and year above written.
G. H., *Justice of the Peace.*

I certify that G. H., before whom the above affidavit purports to have been made, is a Justice of the Peace duly authorized to administer oaths, and that the above is his signature.

[L. s.] In witness whereof I have hereunto set my hand and affixed my official seal, this 25th day of June, in the year one thousand eight hundred and sixty-one, at Washington, in the District of Columbia.

J. K., *Clerk of the Circuit Court.*

DISCHARGE FOR DISABILITY.

Whenever an enlisted man shall become unfit for military service, in consequence of wounds, disease, or infirmity, his captain shall forward to the commander of the Department, or of the army in the field, through the commander of the regiment or post, a statement of his case, with a certificate of his disability signed by the senior surgeon of the hospital, regiment, or post, according to Form 125, p. 252.

If the recommendation for the discharge of the invalid be approved, the authority therefor will be endorsed on the "certificate of disability," which will be sent back to be completed and signed by the commanding officer, who will then send the same to the Adjutant-General's office.

Form 124.—Discharge.

To all whom it may concern:

Know ye, that A. B., a private of Captain C. D.'s Company, (A,) 2d Regiment of Infantry, who was enrolled on the 25th day of June, one thousand eight hundred and fifty-six, to serve five years, is hereby discharged from the service of the United States, this 25th day of June, 1861, at Washington, D. C., by reason of the expiration of the term of his enlistment. (No objection to his being reënlisted is known to exist.*)

Said A. B. was born in Rochester, in the State of New York, is thirty-six years of age, five feet six inches high, dark complexion, black eyes, black hair, and by occupation, when enrolled, a machinist.

Given at Washington, D. C., this 25th day of June, 1861.

C. D., *Capt. 2d Infantry Com'g Company.*

Form 125.— Certificate of Disability for Discharge.
Army of the United States.

A. B., of Captain C. D.'s Company, (I,) of the Third Regiment of United States Artillery, was enlisted by Lieut. E. F., of the Second Regiment of Infantry, at New York, on the 21st day of June, 1860, to serve five years; he was born in Boston, in the State of Massachusetts, is twenty-six years of age, five feet six inches high, dark complexion, dark eyes, black hair, and by occupation when enlisted a miller. During the last two months said soldier has been unfit for duty forty days. The cause of this disability is the loss of a leg from amputation, rendered necessary by a wound received at the battle of Bull Run, on the 21st of July, 1861. C. D., *Com'g Company.*

Station: Fort Washington.
Date: September 10th, 1861.

I certify that I have carefully examined the said A. B., of Captain C. D.'s Company, and find him incapable of performing the duties of a

---

* This sentence will be erased *should there be any thing in the conduct or physical condition* of the soldier rendering him *unfit for the Army.*

soldier because of the amputation of his leg as above stated. The disability is such as to entitle A. B. to a pension. G. H., *Surgeon.*

Discharged this 11th day of September, 1861, at Fort Washington.

J. K., *Commanding the Post.*

A. B.'s address is, Town, New York; County, New York; State, New York.

(DUPLICATES.)

Discharge of Volunteers.

Volunteers discharged previous to the discharge of their companies, receive from their respective company commanders, certificates shown by Form 126, p. 254, to enable them to receive their pay.

Two of these certificates are to be given by the company commander to each discharged volunteer soldier, and the commander of the company will certify to the act of the delivery of the duplicate certificates; on these certificates the soldier is entitled to his *discharge*, and should present his discharge to the paymaster to have the payment endorsed on it.

When the soldier is paid, the paymaster retains the duplicate certificates, and returns the soldier his discharge duly endorsed.

DISABILITY EXISTING PREVIOUS TO MUSTERING INTO SERVICE.

In case a volunteer be discharged for disability that existed at the time he was mustered into the service of the United States, within three months after the muster, he will not receive either pay or allowances, except subsistence and transportation to his home.

DISCHARGE OF COMMISSIONED OFFICERS OF VOLUNTEERS.

The general commanding a separate department, or a detached army, may appoint a military board or commission of not less than three or more than five officers, whose duty it shall be to examine the capacity, qualifications, propriety of conduct, and efficiency of any commissioned officer of volunteers within his department or army, who may be reported to the board or commission, and upon the report of the board, if adverse to the officer, and if approved by the President of the United States, the commission of such officer shall be vacated.

No officer shall sit on such board or commission, whose rank or promotion will in any way be affected by its proceedings, and two members at least, if practicable, will be of equal rank of the officer being examined.

Form 126.

Certificate to be given to Volunteers at the time of their Discharge to enable them to Receive their Pay, etc.

I certify, on honor, that A. B., a private of Captain C. D.'s Company (I) of the Third Regiment of Volunteers, of the State of Maine, born in Bangor, State of Maine, aged 29 years, 5 feet 8 inches high, light complexion, blue eyes, light hair, and by occupation a carpenter, having joined the company on its original organization at Bangor, Me., and enrolled in it at the muster into the service of the United States at Bangor, Me., on the 10th day of May, 1861, (or was mustered in service as a recruit, by   , at
on the   day of   , 186 , to serve in the Regiment) for the term of three years; and having served honestly and faithfully with his company in Virginia, to the present date, is now entitled to a discharge, by reason of wounds received in action.

The said A. B. has pay due him from enrollment to the present date, and also pay for the use of his horse (he having been mounted during the time), and he is entitled to pay and subsistence for travelling to place of enrollment, and whatever other allowances are authorized to volunteer soldiers, or militia, so discharged. He has received six dollars advanced by the United States on account of clothing.

There is to be stopped from him, on account of the State of Maine, or other authorities, for clothing, etc., received on entering service,
dollars; also, for expenses of subsistence, for travelling from place of enrollment to the place of rendezvous, amounting to ten dollars; and on account of the United States for extra clothing received in kind from Captain C. D., and for other stoppages, viz:
amounting to twelve dollars; and he has been subsisted for travelling to his place of enrollment, up to the   186 .
He is indebted to   , Sutler, five dollars.

Given in duplicate, at Washington, D. C., this 12th day of September, 1861.

C. D., *Commanding Company.*

MEDICAL DEPARTMENT.

The Medical Department is under the charge of the Surgeon-General, and the officers thereof, denominated the Medical Staff of the army, consist of *Surgeons* and *Assistant Surgeons*, together with *Medical Cadets* and *Hospital Stewards*, who are non-commissioned officers.

SURGEONS.

Surgeons receive appointment after serving five years and passing an examination for promotion. If an assistant surgeon decline the examination, or be found not qualified by moral habits or professional acquirements, he ceases to be a medical officer of the army.

An applicant for appointment failing at one examination, may be allowed a second, after two years; but never a third.

ASSISTANT SURGEONS.

A board of not less than three medical officers will be appointed from time to time by the Secretary of War, to examine applicants for appointment of assistant surgeons, and assistant surgeons for promotion. And no one shall be so appointed or promoted until so examined and found qualified.

The board will scrutinize rigidly the moral habits, professional acquirements, and physical qualifications of the candidates, and report favorably, either for appointment or promotion, in no case admitting of a reasonable doubt.

The Secretary of War will designate the applicants to be examined for appointment of assistant surgeon. They must be between 21 and 28 years of age. The board will report their respective merits in the several branches of the examination, and their relative merit from the whole; agreeably whereto, if vacancies happen within two years thereafter, they will receive appointments and take rank in the medical corps.

MEDICAL CADETS.

This corps is attached to the medical staff of the army.

It is their duty to act as dressers in the general hospitals, and as ambulance attendants in the field, under the direction and control of the medical officers alone.

They receive the same pay, and have the same rank, as the military cadets at West Point.

Their number is not to exceed fifty, but will be regulated by the exigencies of the service. The corps is to be composed of young men of liberal education, students of medicine, between the ages of eighteen and twenty-three, who have been reading medicine for two years, and have attended at least one course of lectures in a medical college.

Medical cadets are enlisted for one year, and are subject to the rules and articles of war. On the fifteenth day of the last month of their service, the near approach of their discharge is to be reported by them to the Surgeon-General, in order, if desired, that they may be relieved by another detail of applicants.

HOSPITAL STEWARDS.

The Secretary of War will appoint from the enlisted men of the army, or cause to be enlisted, as many competent hospital stewards as the service may require, not to exceed one for each post.

The senior medical officer of a hospital requiring a steward may recommend a competent non-commissioned officer or soldier to be appointed, which recommendation the commanding officer shall forward to the Adjutant-General of the army, with his remarks thereon, and with the remarks of the company commander.

When no competent enlisted man can be procured, the medical officer will report the fact to the Surgeon-General. Applications and testimonials of competency, from persons seeking to be enlisted for hospital stewards, may be addressed to the Surgeon-General.

A commanding officer may reënlist a hospital steward at the expiration of his term of service, on recommendation of the medical officer.

Hospital stewards, appointed by the Secretary of War, whenever stationed in places whence no post return is made to the Adjutant-General's office, or when on furlough, will, at the end of every month, report themselves, by letter, to the Adjutant-General and Surgeon-General, as well as to the medical director of the military department in which they may be serving; to each of whom they will also report each new assignment to duty, or change of station, ordered in their case, noting carefully the number, date, and source of the order directing the same. They will likewise report monthly, when on furlough, to the medical officer in charge of the hospital to which they are attached.

The jurisdiction and authority of courts-martial are the same with reference to hospital stewards as in the cases of other enlisted men. When, however, a hospital steward is sentenced by an inferior court to be reduced to the ranks, such sentence, though it may be approved by the reviewing officer, will not be carried into effect until the case has been referred to the Secretary of War for final action. In these cases of reduction, the application of the man for discharge from service, though not recognized as of right, will generally be regarded with favor, if his offence has not been of too serious a nature, and especially when he has not been recently promoted from the ranks.

As the hospital stewards appointed by the Secretary of War are "permanently attached to the Medical Department," their accounts of pay, clothing, etc., must be kept by the medical officers under whose immediate direction they are serving, who are also responsible for certified statements of such accounts, and correct descriptive lists of such stewards, to accompany them in case of transfer; as, also, that their final statements and certificates of discharge are accurately made out, when they are, at length, discharged from service.

EMPLOYMENT OF PRIVATE PHYSICIANS.

When it is necessary to employ a private physician as medical officer, the commanding officer may do it by written contract, conditioned as in Form 127, p. 259, at a stated compensation not to exceed $50 a month when the number of officers and men, with authorized servants and laundresses, is 100 or more; $40 when it is from 50 to 100, and $30 when it is under 50.

But when he is required to abandon his own business, and give his whole time to the public service, the contract may be not to exceed $80 a month; and not to exceed $100, besides transportation in kind, to be furnished by the Quartermaster's Department, where he is required to accompany troops on marches or transports. But a private physician will not be employed to accompany troops on marches or transports, except by orders from the War Department, or, in particular and urgent cases, by the order of the officer directing the movement; when a particular statement of the circumstances which make it necessary will be appended to the contract.

And when a private physician is required to furnish medicines, he will be allowed, besides the stipulated pay, from 25 to 50 per cent. on it, to be determined by the Surgeon-General.

In all cases, a duplicate of the contract will be transmitted forthwith by the commanding officer to the Surgeon-General; and the commanding officer for the time being will at once discontinue it, whenever the necessity for it ceases, or the Surgeon-General may so direct.

The physicians account of pay due must be sent to the Surgeon-General for payment, vouched by the certificate of the commanding officer that it is correct and agreeable to contract, and that the services have been duly rendered. But when it cannot conveniently be submitted to the Surgeon-General from the frontier or the field, it may be paid on the order of the commanding officer, not to exceed the regulated amount, by a medical disbursing officer or a quartermaster.

When medical attendance is required by officers or enlisted men on service, or for the authorized servants of such officers, and the attendance of a medical officer cannot be had, the officer, or if there be no officer, then the enlisted man may employ a private physician, and a just account therefor will be paid by the Medical Bureau.

The account will set out the name of the patient, the date of and charge for each visit and for medicines. The physician will make a certificate to the account in case of an officer, or affidavit in the case of an enlisted man, that the account is correct, and the charges are the customary charges of the place.

The officer will make his certificate, or the enlisted man his affidavit, to the correctness of the account, that he was on service at the place, and stating the circumstances preventing him from receiving the services of a medical officer.

When the charge is against an officer, he will pay the account if practicable, and transmit it to the Medical Bureau for reimbursement.

FORM 127.

CONTRACT WITH A PRIVATE PHYSICIAN.

This contract, entered into this —— day of ——, 18—, at ——, State of ——, between —— ——, of the United States Army, and Dr. —— ——, of ——, in the State of ——, witnesseth, that for the consideration hereafter mentioned, the said Dr. —— —— promises and agrees to perform the duties of a medical officer, agreeably to the Army regulations, at ——, (*and to furnish the necessary medicines.*) And the said —— promises and agrees, on behalf of the United States, to pay, or cause to be paid, to the said Dr. —— —— the sum of —— dollars for each and every month he shall continue to perform the services above stated, which shall be his full compensation, and in lieu of all allowances and emoluments whatsoever, (*except that for medicines furnished, which shall be at the rate of —— per cent. on his monthly pay, to be determined by the Surgeon-General.*) This contract to continue till determined by the said doctor, or the commanding officer for the time being, or the Surgeon-General.

[SEAL.]

Signed, sealed, and delivered, }
  in presence of—   }

[SEAL.]

I certify that the number of persons entitled to medical attendance, agreeably to regulations, at —— is ——, and that no competent physician can be obtained at a lower rate.

—— ——, *Commanding Officer.*

LIST OF INSTRUMENTS ISSUED TO MEDICAL OFFICERS.

Each medical officer will be supplied with the following surgical instruments for his personal use, which he will retain in his immediate possession so long as he remains in the Army, and for the complete and serviceable condition of which at all times, he will be held responsble:

AMPUTATING.	
1 Capital saw.	1 Large catling.
1 Metacarpal saw.	1 Small "
1 Capital Amputating knife.	1 Scalpel.
1 Medium " "	1 Tenaculum.
1 Small " "	1 Artery needle.
	1 " forceps.
	1 Bone "

LIST OF INSTRUMENTS.

1 Spiral Tourniquet.
12 Surgeon's needles.
1 Mahogany case, brass bound.
1 Gutta Percha pouch.

TREPHINING.

2 Trephines.
1 Scalpel, with Raspitor.
1 Heys' saw.
1 Elevator.
1 Brush.
1 Mahogany case, brass bound.

EXSECTING.

1 Bone forceps, Liston's.
2 " " sharp, assorted.
1 " " for sequestra.
1 Chain saw.
1 Chisel.
1 Gouge.
1 Lenticular knife.
2 Spatulas, protecting.
1 Trephine, small crown.
1 Ecraseur.
1 Mahogany case, brass bound.
1 Gutta Percha pouch.

GENERAL OPERATING.

1 Metacarpal saw.
1 Trocar.
1 Ball forceps.
1 Gullet "
1 Artery "
1 Dressing "
2 Scissors, straight and curved.
1 Artery needle, with 4 points.
12 Surgeon's needles.
1 Tourniquet.
1 Small amputating-knife.
1 " catling.
3 Bistouries.
1 Hernia knife.
3 Scalpels.

1 Cataract knife.
1 " needle.
1 Tenaculum.
1 Double hook.
6 Steel bougies, silvered, double curve, Nos. 1 and 2, 3 and 4, 5 and 6, 7 and 8, 9 and 10, 11 and 12.
6 Wax bougies, Nos. 2, 4, 6, 8, 10.
3 Silver catheters, Nos. 3, 6, 9.
6 Gum-elastic catheters, Nos. 1, 3, 5, 7, 9, 11.
2 Mahogany cases, brass bound.
1 Gutta Percha pouch.

POCKET.

1 Large scalpel.
1 Small "
1 Artery forceps.
1 Bull-dog "
1 Curved "
1 Dressing "
1 Needle.
1 Sharp-pointed bistoury.
1 Probe " "
1 Long probe-pointed bistoury.
1 Straight scissors.
1 Knee "
1 Flat curved "
1 Gum lancet.
1 Tenaculum.
1 Tenotomy knife.
1 Abcess lancet.
1 Exploring-needle.
1 " trocar.
1 Seton-needle.
1 Spatula.
2 Probes.
1 Director.
1 Double canula.
1 Compound silver catheter.
6 Surgeon's needles.
1 Artery needle.
1 Morocco case.
1 Leather trunk.

The transfer of the surgical instruments issued to each medical officer for his own personal use, is positively forbidden. Those instruments will be accounted for to the Surgeon-General, on the 31st day of December, annually. in a special return, in which the true condition of each must be stated; and if any be lost or damaged, a report of the facts and circumstances attending such loss or damage must be given.

MEDICAL SUPPLIES.

The medical supplies of the army are obtained from the medical purveyors, who alone make the regular purchases thereof.

The senior medical officer of each hospital or post, will make requisitions for the supplies required for the ensuing year, in duplicate (Form 128, p. 270), on the Surgeon-General, who will transmit them, with his instructions, to the medical purveyors.

Medical purveyors will furnish medical supplies only on the order of the Surgeon-General, or on a special requisition (Form 129, p. 271 approved by a medical director, or, in particular and urgent cases, by a commanding officer; a like authority will be required in transfers of medical supplies.

When it is necessary to purchase medical supplies, and and recourse can not be had to a medical disbursing officer, they may be procured by the Quartermaster on a special requisition (Form 129, p. 271) and account (Form 130, p. 272).

When any requisition for medical supplies is not according to the supply table, the reason therefor must be set out.

In every case of special requisition, a duplicate of the requisition shall, at the same time, be transmitted to the Surgeon-General.

An officer transferring medical supplies, will furnish a certified invoice to the officer who is to receive them, and transmit a duplicate of it to the Surgeon-General. The receiving officer will transmit duplicate receipts to the Surgeon-General, with a report of the quality and condition of the supplies, and report the same to the issuing officer. A medical officer who turns over medical supplies to a quartermaster for storage or transportation, will forward to the Surgeon-General, with the invoice, the quartermaster's receipt for the packages.

Medical officers will take up and account for all medical supplies of the army that come into their possession, and report, when they know it, to whose account they are to be credited.

In all official lists of medical supplies, the articles will be entered in the order of the Supply Table.

STANDARD SUPPLY TABLE FOR FIELD SERVICE.

ARTICLES.		QUANTITIES.		
		Regiment, 3 mos.	Bat., 3 months.	Comp., 3 months.
MEDICINES.				
Acidi acetici	lb	1	½	½
sulph. aromatici	lb	1	½	¼
tannici	oz	2	1	1
Alcoholis	bott	10	5	3
Aluminis	lb	1	½	¼
Ammoniæ carbonatis	oz	16	8	4
Antimonii et potass. tartratis	oz	2	1	1
Argenti nitratis (crystals)	oz	2	1	½
(fused)	oz	2	1	½
Brominii	oz	1	1	1
Camphoræ	lb	4	2	1
Ceræ albæ	oz	2	2	1
Cerati resinæ	lb	2	1	½
simplicis	lb	8	4	2
Chloroformi	lb	2	1	1
Copaibæ	lb	2	1	¼
Cresoti	oz	2	1	1
Cupri sulphatis	oz	4	2	1
Emplastri adhæsivi	yds	10	5	3
cantharidis	lb	4	2	1
ichthyocollæ	yds	10	5	3
Extracti belladonnæ	oz	1	1	1
buchu fluidi	lb	1	½	¼
chochici acetici	oz	2	1	1
colocynthidis comp	oz	16	8	4
glycyrrhizæ	lb	2	1	½
rhei fluidi	lb	2	1	½
senegæ fluidi	oz	8	4	4
sennæ fluidi	lb	2	1	½
Hydrargyri chloridi corrosivi	oz	½	½	½
mitis	lb	2	1	½
Iodinii	oz	4	2	1
Liquoris ammoniæ	lb	4	2	1
potass. arsenitis	oz	4	2	1
Magnesiæ sulphatis	lb	20	10	5
Massæ pilulæ hydrargyri	oz	16	8	4
Morphiæ sulphatis	drm	4	2	1
Olei caryophylli	oz	1	1	1
menthæ piperitæ	ðz	2	1	1
olivæ	bott	8	4	2

ARTICLES.	QUANTITIES. Regiment, 3 mos.	Bat., 3 months.	Comp., 3 months.
Olei ricini .... qt. bott..	12	6	3
terebinthinæ..................... qt. bott..	8	4	2
tiglii.............................. drm..	2	1	1
Pilul cathartic comp. (U. S.)............ doz..	8	4	2
opii (U. S.)......................... doz..	8	4	2
quiniæ (3 grs.)..................... doz..	8	4	2
Plumbi acetatis........................... lb..	2	1	½
Potassæ bicarbonatis...................... lb..	1	½	¼
chloratis......................... lb..	2	1	½
nitratis.......................... lb..	1	½	¼
Potassii cyanureti....................... drm..	1	1	1
iodidi............................ oz..	8	4	2
Pulveris acaciæ........................... lb..	4	2	1
capsici........................... lb..	½	¼	¼
ferri per sulphatis............... oz..	4	2	1
opii.............................. lb..	2	1	½
ipecacuanhæ....................... lb..	1	½	¼
et opii.............. oz..	8	4	4
lini.............................. lb..	16	8	4
rhei.............................. lb..	½	¼	¼
sinapis nigræ..................... lb..	12	6	3
Quiniæ sulphatis.......................... oz..	24	12	6
Sacchari.................................. lb..	10	5	2
Saponis................................... lb..	8	4	2
Sodæ bicarbonatis......................... lb..	1	½	¼
Spiritus ammoniæ aromatici................ oz..	4	2	2
ætheris compositi................. lb..	1	½	½
ætheris nitrici................... lb..	2	1	½
vini gallici...................... bott..	24	12	6
Strychniæ................................. drm..	1	1	1
Tincturæ aconiti radicis.................. lb..	1	½	¼
ferri chloridi.................... lb..	1	½	¼
Tincturæ opii............................. oz..	16	8	6
veratri viridis................... oz..	8	4	2
Unguenti hydrargyri....................... lb..	1	½	¼
nitratis.............. lb..	½	¼	¼
Zinci acetatis............................ oz..	2	1	1
Zinci sulphatis........................... oz..	2	1	1
INSTRUMENTS.			
Buck's sponge holder for the throat........ no..	1	1	1
Cupping glasses and tins.................. no..	16	8	4
Lancets, spring........................... no..	1	1	1
thumb (with case)................. no..	6	4	2
Pocket.................................... sets..	1	1	1
Probangs, whalebone....................... no..	12	6	2
Scarificators............................. no..	4	2	1
Splints (major)........................... sets..	1	1	1

HOSPITAL STORES.

ARTICLES.		QUANTITIES.		
		Regiment, 3 mos.	Bat., 3 months.	Comp., 3 months.
Stomach pump and case	no..	1	1	1
Syringes, enema	no..	4	2	1
penis, glass	no..	8	4	2
India rubber	no..	8	4	2
Teeth-extracting	sets..	1	1	1
Tongue depressor (hinge)	no..	1	1	1
Tourniquets, field	no..	8	4	2
spiral	no..	2	2	1
Trusses, hernia	no..	6	3	2
BOOKS.				
Anatomy (surgical)	cop..	1	1	1
Medical Practice	cop..	1	1	1
Regulations for Medical Department	cop..	1	1	1
Surgery, (operative)	cop..	1	1	1
Thompson's Conspectus	cop..	1	1	1
Blank	no..	4	4	4
HOSPITAL STORES.				
Arrow root	lb..	10	5	3
Candles (sperm)	lb..	2	1	1
Farina	lb..	10	5	3
Ginger (fluid extract)	lb..	1	½	¼
Nutmegs	oz..	8	4	2
Tea	lb..	30	15	7
Whisky, bottles of	doz..	2	1	½
BEDDING.				
Blankets woolen, brown	no..	20–40	10–20	10
Blanket cases, canvass	no..	1 for 10 blankets.		
Gutta percha cloth	yds..	8	4	2
bedcovers	no..	8	4	2
Musquito bars	no..	12	6	4
FURNITURE AND DRESSINGS.				
Bandages, roller, assorted	doz..	14	7	4
Suspensory, "	no..	12	6	4
Binders, boards (18 by 4 in.)	no..	18	9	5
Buckets, leather	no..	4	2	2
Corks, assorted	doz..	12	6	3
Cork screws	no..	2	1	1
Cotton batting	lb..	2	1	½
wadding	lb..	2	1	½
Flannel, red	yds..	5	3	2
Hatchets	no..	5	1	1
Hones (4 in. by 1, in wood)	no..	1	1	1
Ink, 2-oz. bottles	no..	12	6	3
Knapsack, hospital	no..			

FURNITURE AND DRESSINGS.

ARTICLES.		Regiment, 3 mos.	Bat., 3 months.	Comp., 3 months.
Lanterns	no.	4	2	1
Lint	lb.	8	4	2
Litters and stretchers, hand	no.			
horse	no.			
Measures, graduated, assorted	no.	4	2	2
Medicine chests	no.			
cups and glasses	no.	6	3	2
panniers	no.			
Mess chests (see note)	no.			
Mills, coffee	no.	2	1	1
Mortars and pestles, wedgewood (small)	no.	2	1	1
Muslin	yds.	20	10	5
Needles, sewing (assorted in a case)	no.	25	25	25
Oiled silk, or gutta percha tissue, or India rubber tissue	yds.	8	4	2
Pans, bed	no.	2	1	1
Paper envelopes, assorted	no.	100	50	25
Paper, wrapping	quires.	6	3	1
writing	quires.	12	6	3
Pencils, hair	no.	24	12	6
lead (of Faber's make, No. 2.)	no.	12	6	3
Pens, steel	doz.	4	2	1
Pill Boxes (wood)	papers.	2	1	1
(tin)	no.	6	6	6
Pins, assorted (large and medium)	papers.	4	2	2
Razors	no.	1	1	1
Razor strops	no.	1	1	1
Scales and weights, apothecary's	sets.	1	1	1
Scissors	no.	4	2	2
Sheep skins, dressed	no.	4	2	1
Silk, surgeon's	oz.	½	¼	¼
green	yds.	1	½	½
Spatulas	no.	6	3	2
Sponge, washed	lb.	1	½	¼
Tape	pieces.	4	2	1
Thread, linen	oz.	2	1	1
Tiles	no.	2	1	1
Towels	no.	40	20	10
Twine	lb.	½	¼	¼
Urinals	no.	4	2	1
Vials, assorted (1-oz. and 2-oz.)	doz.	4	2	1
Wafers (half-ounce boxes)	no.	1	1	1
Wax, sealing	sticks.	2	1	1

NOTE TO PRECEDING TABLE.

Furniture of Mess-Chest.

8 Basins, tin.
2 Boxes, pepper and salt.
6 Cups, tin.

4 Canisters (for tea, coffee, sugar, and butter.
2 Dippers and ladles.

1 Grater.	8 Plates (6) and dishes (2), tin.
1 Gridiron.	1 Pot, iron.
1 Kettle, tea, iron.	2 Pots, coffee and tea, tin.
12 Knives and forks	12 Spoons, iron (table [6] and tea [6]).
6 Mugs (Britannia, half-pint.)	
1 Pan, frying.	1 Tray, tin.
1 " sauce.	6 Tumblers, tin.

When the following articles of hospital furniture can not be obtained with the hospital fund, they are to be procured from a quartermaster or medical disbursing officer, by special requisition.

ARTICLES.

Basins, wash.	Mugs.
Bowls.	Pans, frying.
Brushes.	" sauce.
Buckets.	Pitchers.
Candlesticks.	Plates and dishes.
Clothes'-lines.	Pots, chamber and chair.
Cups.	" coffee and tea.
Dippers and ladles.	Sadirons.
Graters.	Shovels, fire.
Gridirons.	Snuffers.
Kettles, tea.	Spoons.
Knives and forks.	Tongs and pokers.
Lamps and lanterns.	Tumblers.
Locks and keys.	Wood-saws.

MUSTER ROLLS.

The muster rolls of hospital attendants and soldiers in hospital are to be prepared according to Form 95, p. 201, and the instructions relating thereto.

Soldiers in hospital, patients or attendants, except stewards, shall be mustered on the rolls of their company, if it be present at the post.

When a soldier in hospital is detached from his company so as not to be mustered with it for pay, his company commander shall certify and send to the hospital his descriptive list and account of pay and clothing, containing all necessary information relating to his accounts with the United States, on which the surgeon shall enter all payments, stoppages, and issues of clothing to him in hospital. When he leaves the hospital, the medical officer shall certify and remit his descriptive list, showing the state of his accounts. If he is discharged from the service in hospital, the surgeon shall make out his final statements for pay and clothing. If he dies in hospital, the surgeon shall take charge of his effects, and make the reports required in the general regulations concerning soldiers who die absent from their companies.

Patients in hospital are, if possible, to leave their arms and accoutrements with their companies, and in no case to take ammunition into the hospital.

When a patient is transferred from one hospital to another, the medical officer shall send with him an account of his case, and the treatment.

The regulations for the service of hospitals apply, as far as practicable, to the medical service in the field.

SURGEON'S CALL.

At surgeon's call the sick then in the companies will be conducted to the hospital by the first sergeants, who will each hand to the surgeon, in his company book, a list of all the sick of the company, on which the surgeon shall state who are to remain or go into hospital; who are to return to quarters as sick or convalescent; what duties the convalescents in quarters are capable of; what cases are feigned; and any other information in regard to the sick of the company he may have to communicate to the company commander.

Medical officers where on duty will attend the officers and enlisted men, and the servants and laundresses authorized by law; and, at stations where other medical attendance cannot be procured, and on marches, the hired men of the army, and the families of officers and soldiers. Medicines will be dispensed to the families of officers and soldiers, and to all persons entitled to medical attendance; hospital stores to enlisted men.

Returns and Accounts to be made by Medical Officers.

RETURN OF MEDICINES, ETC.
Form 131, p. 273.

Medical officers in charge of medical supplies will make yearly returns, on the 31st of December, of medical supplies received, issued, and remaining on hand, and transmit them in duplicate to the Surgeon-General.

These returns are to be made by medical officers when relieved from the duty to which their returns relate.

Medical purveyors are to make these returns quarterly.

The returns are to show the condition of the stores, particularly of the instruments, bedding, and furniture.

ACCOUNT OF CLOTHING, ARMS, ETC., OF PATIENTS.

The effects of patients in hospital are to be numbered and labeled with the patient's name, and registered in a book made pursuant to Form 132, p. 274,

The remarks will note to whom the articles were delivered; what money, etc., were left by those who die, and to whom they were given.

MORNING REPORT.
Form 133, p. 275.

This is to be made every morning to the commanding officer, as soon after sick call as practicable. It will show the number of sick, the number returned to duty since last report, and the number remaining on the sick report.

RETURN OF CLOTHING, CAMP AND GARRISON EQUIPAGE.
Form 87, p 72a.

This return is to be made by all medical officers who receipt for tents or any other article of clothing, camp and garrison equipage.

It must be made quarterly to the Quartermaster-General, so long as the officer has the articles in use, or is accountable for them.

When the officer turns over the property and obtains the receipt of another therefor, he will close his account for this species of property within the quarter.

Other articles of Quartermaster's property for which a medical officer may become accountable, will be accounted for by a return of Quartermaster's property made pursuant to Form 46, p. 92a, at the end of every quarter, as set forth under the head of "*Quartermaster's Department.*"

ACCOUNT CURRENT.

Medical disbursing officers will, at the end of each fiscal quarter, render to the Surgeon-General, in duplicate, a quarterly account current of moneys received and expended, with the proper vouchers for the payments, and certificates that the services have been rendered and the supplies purchased and received for the medical service, and transmit to him an estimate of the funds required for the next quarter.

These accounts are to be made pursuant to Form 38, p. 98.

CORRESPONDENCE.

The Surgeon-General directs that official *letters* addressed to him by medical officers of the army, be written on letter paper (quarto post) whenever practicable, and not on note or foolscap paper. Also, that the letter be folded in three equal folds parallel with the writing, and indorsed on that fold which corresponds with the top of the sheet; thus:

(Post or station and date of letter.)

(Name and rank of writer.)

(Analysis of contents.)

FORM 128.—REQUISITION FOR MEDICAL AND HOSPITAL SUPPLIES.

Station: ———.   Period: ———.
From ——— to ———.
Command: Officers, ———; Enlisted Men, ———; All others entitled to Medicines, ———; Total, ———.

ARTICLES, AND CHARACTERS OR QUANTITIES.	On hand.	Wanted.	ARTICLES, AND CHARACTERS OR QUANTITIES.	On hand.	Wanted.
Acaciæ..................lb.					
Acidi acetici.............lb.					
" arseniosi............lb.					

Date: ———
——————
Surgeon U. S. Army.

N. B.—Requisitions will exhibit the quantity of each and every article "on hand," whether more be wanted or not. They will be transmitted in duplicate, and by different mails.

FORM 129.—SPECIAL REQUISITION FOR SUPPLIES OF MEDICINES, ETC.

Requisition for Medicines (Hospital Stores, etc.) required at ———, for ———

Acet. plumbi, lb. i.
Pulv. cinchonæ, lbs. x.
&c., &c.
&c., &c.

I certify that the medicines above required are necessary for the sick at ———, in consequence of [here state whether from loss, damage, &c., &c.], and that the requisition is agreeable to the supply table.

——— ———, *Surgeon.*

Approved:

——— ———, *Commanding Officer.*

Received, ———, 1861, of ———, the articles above enumerated.

——— ———, *Surgeon.*

FORM 130.—ACCOUNT FOR MEDICINES, ETC., PURCHASED BY A SURGEON OR AN OFFICER OF THE QUARTERMASTER'S DEPARTMENT.

THE UNITED STATES,

To A. B.,   Dr.

Acet. plumb.; lb. i., at 50 cents $0 50
Pulv. cinchon.; lbs. x., at $2 .... 20 00
&c., &c., &c.

I certify that the articles above charged, for the use of the sick at ———, are agreeable to the foregoing requisition, and that the charges are reasonable and just.

——————, Surgeon.

Received, ———, 18—, of ———, ——— dollars and ——— cents, in full of the above account.

A. B.

Form 131.—Return of Medicines, Hospital Stores, Furniture, etc.									
Articles, and characters or quantities.	On hand at last return.	Received since last return.	Total.	Expended with the sick.	Issued.	Lost or destroyed by unavoidable accident.	Worn out, or unfit for use.	Total expended, &c.	On hand.	Remarks.

ACCOUNT OF CLOTHING.

FORM 132.—ACCOUNT OF CLOTHING, ARMS, EQUIPMENTS, ETC., OF PATIENTS IN HOSPITAL.

Date.	Number.	Names.	Rank.	Regiment or corps.	Company.	Coats.	Jackets.	Overalls.	&c.	Muskets.	Knapsacks.	&c.	&c.	&c.	When delivered.	REMARKS.

Form 133.—Morning Report of the Surgeon of a Regiment, Post, or Garrison.												
Date.	Company.	Remaining at last report.		Taken sick.	Total.		Returned to duty.	Discharged.	Sent to general hospital.	Died.	Remaining.		Remarks.
		In hospital.	In quarters.		In hospital.	In quarters.					In hospital.	In quarters.	

BOARDS OF SURVEY.

Boards of Survey are not to be resorted to for the *condemnation* of public property, but only to establish data by which questions of administrative responsibility may be determined, and the adjustment of accounts facilitated, such as to assess the damage which public property has sustained from any extraordinary cause, not ordinary wear, either in transit or in store, or in actual use, and to set forth the circumstances and fix the responsibility of such damage, whether on the carrier or the person accountable for the property or having it immediately in charge; to report from examination the circumstances and amount of the loss or deficiency of public property by accident, unusual wastage, or otherwise, and fix the responsibility of such loss or deficiency; to make inventories of property ordered to be abandoned, when the articles have not been enumerated in the orders; to assess the prices at which damaged clothing may be issued to troops, and the proportion in which supplies shall be issued in consequence of damage that renders them at the usual rate unequal to the allowance which the regulations contemplate; to verify the discrepancy between the invoices and the actual quantity or description of property transferred from one officer to another, and ascertain as far as possible where and how the discrepancy has occurred, whether in the hands of the carrier or the officer making the transfer; and to make inventories and report on the condition of public property in the possession of officers at the time of their death. The action of the Board for the authorized object will be complete with the approval of the commanding officer, but liable to revision by higher authority. In no case, however, will the report of the Board supersede the depositions which the law requires with reference to deficiencies and damage.

Boards of Survey will not be convened by any other than the commanding officer present, and will be composed of as many officers, not exceeding three, as may be present for duty, the commanding officer and the officer responsible in the matter to be reported on being excluded; but in case the two latter only are present, then the one not responsible will perform the duties, and the responsible officer will perform them if no other officer is present. The proceedings of the Board will be signed by each member, and a copy forwarded by the approving officer to the headquarters of the department or army in the field, as the case may be, duplicates being furnished to the officer responsible for the property.

All surveys and reports having in view the *condemnation* of public property, for whatever cause, will be made by the commanding officers of the posts or other separate commands, or by Inspectors-General, or inspectors specially designated by the commander of a department or an army in the field, or by higher authority. Such surveys and reports having a different object from those of Boards of Survey, will be required independently of any action of a Board on the same property.

When public property is received by any officer, he will make a careful examination to ascertain its quality and condition, but without breaking packages until issues are to be made, unless there is cause to suppose the contents defective; and in any of the cases supposed in the first paragraph, he will apply for a Board of Survey for the purposes therein set forth. If he deem the property unfit for use, and that the public interest requires it to be condemned, he will, in addition, report the fact for that purpose to the commanding officer, who will make a critical inspection, or cause it to be made by an Inspector-General or special inspector, according to the nature of his command. If the inspector deem the property fit, it shall be received and used. If not, he will forward a formal inspection report to the commander empowered to give orders in the case. The same rule will be observed, according to the nature of the case, with reference to property already on hand. The person accountable for the property, or having it in charge, will submit an inventory, which will accompany or be embodied in the inspection report, stating how long the property has been in his possession, how long in use, and from whom it was received. The inspector's report will state the exact condition of each article, and what disposition it is expedient to make of it, as, to be destroyed, to be dropped as being of no value, to be broken up, to be repacked or repaired, or to be sold. The inspector will certify on his report that he has examined each article, and that its condition is as stated. If the commanding officer, who ordinarily would be the inspector, is himself accountable for the property, the next officer in rank present for duty will act as the inspector. The authority of inspection and condemnation will not, without special instructions, extend to commanding officers of arsenals with reference to ordnance and ordnance stores, but may in regard to other unserviceable supplies.

An officer commanding a department, or an army in the field, may give orders, on the part of the authorized inspectors, either to sell, destroy, or make such other disposition of condemned property as the case may require, excepting with reference to the sale of ordnance and ordnance stores, for which the orders of the War Department will be requisite; but if the property be of very considerable value, and there is reason to suppose that it could be advantageously applied or disposed of elsewhere than within his command, he will refer the matter to the Chief of the Staff Department to which it belongs for the orders of the War Department. No other persons than those designated, or the General-in-Chief, will order the final disposition of condemned property, excepting in the case of ordnance and ordnance stores which are to be dropped or broken up, horses which should be killed to prevent contagion, and provisions or other stores which are deteriorating so rapidly as to require immediate action. In this last case the inspector may order the destruction or sale of the stores, and in the other cases he may direct the disposition above indicated with reference to them. The inventories will be made out in duplicate—one to be retained by the person accountable, and the other to accompany his accounts. When the action of the inspector has been final, a copy of the inventory will be forwarded through the Department or other superior headquarters, to the Chief of the Staff Department to which the property belongs. When the action of the Department or other superior commander is required, the original inventories will be sent to the headquarters, and returned with the final orders thereon to the person accountable for the property, and a copy of the inventory and orders will be forwarded from the Department, or other superior headquarters, to the Chief of the Staff Department to which they relate.

Every inspector, member of a Board of Survey, and commander acting on their proceedings, shall be answerable that his action has been proper and judicious, according to the regulations and the circumstances of the case.

As far as practicable, every officer in charge of public property, whether it be in use or in store, will endeavor by timely repairs to keep it in serviceable condition, for which purpose the necessary means will be allowed on satisfactory requisitions; and property in store so repaired will be issued for further use. Provisions and other perishable stores will be repacked whenever it may be necessary for their preservation and their value will justify the expense, which will be a legitimate charge against the Department to which they belong. Public animals will not be condemned for temporary disease or want of condition, but may by order of the commanding officer, after inspection, be turned in for rest and treatment, if unfit for service for which they are immediately required.

Public property shall not be transferred gratuitously from one staff department to another; but when offered for sale, and required for public service in another staff department in which its use is allowed by Regulations, it may be bid in on the order of the commanding officer, or purchased at a fair valuation, to be determined by a Board of Survey, if there should be no other bidder.

SETTLEMENT OF ACCOUNTS.

The several returns and accounts made by officers to the Subsistence, Quartermaster's, and Ordnance Departments, are after examination in those departments referred to the following Auditors of the Treasury for final settlement:

All returns and accounts relating to Clothing, Camp and Garrison Equipage and Quartermaster's Stores, to the *Second Auditor.* Ordnance return to the *Second Auditor.* Subsistence accounts to the *Third Auditor.*

After due examination by the respective auditors, the officer receives notice of the final settlement of the accounts, or a statement of differences existing between his accounts and what is considered by the Auditor as correct.

These differences are to be removed by the explanation of the officer, or the accounts are to be modified upon this basis and passed to a final settlement.

Explanations will be made by letter through the department to which the account relates; but should circumstances require it, the officer may be ordered to Washington to attend in person to the settlement of the accounts.

Officers should preserve their duplicate vouchers, and other papers, until they receive the Auditor's letter announcing the final settlement of the account to which they relate.

ASSIGNMENT OF PAY BY VOLUNTEERS.

Congress, by act of July 22d, 1861, authorized the assignment by volunteers of portions of their pay for the benefit of their families. The following is the method of so doing, prescribed by the War Department:

The assignment of pay will be made on a separate roll, to be executed under the supervision of the captain or immediate commander of the recruit at the time of enlistment or of the soldier in camp. When completed, the allotment roll is to be transmitted to the Paymaster-General, by whom the directions will be made on each monthly pay roll, and the aggregate amount of each company's assignment will be transmitted by him to the distributor named in the roll, together with a copy of said roll.

REQUIREMENT OF CAMP AND GARRISON EQUIPAGE FOR A REGIMENT OF INFANTRY ONE THOUSAND STRONG.

Tents.

For officers, 27 wall tents. Hospital tents, 2. Store tent, 1.

To every six non-commissioned officers and privates, 1 servant's tent complete.

Axes, Hatchets, &c.

For officers, 27 axes, 27 hatchets.

To every fifteen enlisted men the following: 2 spades, 2 axes, 2 pickaxes, 2 hatchets, 2 camp kettles, 5 mess pans.

From the foregoing table Regimental Quartermasters will be able to estimate the requirements of their commands on arrival at a depôt.

UNIFORM, DRESS AND HORSE EQUIPMENTS, PRESCRIBED FOR THE ARMY.

COAT.

For Commissioned Officers.

All officers shall wear a frock coat of dark blue cloth, the skirt to extend from two-thirds to three-fourths of the distance from the top of the hip to the bend of the knee; single-breasted for captains and lieutenants; double-breasted for all other grades.

For a Major-General.—Two rows of buttons on the breast, nine in each row, placed by threes; the distance between each row, five and one-half inches at top, and three and one-half inches at bottom; stand-up collar, to rise no higher than to permit the chin to turn freely over it, to hook in front at the bottom, and slope thence up and backward at an angle of thirty degrees on each side; cuffs two and one-half inches deep to go around the sleeves parallel with the lower edge, and to button with three small buttons at the under seam; pockets in the folds of the skirts, with one button at the hip and one at the end of each pocket, making four buttons on the back and skirt of the coat, the hip button to range with the lowest buttons on the breast; collar and cuffs to be of dark blue velvet; lining of the coat black.

For a Brigadier-General.—The same as for a major-general, except that there will be only eight buttons in each row on the breast, placed in pairs.

For a Colonel.—The same as for a major-general, except that there will be only seven buttons in each row on the breast, placed at equal distances; collar and cuffs of the same color and material as the coat.

For a Lieutenant-Colonel.—The same as for a colonel.

For a Major.—The same as for a colonel.

For a Captain.—The same as for a colonel, except that there will be only one row of nine buttons on the breast; placed at equal distances.

For a First Lieutenant.—The same as for a captain.

For a Second Lieutenant.—The same as for a captain.

For a Brevet Second Lieutenant.—The same as for a captain.

For a Medical Cadet.—The same as for a brevet second lieutenant.

A round jacket, according to pattern, of dark blue cloth trimmed with scarlet, with the Russian shoulder-knot, the insignia of rank to be worked in silver in the centre of the knot, may be worn on undress duty by officers of Light Artillery.

For Enlisted Men.

The uniform coat for all enlisted *foot* men, shall be a single breasted frock of dark blue cloth, made without plaits, with a skirt extending one-half the distance from the top of the hip to the bend of the knee; one row of nine buttons on the breast, placed at equal distances; stand-up collar to rise no higher than to permit the chin to turn freely over it, to hook in front at the bottom, and then to slope up and backward at an angle of thirty degrees on each side; cuffs pointed according to pattern, and to button with two small buttons at the under seam; collar and cuffs edged with a cord or welt of cloth as follows, to wit:— scarlet *for Artillery;* sky blue *for Infantry;* yellow *for Engineers;* crimson *for Ordnance* and *Hospital Stewards.* On each shoulder a metallic scale according to pattern; narrow lining for skirt of the coat of the same color and material of the coat; pockets in the folds of the skirts, with one button at each hip to range with the lowest buttons on the breast; no buttons at the end of the pockets.

All Enlisted Men of the Cavalry and Light Artillery shall wear a uniform jacket of dark blue cloth, with one row of twelve small buttons on the breast placed at equal distances; stand-up collar to rise no higher than to permit the chin to turn freely over it, to hook in front at the bottom, and to slope the same as the coat collar; on the collar, on each side, two blind button-holes of lace, three-eighths of an inch wide, one small button on the button-hole, lower button-hole extending back four inches, upper button-hole three and a-half inches; top button and front ends of collar bound with lace three-eighths of an inch wide, and a strip of the same extending down the front and around the whole lower edge of the jacket; the back seam laced with the same, and on the cuff a point of the same shape as that on the coat, but formed of the lace; jacket to extend to the waist, and to be lined with white flannel; two small buttons at the under seam of the cuff, as on the coat cuff; one hook and eye at the bottom of the collar; color of lace (worsted), yellow for *Cavalry*, and scarlet for *Light Artillery*.

For all Musicians.—The same as for other enlisted men of their respective corps, with the addition of a facing of lace three-eighths of an inch wide, on the front of the *coat or jacket*, made in the following manner: bars of three-eighths of an inch worsted lace placed on a line with each button, six and one-half inches wide at the bottom, and *thence* gradually expanding upwards to the last button, counting from the waist up, and contracting from thence to the bottom of the collar, where it will be six and one-half inches wide, with a strip of the same lace following the bars at their outer extremity—the whole presenting something of the herring-bone form; the color of the lace facing to correspond with the color of the trimming of the corps.

For Fatigue Purposes.—A sack coat of dark blue flannel extending half way down the thigh, and made loose, without sleeve or body lining, falling collar, inside pocket on the left side, four coat buttons down the front.

For Recruits.—The sack coat will be made with sleeve and body lining, the latter of flannel.

On all occasions of duty, except fatigue, and when out of quarters, the coat or jacket shall be buttoned and hooked at the collar.

BUTTONS.

For General Officers and Officers of the General Staff.—Gilt, convex, with spread eagle and stars, and plain border; large size, seven-eighths of an inch in exterior diameter; small size, one-half inch.

For Officers of the Corps of Engineers.—Gilt, nine-tenths of an inch in exterior diameter, slightly convex; a raised bright rim, one-thirtieth of an inch wide; device, an eagle holding in his beak a scroll, with the word "*Essayons*," a bastion with embrasures in the distance surrounded by water, with a rising sun—the figures to be of dead gold upon a bright field. Small buttons of the same form and device, and fifty-five hundredths of an inch in exterior diameter.

For Officers of the Corps of Topographical Engineers.—Gilt, seven-eighths of an inch exterior diameter, convex and solid; device, the shield of the United States, occupying one-half the diameter, and the letters 𝕮. 𝕰. in old English characters the other half; small buttons, one-half inch diameter, device and form the same.

For Officers of the Ordnance Department.—Gilt, convex, plain border, cross cannon and bombshell, with a circular scroll, over and across the cannon, containing the words "Ordnance Corps," large size, seven-eighths of an inch in exterior diameter; small size, one-half inch.

For Officers of Artillery, Infantry, and Cavalry.—Gilt, convex; device, a spread eagle with the letter A, for Artillery; I, for Infantry; C, for Cavalry, on the shield; large size seven-eighths of an inch in exterior diameter; small size, one-half inch.

Aides-de-Camp may wear the button of the general staff, or of their regiment or corps, at their option.

For Medical Cadets.—The same as for officers of the General Staff.

For all Enlisted Men, yellow, the same as is used by the artillery, etc., omitting the letter on the shield.

TROWSERS.

For General Officers and Officers of the Ordnance Department.—Of dark blue cloth, plain, without stripe, welt, or cord down the outer seam.

For Officers of the General Staff and Staff Corps, except the Ordnance—dark blue cloth, with a gold cord, one-eighth of an inch diameter, along the outer seam.

For Medical Cadets.—The same as for officers of the General Staff, except a welt of buff cloth instead of a gold cord.

For all Regimental Officers.—Sky-blue cloth, with a welt let into the outer seam, one-eighth of an inch in diameter, of colors corresponding to the facings of the respective regiments, viz: *Cavalry*, yellow; *Artillery*, scarlet; *Infantry*, dark-blue.

For Enlisted men, except companies of light artillery—dark blue cloth; *sergeants*, with a stripe one and one-half inch wide; *corporals*, with a stripe one-half inch wide, of worsted lace, down and over the outer seam, of the color of the facings of the respective corps.

Ordnance Sergeants and Hospital Stewards.—Stripe of crimson lace, one and one-half inch wide.

Privates.—Plain, without stripe or welt.

For Companies of Artillery, equipped as Light Artillery,—Sky-blue cloth.

All trowsers to be made loose, without plaits, and to spread well over the boot; to be re-inforced for all enlisted mounted men.

HAT.

For Officers.—Of best black felt. The dimensions of medium size to be as follows:

Width of brim, $3\frac{1}{4}$ inches.
Height of crown, $6\frac{1}{4}$ inches.
Oval of tip, $\frac{1}{2}$ inch.
Taper of crown, $\frac{3}{4}$ inch.
Curve of head, $\frac{3}{8}$ inch.

The binding to be $\frac{1}{2}$ inch deep, of best black ribbed silk.

For Enlisted Men.—Of black felt, same shape and size as for officers, with double row of stitching instead of binding around the edge. To agree in quality with the pattern deposited in the clothing arsenal.

Medical Cadets will wear a forage cap according to pattern.

TRIMMINGS.

For General Officers.—Gold cord, with acorn-shaped ends. The brim of the hat looped up on the right side, and fastened with an eagle attached to the side of the hat; three black ostrich feathers on the left side; a gold embroidered wreath in front, on black velvet ground, encircling the letters U. S. in silver, old English characters.

For Officers of the Adjutant-Genral's, Inspector-General's, Quartermaster's, Subsistence, Medical and Pay Departments, and the Judge-Advocate, above the rank of Captain.—The same as for General officers, except the cord, which will be of black silk and gold.

For the same Departments, below the rank of Field Officers.—The same as for Field Officers, except that there will be but two feathers.

For Officers of the Corps of Engineers.—The same as for the General Staff, except the ornament in front, which will be a gold embroidered wreath of laurel and palm, encircling a silver turreted castle on black velvet ground.

For Officers of the Topographical Engineers.—The same as for the General Staff, except the ornament in front, which will be a gold embroidered wreath of oak leaves, encircling a gold embroidered shield, on black velvet ground.

For Officers of the Ordnance Department.—The same as for the General Staff, except the ornament in front, which will be a gold embroidered shell and flame, on black velvet ground.

For Officers of Cavalry.—The same as for the General Staff, except the ornament in front, which will be two gold embroidered sabres crossed, edges upward, on black velvet ground, with the number of the regiment in silver in the upper angle.

For Officers of Artillery.—The same as for the General Staff, except the ornament in front, which will be gold embroidered cross cannon, on black velvet ground, with the number of the regiment in silver at the intersection of the cross cannon.

For Officers of Infantry.—The same as for Artillery, except the ornament in front, which will be a gold embroidered bugle, on black velvet ground, with the number of the regiment in silver within the bend.

For Enlisted Men, except companies of Light Artillery. —The same as for officers of the respective corps, except that there will be but one feather; the cord will be of worsted, of the same color as that of the facing of the corps, three-sixteenths of an inch in diameter, running three times through a slide of the same material, and terminating with two tassels, not less than two inches long, on the side of the hat opposite the feather: For *Hospital Stewards* the cord will be of buff and green mixed. The insignia of the corps, in brass, in front of the hat, corresponding with those prescribed for officers, with the number of regiment, five-eighths of an inch long, in brass, and letter of company, one inch, in brass, arranged over insignia. Brim to be looped up to side of hat with a brass eagle, having a hook attached to the bottom to secure the brim, —on the right side for mounted men, and left side for foot men. The feather to be worn on the side opposite the loop.

All the trimmings of the hat are to be made so that they can be detached; but the eagle, badge of corps, and letter of company, are to be always worn.

For companies of Artillery equipped as Light Artillery, the old pattern uniform cap, with red horse-hair plume, cord and tassel.

Officers of the General Staff and Staff Corps, may wear, at their option, a light French chapeau, either stiff crown or flat, according to the pattern deposited into the Adjutant-General's office. Officers below the rank of Field Officers to wear but two feathers.

FORAGE CAPS.

For fatigue purposes, forage caps, of pattern in the Quartermaster-General's office: Dark blue cloth, with a welt of the same around the crown, and yellow metal letters to designate companies.

Commissioned officers may wear forage caps of the same pattern, with the distinctive ornament of the corps and regiment in front.

CRAVAT OR STOCK.

For all Officers.—Black; when a cravat is worn, the tie not to visible at the opening of the collar.

For all Enlisted Men.—Black leather, according to pattern.

BOOTS.

For all Officers.—Ankle or Jefferson.

For Enlisted Men of Cavalry and Light Artillery.—Ankle and Jefferson rights and lefts, according to pattern.

For Enlisted Men of Artillery, Infantry, Engineers and Ordnance.—Jefferson rights and lefts, according to pattern.

SPURS.

For all Mounted Officers.—Yellow metal, or gilt.

For all Enlisted Mounted Men.—Yellow metal, according to pattern hereafter described.

GLOVES.

For General Officers, and Officers of the General Staff and Staff Corps.—Buff or white.

For Officers of Artillery, Infantry, and Cavalry.—White.

SASH.

For General Officers.—Buff, silk net, with silk bullion fringe ends; sash to go twice around the waist, and to tie behind the left hip, pendent part not to extend more than eighteen inches below the tie.

For Officers of the Adjutant-General's, Inspector General's, Quartermaster's and Subsistence Departments, Corps of Engineers, Topographical Engineers, Ordnance, Artillery, Infantry, and Cavalry, and the Judge Advocate of the Army.—Crimson silk net. *For Officers of the Medical Department.*—Medium or emerald green silk net, with silk bullion fringe ends; to go around the waist and tie as for General Officers.

For all Sergeant Majors, Quartermaster Sergeants, Ordnance Sergeants, First Sergeants, Principal or Chief Musicians and Chief Buglers.—Red worsted sash, with worsted bullion fringe ends; to go twice around the waist and to tie behind the left hip, pendent part not to extend more than eighteen inches below the tie.

The sash will be worn (over the coat) on all occasions of duty of every description, except stable and fatigue.

The sash will be worn by "*Officers of the Day*" across the body, scarf fashion, from the right shoulder to the left side, instead of around the waist, tying behind the left hip as prescribed.

SWORD BELT.

For all Officers.—A waist belt not less than one and one half inch, nor more than two inches wide; to be worn over the sash; the sword to be suspended from it by slings of the same material as the belt, with a hook attached to the belt, upon which the sword may be hung.

For General Officers.—Russia leather, with three stripes of gold embroidery; the slings embroidered on both sides.

For all other Officers.—Black leather, plain.

For all Non-Commissioned Officers.—Black leather, plain.

SWORD-BELT PLATE.

For all Officers and Enlisted Men.—Gilt, rectangular, two inches wide, with a raised bright rim; a silver wreath of laurel encircling the "Arms of the United States;" eagle, shield, scroll, edge of cloud and rays bright. The motto, "E PLURIBUS UNUM," in silver letters, upon the scroll; stars also of silver, according to pattern.

SWORD AND SCABBARD.

For General Officers.—Straight sword, gilt hilt, silver grip, brass or steel scabbard.

For Officers of the Adjutant-General's, Inspector General's, Quartermaster's and Subsistence Departments, Corps of Engineers, Topographical Engineers, Ordnance, the Judge Advocate, of the Army, Aides-de-Camp, Field Officers of Artillery, Infantry and Foot Riflemen, and for the Light Artillery.—The sword of the pattern adopted by the War Department April 9, 1850; or the one described in the G. O. No. 21, of August 28, 1860, for officers therein designated.

For the Medical and Pay Departments.—Small sword and scabbard according to pattern in the Surgeon-General's office.

For Medical Cadets.—The sword and belt and plate will be the same as for non-commissioned officers.

For Officers of Cavalry.—Sabre and scabbard now in use, according to pattern in Ordnance Department.

For the Artillery, Infantry and Foot Riflemen, except the Field Officers.—The sword of the pattern adopted by the War Department, April 9, 1850.

The sword and sword belt will be worn upon all occasions of duty, without exception.

When on foot, the sabre will be suspended from the hook attached to the belt.

When not on military duty, officers may wear swords of honor, or the prescribed sword with a scabbard, gilt, or of leather with gilt mountings.

SWORD-KNOT.

For General Officers.—Gold cord with acorn end.

For all other Officers.—Gold lace strap with gold bullion tassel.

BADGES TO DISTINGUISH RANK.

Epaulettes.

For the Major-General Commanding the Army.—Gold, with solid crescent; device, three silver embroidered stars, one, one and a half inches in diameter, one, one and one-fourth inches in diameter, and one, one and one-eighth inches in diameter, placed on the strap in a row, longitudinally, and equidistant, the largest star in the centre of the crescent, the smallest at the top; dead and bright gold bullion, one half inch in diameter, and three and one-half inches long.

For all other Major-Generals.—The same as for the Major-General Commanding the Army, except that there will be two stars on the strap instead of three, omitting the smallest.

For a Brigadier-General.—The same as for a Major-General, except that, instead of two there shall be one star, omitting the smallest, placed upon the strap, and not within the crescent.

For a Colonel.—The same as for a Brigadier-General, substituting a silver embroidered spread eagle for the star, upon the strap; and within the crescent for the *Medical Department*—a laural wreath embroidered in gold, and the letters 𝔐. 𝔖., in old English characters, in silver, within the wreath; *Pay Department*—same as Medical Department, with the letters 𝔓. 𝔇., in old English characters; *Corps of Engineers*—a turreted castle of silver; *Corps of Topographical Engineers*—a shield, embroidered in gold, and below it the letters 𝔗. 𝔈., in old English characters, in silver; *Ordnance Department*—shell and flame in silver embroidery; *Regimental Officers*—the number of the regiment embroidered in gold, within a circle of embroidered silver, one and three-fourths inches in diameter, upon cloth of the following colors: for *Artillery*, scarlet; *Infantry*, light or sky blue; *Cavalry*, yellow.

For a Lieutenant-Colonel.—The same as for a Colonel, according to corps, but substituting for the eagle a silver embroidered leaf.

For a Major.—The same as for a Colonel, according to corps, omitting the eagle.

For a Captain.—The same as for a Colonel, according to corps, except that the bullion will only be one-fourth of an inch in diameter, and two and one-half inches long, and substituting for the eagle, two silver embroidered bars.

For a First Lieutenant.—The same as for a Colonel, according to corps, except that the bullion will be only one-eighth of an inch in diameter, and two and one-half inches long, and substituting for the eagle one silver embroidered bar.

For a Second Lieutenant.—The same as for a First Lieutenant, omitting the bar.

For a Brevet Second Lieutenant.—The same as for a Second Lieutenant.

All officers having military rank, will wear an epaulette on each shoulder.

The epaulette may be dispensed with when not on duty, and on certain duties off parade, to wit:—at drills, at inspection of barracks and hospitals, on Courts of Inquiry and Boards, at inspection of articles and necessaries, on working parties and fatigue duties, and upon the march, except when, in war, there is immediate expectation of meeting the enemy; and also when the overcoat is worn.

Shoulder Straps.

For the Major-General Commanding the Army.—Dark blue cloth, one and three eighths inches wide, by four inches long; bordered with an embroidery of gold one-fourth of an inch wide; three silver embroidered stars of five rays, one star on the centre of the strap, and one on each side, equidistant between the centre and the outer edge of the strap; the centre star to be the largest.

For all other Major-Generals.—The same as for the Major-General Commanding the Army, except that there will be two stars instead of three; the centre of each star to be one inch from the outer edge of the gold embroidery on the ends of the strap; both stars of the same size.

For a Brigadier-General.—The same as for a Major-General, except that there will be one star instead of two; the centre of the star to be equidistant from the outer edge of the embroidery on the ends of the strap.

For a Colonel.—The same size as for a Major-General, and bordered in like manner with an embroidery of gold; a silver embroidered spread eagle on the centre of the strap, two inches between the tips of the wings, having in the right talon an olive branch, and in the left a bundle of arrows; an escutcheon on the breast, as represented in the arms of the United States; cloth of the straps as follows: for the *General Staff and Staff Corps*—dark blue; *Artillery*, scarlet; *Infantry*, light or sky blue; *Cavalry*, yellow.

For a Lieutenant-Colonel.—The same as for a Colonel, according to corps, omitting the eagle, and introducing a silver embroidered leaf at each end, each leaf extending seven-eighths of an inch from the end border of the strap.

For a Major.—The same as for a Colonel, according to corps, omitting the eagle, and introducing a gold embroidered leaf at each end, each leaf extending seven-eighths of an inch from the end border of the strap.

For a Captain.—The same as for a Colonel, according to corps, omitting the eagle, and introducing at each end two gold embroidered bars, of the same width as the border, placed parallel to the ends of the strap; the distance between them and from the border equal to the width of the border.

For a First Lieutenant.—The same as for a Colonel, according to corps, omitting the eagle, and introducing at each end one gold embroidered bar, of the same width as the border, placed parallel to the width of the border.

For a Second Lieutenant.—The same as for a Colonel, according to corps, omitting the eagle.

For a Brevet Lieutenant.—The same as for a Second Lieutenant.

For a Medical Cadet.—A strip of gold lace, three inches long, and half an inch wide, placed in the middle of a strap of green cloth, three and three-quarter inches long, by one and one-quarter inches wide.

The shoulder strap will be worn whenever the epaulette is not.

CHEVRONS.

The rank of non-commissioned officers will be marked by chevrons upon both sleeves of the uniform coat and overcoat, above the elbow, of silk or worsted binding, one-half an inch wide, same color as the edging on the coat, points down, as follows:

For a Sergeant-Major.—Three bars and an arc, in silk.

For a Quartermaster-Sergeant.—Three bars and a tie, in silk.

For an Ordnance-Sergeant.—Three bars and a star, in silk.

For a Hospital Steward.—A caduceus two inches long, embroidered in yellow silk on each arm above the elbow, in the place indicated for a chevron, the head toward the outer seam of the sleeve.

For a First Sergeant.—Three bars and a lozenge, in worsted.

For a Sergeant.—Three bars, in worsted.

For a Corporal.—Two bars, in worsted.

For a Pioneer.—Two crossed hatchets of cloth, same color and material as the edging of the collar, to be sewed on each arm above the elbow, in the place indicated for a chevron, (those of a corporal to be just above and resting on the chevron,) the head of the hatchet upward, its edge outward, of the following dimensions, viz: *Handle*—four and one half inches long, one fourth to one third of an inch wide. *Hatchet*—two inches long, one inch wide at the edge.

To indicate service.—All non-commissioned officers, musicians, and privates, who have served faithfully for the term of five years, will wear, as a mark of distinction, upon both sleeves of the uniform coat, below the elbow, a diagonal half chevron, one-half an inch wide, extending from seam to seam, the front end nearest the cuff, and one-half an inch above the point of the cuff, to be of the same color as the edging on the coat. In like manner, an additional half chevron, above and parallel to the first, for every subsequent five years of faithful service; difference between each chevron one-fourth of an inch. Service in war will be indicated by a light or sky-blue stripe on each side of the chevron for Artillery, and a red stripe for all other corps, the stripe to be one-eighth of an inch wide.

OVERCOAT.

For Commissioned Officers.

A "*cloak coat,*" of dark blue cloth, closing by means of four frog buttons of black silk and loops of black silk cord down the breast, and at the throat by a long loop *à échelle*, without tassel or plate, on the left side, and a black silk frog button on the right; cord for the loops fifteen-hundredths of an inch in diameter; back, a single piece, slit up from the bottom, from fifteen to seventeen inches, according to the height of the wearer, and closing at will, by buttons and button-holes cut in a concealed flap; collar of the same color and material as the coat, rounded at the edges, and to stand or fall; when standing, to be about five inches high; sleeves loose, of a single piece, and round at the bottom, without cuff or slit; lining, woolen; around the front and lower border, the edges of the pocket, the sleeves, collar, and slit in the back, a flat braid of black silk one-half an inch wide; and around each frog button on the breast, a knot two and one-quarter inches in diameter, arranged according to drawing; cape of the same color and material as the coat, removable at the pleasure of the wearer, and reaching to the cuff of the coat-sleeve when the arm is extended; coat to extend down the leg from six to eight inches below the knee, according to height. *To indicate rank*, there will be on both sleeves, near the lower edge, a knot of flat black silk braid not exceeding one-eighth of an inch in width, arranged according to drawing, and composed as follows:

For a *General*.—Of five braids, double knot.
For a *Colonel*.—Of five braids, single knot.
For a *Lieutenant Colonel*.—Of four braids, single knot.
For a *Major*.—Of three braids, single knot.
For a *Captain*.—Of two braids, single knot.
For a *First Lieutenant*.—Of one braid, single knot.
For a *Second Lieutenant and Brevet Second Lieutenant*.—A plain sleeve without knot or ornament.

For Enlisted Men.

Of all *Mounted Corps*.—Of sky-blue cloth; stand and fall collar; double breasted; cape to reach down to the cuff of the coat when the arm is extended, and to button all the way up; buttons (24).

All other *Enlisted Men*.—Of sky-blue cloth; stand-up collar; single-breasted; cape to reach down to the elbows when the arm is extended, and to button all the way up; buttons (24).

For *Cavalry*.—A gutta percha talma or cloak, extending to the knee, with long sleeves.

MILITARY STOREKEEPERS.

A citizen's frock coat of blue cloth, with buttons of the department to which they are attached; round black hat; pantaloons and vest, plain, white, or dark blue; cravat or stock, black.

MISCELLANEOUS.

General Officers, and Colonels having the brevet rank of General Officers, may, on occasions of ceremony, and when not serving with troops, wear the "dress" and "undress" prescribed by existing regulations.

Officers below the grade of Colonel having brevet rank,

will wear the epaulettes and shoulder straps distinctive of their army rank. In all other respects, their uniform and dress will be that of their respective regiments, corps, or departments, and according to their commissions in the same. Officers above the grade of Lieutenant-Colonel by ordinary commissions, having brevet rank, may wear the uniform of their respective regiments or corps, or that of General Officers, according to their brevet rank.

Officers are permitted to wear a plain dark blue body coat, with the button designating their respective corps, regiments, or departments, without any other mark or ornament upon it. Such a coat, however, is not to be considered as a dress for any military purpose.

In like manner, officers are permitted to wear a buff, white, or blue vest, with the small button of their corps, regiment, or department.

Officers serving with mounted troops are allowed to wear, for stable duty, a plain dark blue cloth jacket, with one or two rows of buttons down the front, according to rank; stand-up collar, sloped in front as that of the uniform coat; shoulder straps according to rank, but no other ornament.

The hair to be short; the beard to be worn at the pleasure of the individual; but when worn, to be kept short and neatly trimmed.

A Band will wear the uniform of the regiment or corps to which it belongs. The commanding officer may, at the expense of the corps, sanctioned by the Council of Administration, make such additions in ornaments as he may judge proper.

OTHER ARTICLES OF CLOTHING AND EQUIPMENT.

Flannel Shirt, Drawers, Stockings and Stable Frock.—The same as now furnished.

Blanket.—Woolen, grey, with letters U. S. in black, four inches long, in the centre; to be seven feet long, and five and a half feet wide, and to weigh five pounds.

Canvas Overalls for Engineer Soldiers.—Of white cotton; one garment to cover the whole of the body below the waist, the breast, the shoulders and the arms; sleeves loose, to allow a free play of the arms, with narrow wristband buttoning with one button; overalls to fasten at the neck behind with two buttons, and at the waist behind with buckle and tongue.

Belts of all Enlisted Men.—Black leather.

Cartridge box.—According to pattern in the Ordnance Department.

Drum sling.—White webbing; to be provided with a brass drum-stick carriage, according to pattern.

Knapsack.—Of painted canvas, according to pattern now issued by the Quartermaster's Department; the great coat, when carried, to be neatly folded, not rolled, and covered by the out flap of the knapsack.

Haversack.—Of painted canvas, with an inside sack unpainted, according to the pattern now issued by the Quartermaster's Department.

Canteen.—Of tin, covered with woolen cloth, of the pattern now issued by the Quartermaster's Department.

TENTS.

For all *Commissioned Officers*—Wall tent, with a fly, pattern now issued by the Quartermaster's Department.

For *Hospital purposes.*—Pattern described in "General Orders, No. 1," of January 19, 1860.

For all *Enlisted Men.*—Sibley's patent, according to the pattern now issued by the Quartermaster's Department, at the rate of one tent to 17 mounted or 20 foot men. Sheet-iron stoves will be issued with the tents in cold climates, or when especially ordered.

For *Officers' Servants and Laundresses.*— Small common tent, old pattern.

HORSE FURNITURE.

For General Officers and the General Staff.

Housing for General Officers—to be worn over the saddle. Of dark blue cloth, trimmed with two rows of gold lace, the outer row one inch and five-eighths wide, the inner row two inches and one-fourth; to be made full, so as to cover the horse's haunches and forehands, and to bear on each flank corner the following ornaments, distinctive of rank, to wit: for the *Major-General Commanding the Army*—a gold-embroidered spread eagle and three stars; for other *Major-Generals*—a gold-embroidered spread eagle and two stars; for a *Brigadier-General*—a gold-embroidered spread eagle and one star.

Saddle Cloth for General Staff Officers—dark blue cloth, of sufficient length to cover the saddle and holsters, and one foot ten inches in depth, with an edging of gold lace one inch wide.

Surcingle—blue web.

Bridle—black leather; bent branch bit, with gilt bosses; the front and roses yellow.

Collar—yellow.

Holsters—black leather, with gold mountings.

Stirrups—gilt or yellow metal.

For Officers of the Corps of Engineers and Topographical Engineers.

The same as for General Staff Officers.

In time of actual field service, General Officers and Officers of the General Staff and Staff Corps are permitted to use the horse equipments described for mounted service.

HORSE EQUIPMENTS FOR THE MOUNTED SERVICE.

A complete set of horse equipments for mounted troops consists of 1 bridle, 1 watering bridle, 1 halter, 1 saddle, 1 pair saddle bags, 1 saddle blanket, 1 surcingle, 1 pair spurs, 1 currycomb, 1 horse brush, 1 picket pin, and 1 lariat; 1 link and 1 nose bag when specially required.

HEAD GEAR.

All the *leather* is black bridle leather, and the buckles are malleable iron, flat, bar buckles, blued.

BRIDLE—It is composed of 1 *head-stall*, 1 *bit*, 1 *pair of reins*.

HEADSTALL—1 *crown piece*, the ends split, forming 1 *cheek strap* and one *throat lash billet* on one side and on the other, 1 *cheek strap* and 1 *throat lash*, with 1 *buckle*, .625 inch, 2 *chapes*, and 2 *buckles*, .75 inch, sewed to the ends of cheek piece to attach the bit; 1 *brow band*, the ends doubled and sewed form 2 loops on each end through which the cheek straps and throat lash billet pass.

BIT—(shear steel, blued,) 2 *branches*, S shaped, pierced at top with an *eye* for the cheek strap billet, and with a small hole near the *eye* for the curb chain, terminated at the bottom by 2 *buttons*, into which are welded 2 *rings*, 1 inch, for the reins; 1 *mouth piece*, curved in the middle, its ends pass through the branches and are rivetted to them; 1 *cross bar*, rivetted to the branches near the lower ends; 2 *bosses*, (cast brass,) bearing the number and letter of the regiment and the letter of the company, rivetted to the branches with 4 *rivets*; 1 *curb chain hook*, steel wire, No. 10, fastened to the *near* branch; 1 *curb-chain*, steel wire, No. 11, curb-chain links 0.7 inch wide, with 1 loose ring in the middle, fastened to the *off* branch by a S hook, cold-shut; 1 *curb strap*, (leather,) fastened to the curb-chain by 2 *standing loops*.

1 *curb-ring* for bit No. 1 replaces the curb-chain and curb-strap. They are of two sizes: No. 1 has an interior diameter of 4 inches; No. 2, of 3.75 inches. The number is marked on the outside of the swell, No. 1 is the larger size.

There are four bits, differing from each other in the arch of the mouth piece, and in the distance from the mouth piece to the eye for the cheek strap. The branches are alike below the mouth piece. No. 1 is a Spanish bit, No. 2 is the next severest, and No. 4 is the mildest. Height of arch is $2\frac{1}{4}$ inches in No. 1, 2 inches in No. 2, $1\frac{1}{2}$ inch in No. 3, and $\frac{1}{2}$ inch in No. 4. The distance between the branches is 4.5 inches in all the bits.

REINS—2 *reins* sewed together at one end, the other ends sewed to the rings of the bit.

WATERING BRIDLE.

The watering bridle is composed of 1 *bit* and 1 *pair of reins*.

BIT (wrought iron, blued) 2 *mouth piece sides* united in the middle by a loop hinge; their ends are pierced with 2 holes to receive 2 *rings* 1.7 inches diameter for the reins. 2 *chains and toggles*, 3 links, each 1 inch by 0.55 inch, welded into the rein rings.

REINS—2 *reins* sewed together at one end, the other end sewed to rings of the bit.

HALTERS.

2 *cheek pieces*, sewed at one end to 2 *square loops* 1.6 inches diameter, and the other to *cheek rings* 1.6 inches diameter; 2 *standing loops* for the toggles of the watering bridle sewed to the cheek piece near to the square loops; 1 *crown piece* sewed to the *off* check ring, 1 buckle 1.12 inches, and *chape* sewed to the near cheek ring; 1 *nose band*, the ends sewed to the square loops; 1 *chin strap*, the ends sewed to the square loops and passing loose through the hitching-strap ring.

1 *throat strap*, folded on itself making two thicknesses and forming at top a loop for the throat band to pass through, and embracing in the fold at the other end 1 *bolt* which holds 1 *hitching-strap ring;* 1 *throat band* passes loose through the loop in the throat strap, and is sewed to the cheek rings; 1 *hitching-strap* 6½ feet long, 1 *buckle* 1.25 inches, and 1 *standing loop*, 1 *billet* sewed to the buckle end by the same seam which holds the buckle.

SADDLE.

All the *leather* is black bridle or harness leather, and the buckles are blued malleable iron.

The *saddle* is composed of 1 *tree*, 2 *saddle-skirts*, 2 *stirrups*, 1 *girth* and *girth-strap*, 1 *surcingle*, 1 *crupper*.

SADDLE TREE.

WOOD (beech) 1 *pommel* made of 2 pieces framed together at top and glued; 1 *cantle* formed of 2 pieces like the pommel; 2 *side bars* (poplar) each made of 3 pieces glued together; they are glued to the pommel and cantle, and fastened by 2 *rivets;* 2 *burrs, and* 4 *nails*, the burrs let in on the underside; 1 *strap mortice* in the pommel, 3 *strap mortices* in the cantle.

There are three sizes of trees, varying in the length of the seat. The number is marked on the pommel ornament.

No. 1. 11 inches length of seat. 15 per cent.
No. 5. 11½   "   "   50   "
No. 3. 12   "   "   35   "

IRON—1 *pommel arc* 0.1 inch thick, with three small holes on top, fastened to the side bars by 4 *rivets;* 1 *pommel plate* 0.1 inch thick, semi-circular, fastened to the front of the pommel by 4 *rivets;* 1 *cantle arc* 0.1 inch thick, with three small holes on top, fastened to the side bars by 4 *rivets;* 1 *cantle plate* 0.1 inch thick fastened to the rear of the cantle by 4 *rivets;* 2 *stirrup loops* hinged in 2 *holdfasts* which are fastened to the side bars by 6 *rivets.*

The tree is painted with one coat of white lead. It is covered with best quality kip skin raw hide, put on wet, sewed with thongs of the same and held in place by stitches through the wood along the junction of the pommel and cantle with the side bars. The seams are made on the edges of the side bars where they will not chafe the horse or rider.

2 *crupper rings,* held by staples driven into the front ends of side bars; 2 *foot staples* for coat straps fastened to the front of the pommel by 4 *brass screws,* ¾ inch; 2 *crupper rings,* (japanned black,) fastened by staples driven into the rear ends of side bars; 2 *foot staples,* fastened to the rear of cantle by 4 brass screws, ¾ inch; 1 *guard plate,* 1 *pommel ornament,* shield-shaped, (sheet brass,) fastened to the pommel, each by 3 brass screw pins; 6 *guard plates,* fastened to the cantle by 12 *screw pins;* 2 *foot staples,* fastened on the back strap by 4 *brass screws,* ¾ inch; 1 *saddle-bags stud,* fastened on the back strap to the cantle arc by 2 copper rivets.

Two SADDLE SKIRTS, (thick harness leather,) fastened to the side bars by 38 brass screws, ¾ inch; 2 *stay loops* for the saddle-bag straps sewed to the rear edge of the skirts.

Two STIRRUPS, (hickory or oak,) made of one piece bent, the ends separated by 1 *transom* and fastened by 2 *iron rivets,* each 4 burrs; 2 *leather hoods,* fastened to the stirrups by 12 *copper rivets and burrs*—distance of hood from rear of stirrups 6 inches; 2 *stirrup straps,* 2 *brass buckles,* 1.375 inches, 2 *sliding loops* pass through the stirrup loops and through a hole cut in the skirts; 2 *sweat leathers,* each has 2 *standing loops.*

GIRTH—2 *girth straps* pass over the pommel and cantle arcs, to which they are fastened by 4 *copper rivets* and 4 *burrs;* they are fastened to the side bars by 4 *brass screws,* ¾ inch; the ends are sewed into 2 D rings, 1.85 inches; 2 *girth billets,* sewed to the straight side of the D rings; 1

girth, 1.5 inches, blue woollen webbing; 1 *chape*, 1 *buckle*, 3 inches, 1 *standing loop*, and 1 *safe* on the off end; and 1 *chape*, 1 *buckle*, 1.5 inches, 1 D *ring*, 1.85 inches, 1 *standing loop*, 1 *safe* on the near side; 1 *standing loop* on the middle.

SIX COAT STRAPS, 6 *buckles*, 0.625 inch, and stops. They pass through the mortices in the pommel and cantle and the foot staples.

ONE CARBINE SOCKET, 1 *strap*, 1 *buckle*, 0.75 inch, sewed to the socket. The socket is buckled to the D ring on the off side of the saddle.

ONE SURCINGLE, 3.25 inches, blue woollen webbing; 1 *chape*, 1 *buckle*, 1.5 inches, 1 *standing loop* on one end, and 1 *billet* on the other; 1 *billet* lining sewed over the end of webbing to the billet; 2 *standing loops* near the buckle end.

CRUPPER—1 *dock*, made of a single piece and stuffed with hair, the ends sewed to the body of the crupper; 1 *body*, split at one end, has sewed to it 1 *chape*, 1 *ring*, 1.25 inches, 2 *back straps*—each ·has one buckle, 0.75 inch, and 2 *sliding loops*—they pass through the rings of the side bars and the ring on the body of the crupper.

SADDLE BAGS, (bag leather)—They are composed of 2 *pouches* and 1 *seat;* the ends of the seat are sewed to the the pouches. Each pouch has 1 *back*, sewed to the gusset and upper part of inner front with a *welt;* 1 *gusset*, sewed to the back and to 1 *outer* and 1 *inner front* with a *welt;* 1 *flap* sewed to the top of the back and to the seat by 2 seams; 1 *flap billet*, sewed to the point of the flap; 1 *chape* and 1 *buckle*, 0.625 inch, sewed to the outer front; 1 *billet*, 1 *buckle*, 0.625 inch, sewed to the chape. The seat is sewed to the pouch by the same seams which join the flap to the back of the pouch. It has 2 *holes* for the foot staples and 1 *hole* for the saddle-bag stud; 2 *key straps*, sewed to the seat near its ends; 4 *lacing thongs* for the pouches.

SADDLE BLANKET—To be of pure wool, close woven, of stout yarns of an indigo blue color, with an orange border 3 inches wide, 3 inches from the edge. The letter U. S., 6 inches high, of orange color, in the centre of the blanket. *Dimensions:* 75 inches long, 67 inches wide; weight, 3.1875 pounds; variation allowed in weight, 0.1875 pounds.

SPURS, (brass)—2 *spurs*, 2 *rowels*, 2 *rivets*, 2 *spur straps*, 19 inches long, 2 *roller buckles*, 0.625 inch, 2 *standing loops*,

Length of heel for No. 1, 3½ inches; for No. 2, 3¼ inches—inside measure.

Width of heel for No. 1, 3¼ inches; for No. 2, 3 inches—inside measure.

Length of shank to centre of rowel, 1 inch.

Diameter of rowel, 0.85 inch.

ONE HORSE BRUSH—1 *body*, (maple,) *Russia* bristles; 1 *cover*, glued and fastened to the body by 8 brass screws; 1 *hand strap*, fair leather, fastened to the sides of the body by 6 screws, 2 *leather washers* under the heads of screws. *Dimensions:* Body 9.25 inches long, 4 inches wide, 0.5 inch thick; cover 0.1 inch thick; bristles project 0.9 inch; hand strap 2 inches wide.

ONE CURRY COMB.—(iron, japanned black.) The pattern of "Carpenter's, No. 333." 1 *body*, (sheet iron, 0.4,) the top and bottom edges turned at right angles, forming two rows of teeth; 3 *double rows* of teeth, rivetted to the body by *six rivets;* 1 *cross bar*, rivetted across the top by 2 rivets; 1 *handle shank*, rivetted to the body by 3 rivets; 1 *handle*, (wood) turned and painted, passes over the shank and is held by the rivetted end of the shank; 1 *ferrule*, sheet iron. *Dimensions:* length, 4 inches; width, 4.75 inches; thickness, 0.75 inch; length of handle, 4 inches; weight, 0.84 pound.

ONE PICKET PIN, (iron, painted black)—The parts are: *the body, the neck, the head, the swell, the point;* 1 *lariat ring* around the neck, 8-shaped, the larger opening for the lariat. *Dimensions:* length, 14 inches; diameter at swell, 4 inches; from point, 0.75 inch; at neck, 0.5 inch; at head, 1 inch: lariat ring, 0.2 inch wire, welded, interior diameter 1 inch; weight of pin, 1.29 pounds.

ONE LARIAT—Best hemp 1¾ inch rope, 30 feet long, of 4 strands; an eye spliced in one end, the other end whipped with small twine; weight, 2.38 pounds.

ONE LINK—1 *strap*, embracing in the fold at one end 1 *spring hook*, and at the other 1 *buckle*, 0.75 inch, and 1 *billet*.

ONE NOSE BAG—Same as for Light Artillery.

INDEX.

	PAGE
Abstract of provisions issued	15
extra issues	15
articles paid for	83
payments	83
advances to officers	84
disbursements on account of contingencies	84
supplies purchased	84
property rec'd from officers	85
fuel issued	85
forage issued	85
straw issued	85
stationery issued	85
all other issues	86
articles expended, etc	86
transfers	86
property not otherwise accounted for	87
Accounts current, subsistence department	18
quartermaster's department	89
quartermaster's department, contingencies	89
recruiting service	212
medical department	208
Accounts, settlement of	279
Accoutrements, prices of	154
Adjutant-General, has charge of	6
Ammunition, not to be wasted	5
Army, composed of	5
supplied with provisions by	5
supplied with clothing by	5
supplied with transport'n by	5
supplied with fuel by	5
supplied with quarters by	5
paid by	5
supplied with arms by	6
Arms, care of	10
not to be taken apart	10
sales of, to officers	150
receipt for	151
prices of	151
Battery, composition of	154
ammunition for	155
harness required for	155
implements for	155
smith's tools for	156
saddler's tools for	157
stores for	157
requisition for	158
Books, regimental	9
acknowledgment of	193
Boards of survey	276
Brevet rank, when exercised	7
Captains, subject to detail	8
Cadets, medical	255
number of	256
how appointed	256

	PAGE
Cadets, pay of	256
Camp and garrison equipage	66
worn out	65
cost of	65
allowance of	69
return of	70
Clothing, by whom issued	65
how issued	65
extra issues of	65
allowance of	66
losses of	66
cost of	67
requisitions for	72
receipt rolls	69
soldiers' account of	69
how obtained by officers	70
return of	70
Companies, how designated	8
police regulations of	10
Company return	188
how prepared	188
to whom sent	189
Company morning report	189
how prepared	189
to whom sent	189
Company fund	198
return of	190
Commissary of subsistence	13
sergeant	13
acting assistant	14
Commissary property	14
return of	17
Commissary returns	16
Courts-martial, expenses of	81
accounts for	106
pay of members	81
pay of witnesses	81
Descriptive list	221
of men joining	187
Deceased soldiers, return of	186
regimental return of	192
final statement of	186
inventory of effects of	186
Disbursements, abstract of, subsistence department	18
Discharge, for disability	251
form of	252
certificate of disability for	252
of volunteers	253
of officers of volunteers	253
certificate to volunteers for	254
Form of ration return	81
consolidated ration return	82
receipt for subsistence funds	14
abstract of provisions issued	83
abstract of issues to citizens	34
abstract of extra issues	35
abstract of issues to hospital	36

(303)

304 INDEX.

Entry	Page
Form of abstract of sales to officers,	38
abstract of purchases of subsistence	39
monthly return of provisions	43a
monthly summary of statement	40
return of commis'y property	41
abstract of purchases	42
abstract of disbursements on account of contingencies	43
account current	44
account for commutation of rations	45
account commutation, soldier on furlough	46
voucher for services	47
pay roll	48
voucher for purchases for hospital	49
voucher for purchase of company savings	50
voucher for supplies paid for	51
voucher for supplies purch'd	52
receipt for stores transferred	53
invoice of stores transferred	54
quartermaster's receipt	55
invoice to quartermaster	56
requisition for stores	57
estimate of funds	58
contractor's account	59
contractor's abstract	60
contract for complete rations	61
contract for beef	62
of bond	63
clothing receipt roll	71
special requisition	72
return of clothing, camp and garrison equipage	72a
requisition for forage for public animals	122
requisition for forage for private horses	123
requisition for straw	126
requisition for stationery	128
requsition for fuel	119
requisition for fuel for officers	120
commutation account for fuel and quarters	102
account for mileage	103
account for actual transportation expenses	104
transportation account for civilian	105
account for court-martial expenses	106
account for postage paid	107
pay roll of quartermaster's men	108
descriptive list of persons transferred	148
account current of contingencies	110
voucher for purchases	100
invoice	117
account current, expenditures of quartermaster's dep't	98
list of articles expended	131
list of articles lost, etc	132
Form of account sales	183
voucher to abstract of purchases	115
voucher for miscellaneous disbursements	147
voucher to abstract C	113
abstract A	99
abstract B	101
abstract Bb	109
abstract C	111
abstract D	114
abstract E	116
abstract F	118
abstract G	121
abstract H	125
abstract I	127
abstract K	129
abstract L	130
abstract M	134
abstract N	135
return of quarterm's stores	114a
report of persons and articles	133
monthly summary statement	137
roll of extra duty men	140
report of stores for transport'n	141
return of animals	142
report of forage	143
report of fuel and quarters commuted	144
report of pay due	145
estimate for funds	146
requisition for ordnance for militia	161
report of allowances paid to officers	136
special requisit'n for ordnance	162
return of ordnance	153
officers' pay account	174
pay account of discharged soldiers	167
pay roll of militia	176
muster roll	201
muster and pay roll	202
return of men joined	207
company return	202a
morning report of company	202b
monthly return of regiment	202c
quarterly return of deceased soldiers	204
annual return of casualties	202d
regimental morning report	203
post return	206a
return of post and comp. fund	206
division return	206b
recruiting account current	225
abstract of disbursements of recruiting service	212
voucher for disbursements of recruiting service	213
tri-monthly report	228
monthly return of recruits	229
muster and descriptive roll of recruits	232
account of clothing	234
enlistment	217
descriptive list	235
return of regimental recruiting party	236

INDEX. 305

	PAGE
Form of return of recruits enlisted,	237
regimental recruiting return.	238
muster-in roll	239
muster-out roll	240
discharge	252
certificate of disability	252
certificate to volunteers	254
contract with private physician	259
requisition for medicine	270
special requis'n for medicine.	271
account for purchase of medicine	272
return of medicines	273
account of arms of soldiers in hospital	274
surgeon's morning report	275
Forage	74
allowance of	74
not to be sold	74
requisition for	74
commutation of	74
Fuel, allowance of	77
by whom furnished	77
commutation of	77
Hospital, purchases for	22
abstract of issues to	16
fund	20
ration, cost of	20
stewards	256
how appointed	256
how mustered	257
Horses	73
how condemned	73
how obtained	73
by whom issued	73
Laundresses, rations of	19
temporarily separated	19
Medical department	255
under charge of	5
correspondence of	269
Medical officers, instrum'ts issued to	259
return of same	260
Medical supplies, by whom issued	261
how issued	261
standard table of	262
Militia	242
how mustered in service	242
Monthly summary statement	90
Muster rolls	178
how prepared	179
certificate on	184
recapitulation of	182
certificate of mustering officer	185
of field and staff	155
Muster and pay rolls	181
how prepared	181
Muster-in rolls	242
how prepared	242
captain's certificate to	243
appraiser's certificate to	243
mustering officer's certificate to	243
number of rolls required	244
Muster-out rolls	244
how prepared	245
captain's certificate to	246
number of rolls	247

	PAGE
Muster rolls for pay	247
Non-commissioned officers	8
how to be treated	8
how reduced	8
Ordnance	149
what comprehended by	149
losses of	149
how issued	150
requisitions for	150
when repairs needed to	150
delivery to states	150
receipt for	159
return of	159
Pay, table of	164
of officers' servants	166
of officers, how made up	166
of acting assistant commiss'y	166
of discharged soldiers	167
roll of quartermaster	92
assignment of	280
Payment of soldiers	168
of volunteers	169
Postage	82
account for	107
Post return	194
to whom sent	194
how prepared	195
Post fund	198
accounts	198
Provision return	13
consolidated	13
Provisions, how drawn	13
issues to soldiers	15
to citizens	15
to hospital	15
sales to officers	16
monthly return of	48a
wastage on issues	12
abstract of, sold to officers	18
Private physicians, employment of	257
compensation to	258
contract with	259
Purchases, subsistence department, abstract of	18
Quarters, allowance of	77
commutation of	78
commutation account	102
Quartermaster's department	82
returns of	82
list of monthly returns	82
articles furnished by	93
Rank of officers	6
brevet	6
Rations of the army	11
extra issues	11
commutation of	20
Resignations, to take effect	8
Regiments	8
Regiment, return of	190
to whom sent	190
how prepared	191
Regimental recruiting return	191
return of deceased soldiers	192
morning report	194
fund accounts	198
Regimental recruiting service	222
Return of quartermaster's stores	87
of animals, etc.	91

INDEX.

	PAGE
Return of clothing, camp and garrison equipage	70
of ordnance	159
of regiment	190
of regimental recruit'g service	191
of casualties	192
of department	199
of division	199
of army corps	199
of brigade	199
from commanders of recruits	220
of medicine	267
Report of persons and articles	90
of stores for transportation	91
of forage	91
of fuel and quarters com'uted	91
of damaged arms	187
of regimental appointments	198
of arrival and departure of troops	196
of condition of buildings	196
Retired list	249
pay of officers on	249
how placed on	249
promotion consequent to	250
Recruiting service	208
parties	208
stationery for	208
Recruiting accounts current	212
return of property	213
monthly summary statement	213
tri-monthly report	214
muster roll	214
return of recruits	214
return of clothing	214
return of arms	215
estimate for funds	215
regimental	222
returns of	222
Recruiting of volunteers	223
expenses allowed	224
Recruits	209
examination of	210
muster and descriptive roll of	215
how prepared	215
to whom sent	216
account of clothing	216
enlistment, form of	217
transportation of	218
boards of inspection of	219
Recruiting blanks	219
Roll of extra-duty men	91
Rolls, returns and reports	178
Soldiers, discharge of	251
Straw	74
allowance of	75
requisition for	126
Stationery	75
allowance of	75
for courts-martial	76
for officers	76
requisition for	128
purchase of	76

	PAGE
Stationery, blanks	76
Swords and sabres, prices of	153
Surgeons	255
how appointed	255
assistant	255
how appointed	255
account of clothing	268
morning report	268
Surgeon's call	267
Tents, hospital	68
Transportation, by whom furnished	78
allowance of	79
commutation of	78
account for commutation of	103
account for actual expenses	104
account of civilian for	105
for hospital service	80
of officers' horses	80
to cash drafts	80
changes of station	80
paymaster's clerk	81
to courts-martial	81
Uniform of the army, coat	281
buttons	283
trowsers	284
hat	285
forage cap	287
cravat	287
boots	287
spurs	287
gloves	287
sash	287
sword belt	288
sword belt plate	288
sword knot	289
epaulettes	289
shoulder straps	291
chevrons	292
overcoat	293
for military storekeepers	294
of bands	295
equipment	296
tents	296
horse furniture	296
head gear	297
bit	298
watering bridle	298
halters	299
saddle	299
saddle bags	301
spurs	301
curry comb	302
nose bag	302
Vouchers to abstract D	88
E	88
K	88
L	88
A	89
B	89
C	90
Volunteers, allowances to	247
pensions to	248

PATTEN'S
APPROVED MILITARY WORKS,

Price Twenty-five cents.

ARTILLERY DRILL,

CONTAINING THE

Manual of the Piece and Light Battery Manœuvres.

160 pages and 72 Engravings.

OFFICE OF CHIEF OF ARTILLERY, ARMY OF POTOMAC,
WASHINGTON, *March* 5, 1862.

COLONEL:—It gives me great pleasure to state that your little book, entitled "PATTEN'S ARTILLERY DRILL," is, in my opinion, most admirably adapted to the use of non-commissioned officers and soldiers of the regular and volunteer batteries of field artillery. I should be glad to see it officially introduced into the service, particularly at the present time. I am, Colonel, very respectfully your obedient servant,

WM. F. BARRY, Brig.-Gen., Ch. of Artillery.

HEADQUARTERS MILITARY DEFENCES,
WASHINGTON, D. C., *March* 5, 1862.

I consider your work, called "PATTEN'S ARTILLERY DRILL," an excellent manual for the use of our artillery soldiers, on account of its portability, easy references and full illustrations of every movement.

Yours very truly, A DOUBLEDAY,
Brigadier-General of Volunteers.
To COLONEL PATTEN.

JAMES W. FORTUNE, Publisher,
NEW YORK.

PATTEN'S
APPROVED MILITARY WORKS,

Price fifty cents.

INFANTRY TACTICS.

Containing the School of the Soldier, Manual of Arms for both Musket and Rifle, School of the Company, and Battalion Instruction for Skirmishers, Bayonet Drill and the Small Sword Exercise. Illustrated.

Price twenty-five cents.

INFANTRY TACTICS.

Containing the School of the Soldier, Manual of Arms for both Musket and Rifle, School of the Company, Instruction for Skirmishers, Bayonet Drill and the Small Sword Exercise. 164 pages and 92 Engravings.

Price twenty-five cents.

CAVALRY DRILL,

CONTAINING THE

Schools of the Trooper, Platoon and Squadron.

160 *pages and* 93 *Engravings.*

COLONEL PATTEN'S MILITARY BOOKS are compiled in accordance with the authorizations of the War Department of the United States, expressly to impart instruction to the recruit and the officer in the simplest and most approved manner.

COLONEL PATTEN'S MILITARY BOOKS are profusely illustrated, and got up regardless of cost, no works of their size or price yet published in the United States having cost such large sums in their production.

JAMES W. FORTUNE, Publisher,
NEW YORK.

www.ingramcontent.com/pod-product-compliance
Lightning Source LLC
Chambersburg PA
CBHW031852220426
43663CB00006B/596